TEXTUAL
Orientations

D1238563

TEXTUAL ORIENTATIONS

*Lesbian and Gay Students
and the Making of
Discourse Communities*

HARRIET MALINOWITZ

Boynton/Cook Publishers
HEINEMANN
Portsmouth, NH

Boynton/Cook Publishers
A subsidiary of Reed Elsevier Inc.
361 Hanover Street
Portsmouth, NH 03801–3912

Offices and agents throughout the world

Acknowledgments for borrowed material are continued on page x.

Library of Congress Cataloging-in-Publication Data

Malinowitz, Harriet.
  Textual orientations: lesbian and gay students and the making of discourse communities / Harriet Malinowitz.
    p. cm.
  Includes bibliographical references and index.
  ISBN 0–86709–353–6 (acid-free paper)
  1. English language—Rhetoric—Study and teaching—Social aspects—United States.
2. Gay college students—United States—Social conditions. 3. Lesbian students—United States—Social conditions. 4. English language—Discourse analysis. 5. Lesbians—United States—Language. 6. Gays—United States—Language. 7. Group identity. I. Title.
PE1405.U6M34 1995   94-36734
378.1 982664—dc20   CIP

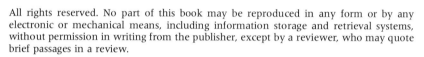

Editor: Peter R. Stillman
Production: Vicki Kasabian
Cover design: Jenny Jensen Greenleaf

Printed in the United States of America on acid-free paper
99 98 97 96 95 EB 1 2 3 4 5

For Sara Cytron,

life partner par excellence

Contents

Chapter Five
**The Politics of Outsiderhood Go to
School: Liberatory Pedagogy**

Part Three
The Lesbian- and Gay-Themed Writing Class

Chapter Six
**Construing and Constructing Knowledge as a Lesbian or Gay
Student Writer: Reflections on an Identity-Based Course**

Chapter Seven
The Course of Study/Study of the Course

Part Four
Portraits of Four Student Writers

Chapter Eight
Adrian O'Connor: "It's a Social World"

Chapter Nine
Isabel Serrano: "Setting the Record Straight"

Chapter Ten
John Lee: Writing Fractured Identity

Chapter Eleven
Mary Donoghue: "Let's Assume These Things Are True"

Part Five
Conclusion

The author and publisher wish to thank those who have generously given permission to reprint borrowed material:

Excerpts from "Inventing the University" by David Bartholomae from *When a Writer Can't Write* (1985), Mike Rose, ed. Copyright © 1985. Published by Guilford Press. Reprinted by permission.

Excerpts from "Notes Toward a Politics of Location" are reprinted from *Blood, Bread, and Poetry: Selected Prose 1979–1985* by Adrienne Rich, by permission of the author and W. W. Norton & Company, Inc. Copyright © 1986 by Adrienne Rich.

"AIDS: 1 in 61" (page 42); "Riot" (page 99); "American Flag" (page 108); and "Know Your Scumbags" (page 134) from *AIDS demo graphics* by Douglas Crimp with Adam Rolston. Copyright © 1990. Published by Bay Press, 115 West Denny Way, Seattle, WA 98119. Reprinted by permission.

Excerpts from "The Rhetoric of Empowerment in Writing Programs" by Harriet Malinowitz from *The Right to Literacy*, Andrea Lunsford, Helene Moglen, and James Slevin, eds. Copyright © 1990. Published by the Modern Language Association. Reprinted by permission.

Excerpts from "Construing and Constructing Knowledge as a Lesbian or Gay Student Writer" by Harriet Malinowitz from Queer Rhetoric double issue of *Pre/Text*, Margaret Morrison, guest ed. Published by University of Texas. Reprinted by permission of *Pre/Text*.

Excerpts from "Queer Theory: Whose Theory?" by Harriet Malinowitz from *Frontiers* Volume 13, Number 2. Published by *Frontiers: A Journal of Women Studies*. Reprinted by permission.

Excerpts from "Extending Our Concept of Multiculturalism: Lesbian and Gay Reality and the Writing Class" copied by permission of Harriet Malinowitz. In *Vital Signs 3: Restructuring the English Classroom*, edited by James L. Collins (Boynton/Cook Publishers Inc., Portsmouth, NH, 1992).

Excerpts from a commentary by Harriet Malinowitz from *HOT WIRE: The Journal of Women's Music and Culture*. Published by Empty Closet Enterprises, Inc. Reprinted by permission of *HOT WIRE: The Journal of Women's Music and Culture*.

"The Bridge Poem" by Kate Rushin from *This Bridge Called My Back: Writings by Radical Women Of Color*, edited by Cherrie Moraga and Gloria Anzaldua, 1983. Used by permission of the author and of Kitchen Table Press, P. O. Box 908, Latham, NY 12110.

Acknowledgments

In her book *Families We Choose: Lesbians, Gays, Kinship,* Kath Weston demonstrates that chosen, as opposed to biological, families are frequently "families of friends" with fluid boundaries—galaxies of people "in a cluster surrounding a single individual, rather than taking couples or groups as units of affiliation." The cluster surrounding me has grown larger over the years that I have worked, first on my doctorate and then on this book, and even people one customarily thanks formally in an acknowledgments section have come to feel like vital parts of my family of friends.

First and foremost, I owe the students who participated in my study as well as those who participated in the two classes described herein an enormous debt. Their energy and enthusiasm, their willingness to give of their time and share their work, and their ongoing interest in this endeavor will always be appreciated. I know that they did it partly to help me, but also very much out of their desire to change the academic environment for students who will follow them. Their participation was an act of activism, and I will always remember them with immense warmth.

Many thanks go to John Mayher, Barbara Danish, Martin Duberman, and Berenice Fisher. All have provided crucial conversations, contexts, models for teaching and thinking, and encouragement. I also owe much to my dissertation support group, who helped this project take form from its inception: Nancy Biederman, Joyce Harte, Deborah Mutnick, and Sue Ruskin. Thanks for various forms of practical help and shots of spiritual uplift from Allan Brick, Eleonore Pepin, Lou Timmons, Charles Schuster, Mary Elliott, Marguerite Helmers, and Hilary Roberts. Certain spare but apt utterances from Jo Barrett Grellong and Lee Zevy over the years enabled me to locate myself in this project. This work could not have come to fruition without vital input from Scott Bane, Christopher Godfrey, David Murphy, Jacquie Bishop, Laura Roemer, Cari Daly, Leticia Montalvo, David Rain, Nika Hedges, Julia Storke, Kerri Leas, Kevin Ray, Scott Ebersold, and Cristina Lugo.

I have benefited greatly from colloquia and discussions at the Lesbian and Gay Studies group at Columbia and at CUNY's Center for Lesbian and Gay Studies. The Lesbian and Gay Caucus of CCCC has provided a wonderful network of friendship and scholarly camaraderie, as well as a forum for thinking about the connections between composition and lesbian and gay studies. I am especially grateful for the active presence there of Sarah-Hope Parmeter, Paul Puccio, Ellen Louise Hart, Joe Marchesani, Lisa Albrecht, and Scott Stoddart, who can make any bland convention site feel like home. (Special thanks to Paul for graciously allowing me to appropriate a paragraph of joint intellectual property.) Seated at mission control of CCCC, Debbie Fox has been a wonderful presence at the other end of the telephone line—whether helping convey to Oregon and Colorado that CCCC wouldn't hold conventions in states that mandate homophobia or simply rooting for me when I needed it. Eternal thanks go to Peter Stillman at Boynton/Cook for dangling a book contract in front of me when I needed such inspiration, and for always being there in the woods when I was trying to get out of the woods.

I thank my loyal long-distance friends—many of whom are not academics and think the way I live is my own personal sickness—for their patience and support during this period: Lisa Gross, Marc Donaldson, Bronwyn Jones, Priscilla Lynch, Cindy Lanane, Gail Nankin, Amy Horton, Charles Levitan, Jacquie Morris, Jed Rosenstein, Marcey Jacobson, Janet Marren, Stephanie Roth, Kim Klein, Judith Branzburg (with whom I had discussions of lifelong importance at Puffers Pond in 1978 about what it means to collapse the border between work and pleasure) and Amy Ryan (who will hopefully be the first out lesbian in space). Ditto my local friends: Seymour Kleinberg, Mimi Brown, Stephanie Davies, Sharon DuPree, Patrick Horrigan, and Paul Wasserman. The friends who most actively supported me in taking the time I needed to be reclusive were Esther Hyneman and Gloria Jean Jenkinson. Esther would frequently command me to hang up when she called if I said I was at my computer (though she told me to call her the minute I finished, even if it was in the middle of the night, which I did and it was). Gloria Jean showed the utmost spiritual generosity in forgiving me for missing both her graduation and forty-fifth birthday parties; her own experience as a returning student had left her convinced of the importance of prioritizing one's work.

I am very fortunate to have a biological family who genuinely feels like part of my family of friends. Fred Pauker, Sura Ruth, the Meirs, and the Toronto Paukers heard me say, "My life is out of control!" so many times during this project as a reason for not seeing them that I'm lucky they didn't disown me. Above all, Stan Malinowitz, whose thinking I respect more than anyone's in the world, is the most perceptive, witty, loving, and politically astute brother with whom one could ever hope to analyze the complexities of the academic and extra-academic world.

As a New Yorker *and* an academic, I haven't had a chance to cook since 1986. A million thanks to those establishments in my neighborhood whose take-out menus kept me alive: Dojo's, B-B-Q Restaurant, Charlie Mom, Pane & Cioccolato, the Waverly Coffee Shop, and Eden Farm's salad bar.

Finally—what can I say about Sara Cytron, who has lived with me through all this? I can't just acknowledge her patience and fortitude, as per tradition, because that hardly conveys the whole story. Sara has said that when this project is over, we will need readjustment counseling—the kind families have when a member who has been missing in action for seven years suddenly returns. Yet, Sara didn't just wait in the wings while I worked. She made this project feel almost like a collaborative enterprise (or a codependent one, depending on your perspective) because she learned the language of my field; she read, discussed, and edited my papers and drafts; she came to a few conferences (though I wouldn't let her come to others because of her tendency to sit there and beam at me embarrassingly while I read papers); she took graduate courses so that our fights could be informed by theory; and she talked with me about writing theory, feminist theory, and lesbian and gay studies over dinners, on beaches, on car trips, and on walks in the country. At the same time, she kept me from getting monotonically academic and theoretical by luring me into what *she* was involved with—theatre and stand-up comedy. I've always said that what I wanted in life was a John-and-Yoko relationship, by which I meant one informed by a shared sense of creative energy and excitement, a passion that was charged on multiple levels. I've definitely had this with Sara. In addition, she has sustained me during my long work hauls by making me hundreds of the most wonderful salads I've ever eaten. I can never recount here the ways that Sara's presence, support, sensibility, and love have informed every step of this book's process. A greater and more cherished life partner there never was.

Preface

Imagine that we are at a conference about college writing pedagogy, and that instead of being positioned in relative mutual obscurity at opposite ends of the publishing process's digestive tract, we are gazing at each other across a dais in a session on discourses of the classroom. You are hearing a paper that I am "delivering" to you, one whose actual moment of composition anticipated this event. You watch my face as I speak, and I register some measure of your response through your nods, your laughter, your fidgeting, or your silence.

Let's say my paper, called "Textual Orientations: Lesbian and Gay Students and the Making of Discourse Communities," is the only one listed on the conference schedule that includes the words "lesbian" and "gay" in its title. That means that I am inserting a discourse of sexuality into a realm that otherwise fences it out, and whose flexible parameters are now first shifting in some way to accommodate it. Because I don't really know my audience and my audience doesn't know me, I can't begin to know, until the point of utterance, what the initiation of this discourse will mean, and what risks I incur as the only visible speaking subject of the discourse. And yet, because the subject of my paper is in print on the program, preceding my presentation of it, you can't claim that it surprises you—whoever "you" are—and this places me in a different discursive space that I would have been in if you had had no idea what you were going to hear. You may in fact be hostile, but at least I can expect not to hear the gasp of your shock (which may have occurred in private, in which case it must have been succeeded by some sort of intervention leading to your presence here) or see you walk out in protest. And even if you do hate me, it's too late for you to terrorize me into silence. I'm not hovering at that threshold of indecision where the benefits of being out can be swiftly weighed against the liabilities. I'm already out; when I walk into this room it's into an existing discourse that I have already instigated. And so I proceed with the freedom to say what I want, my trajectory unweighted by fears of repercussions and hopes that my silence will protect me.

And yet, even while unafraid to speak, I still feel hobbled by a wave of rhetorical confusion. Because composition theorists don't usually talk about lesbian and gay issues, I don't really know, for the purposes of my paper, who you are, what you know, or what you believe, so that in constructing the text that I am now presenting I have had to entertain a daunting range of conjectured possibilities. As writing instructors, we're used to urging writers to claim authority, to feel powerful in writing what they are knowledgeable about. Yet if, as a lesbian writing teacher, I know more than you do about issues facing lesbian and gay writers as they compose, does that give me power? I'm thinking of what Eve Kosofsky Sedgwick (1990) has said about knowledge *not*, in fact, being power, but rather something that puts one in a vulnerable position. It is ignorance, after all, that most often tyrannizes us, says Sedgwick, offering by way of example:

> If M. Mitterrand knows English but Mr. Reagan lacks—as he did lack—French, it is the urbane M. Mitterrand who must negotiate in an acquired tongue, the ignorant Mr. Reagan who may dilate in his native one. (4)

These features of this hypothetical writing context are at play, in some form, for our lesbian and gay students all the time. Ann Berthoff (1982) says that "[w]riting involves the same acts of mind as does making sense of the world: you construct the way you construe" (87). Paulo Freire (Freire and Macedo 1987) sees "reading the word and the world" as allied activities, both of which depend on our understanding the relationship between text and context. A few years ago, then, I decided that I wanted to create a course in which lesbian and gay students could experiment with publicly and academically constructing knowledge within the rubrics that they construed it, and in which they could compose texts that reflected, rather than worked against, their sense of contexts.

This book is the result of research centering on an unusual situation: lesbian, gay, bisexual, and heterosexual writers gathered together in a class in which lesbian and gay experience is the thematic material, issues involving lesbian and gay identity and life are foregrounded, and many of the usual constraints on the open discussion of lesbian and gay life are removed. My investigation is partly an attempt to answer the question: What can happen to lesbian and gay writers in such a situation? What happens to them as readers and writers when the assigned course texts include theory, narratives, political arguments, debates from the gay popular press, historical essays, and cultural artifacts of lesbian and gay life? How do they write when assignments ask them to respond to these texts; to analyze the relationship between social practices, policies, and rituals and sexual identity; to theorize about the connections between sexual identity and acts of reading and writing; to use their own and others' experiences with homophobia to reread ideology about the nuclear family?

Perhaps most important, what happens to these students as readers, writers, and reviewers of peers' work when the majority of those "peers" are lesbian and gay students? What kind of discourse community gets formed here, and what new kind of work does it enable? What kind of interpretive framework does such a setting provide? How does such a changed sense of audience affect a lesbian or gay writer's work? What kinds of intertextuality emerge in such a situation? What is the relationship between the lifting of usual taboos, a writer's sense of intellectual and creative freedom, a writer's sense of confidence, and the work that gets produced? How do these issues become further complicated for students of multiple Otherhood—for example, a Latina lesbian? In what ways might such a class enhance a writer's awareness of rhetorical processes and of the dynamics of the composing process? In what ways might a lesbian or gay writer begin to engage with *other* subjects differently after having experienced a class such as this?

These are some of the questions this book will address. Yet in the process of trying to answer them I can't help but engage with other questions which may ultimately be of more immediate interest to teachers of mainstream writing classes: What gaps exist in composition theory and practice that are significant for lesbian and gay students in a mainstream writing class? More specifically, to what extent and in what ways might homophobia in society, and as it is reproduced in the writing class, constitute a basic form of interference in lesbian and gay students' abilities to manifest significant expressive and epistemic aspects of writing processes and performances? What factors might they have to weigh when deciding whether or not to disclose their sexual identity in their writing, and what are the risks and costs of either choice? What tensions surround the naming of that identity, and what are their effects likely to be on writers who are asked to compose reflectively and critically?

How are the strategies contemporary writing theory offers—such as freewriting, peer collaboration, critical revision—likely to help, hinder, or complicate the composing processes of lesbian and gay writers? How, in particular, do social constructionist and liberatory pedagogies stop short of fully realizing their intentions where lesbian and gay students are concerned? To what extent does or doesn't the language of writing assignments acknowledge lesbian and gay existence and facilitate its expression? Most of our theories of writing, although abstractly acknowledging that social context frames the writing act, nevertheless tend to address the needs and purposes of generic writers.

How do they translate when we insert instead "lesbian or gay writers"? What can change for lesbian and gay writers when they are in a writing class in which lesbian and gay existence is acknowledged and affirmed?

This inquiry also draws heavily on a body of work that has emerged—largely in the past decade—within the field of lesbian and gay studies. What new perspectives does lesbian and gay theory offer that are pertinent to writing instruction? What perceptions about identity itself does the field suggest, and how do they relate to the aims of current composition pedagogy? What does sexuality have to do with writing? How might knowledge about lesbian and gay identities further illuminate our developing understanding of the role of gender in the writing act? In short, what may lesbian and gay studies offer composition?

My focus here is on the processes by which lesbian or gay writers generate and authorize knowledge, and the conditions which affect their composing processes in collaborative classrooms. I would contend, though, that this work has implications for all student writers constructing knowledge within the context of a homophobic society, and that effacing lesbian and gay existence in the composition class is pedagogically reductive for heterosexual writer-learners as well. Ultimately, I hope that my research will help to establish a place for lesbian and gay discourses within the multiple and overlapping discourses that are the interpretive and collaborative bases of our writing classes. I hope to show that beyond serving the needs only of a particular segment of our student population, this inclusion will more generally augment the effectiveness of writing instruction as current theory has shaped it.

Part One

Introduction

Chapter One

Queer Texts, Queer Contexts

I have come increasingly to recognize that most learning in most settings is a communal activity, a sharing of the culture. It is not just that the child must make his knowledge his own, but that he must make it his own in a community of those who share his sense of belonging to a culture. It is this that leads me to emphasize not only discovery and invention but the importance of negotiating and sharing—in a word, of joint culture creating as an object of schooling and as an appropriate step en route to becoming a member of the adult society in which one lives out one's life.

Jerome Bruner, *Actual Minds, Possible Worlds*

Axiom 1: People are different from each other. It is astonishing how few respectable conceptual tools we have for dealing with this self-evident fact.

Eve Kosofsky Sedgwick, *Epistemology of the Closet*

While taking a writing course several semesters ago, I was inhibited about writing any pieces involving gay subject matter which would then have to be read to the class. I believe all gay and lesbian writers confront this in their writing and in writing workshops, and at times compromise. However, it is the act of compromising that is lethal to the writer. It stunts our growth and maturity as writers. In this class, I hope to continue searching for the voice I have spent years trying to develop and allow the person I kept stifled to grow.

Student in a lesbian/gay writing class

*I want to be able to express myself as a gay man without fear of
ridicule (or physical violence) by fellow classmates.*
                                 Student in a lesbian/gay writing class

We're here. We're queer. Get used to it.
                                            Queer Nation chant

In the last few years, there has been a subtle but persistent change in
the classroom climate around the subject of sexual orientation. It's not
that students have suddenly and universally become empathetic and
comfortable with lesbian and gay existence; but they do seem to regard
the issue itself with much less suspicion or surprise than they used to.
In fact, students often introduce the subject themselves, either in
classroom discussions or essay topics. Although five years ago, for
instance, participants at the Conference for College Composition and
Communication (CCCC) were arguing for the "inclusion" of lesbian and
gay issues in the writing classroom, teachers now are recognizing that
lesbian and gay issues are already *in* the writing classroom—because
they have become a part of our students' collective consciousness.

Like the eighteenth-century narrator of Laurence Sterne's *Tristram
Shandy*—who could not write his autobiography fast enough because,
while he attempted to recount the events of his past, the present
continuously heaped more material upon him which itself had to be
recorded—I have found that my writing of this book couldn't keep up
with the rapid pace of the lesbian and gay movement in the world
outside my study. I began, three years ago, intending to create a classic
argument for "inclusion" based on widespread lesbian and gay invisibility in composition and its contexts, academy and society. Yet in the
ensuing time, mainstream media, responding to various social forces,
have produced dramatically different coverage of lesbian and gay issues
than they ever did before, changing the conceptual landscape for
everyone. At one time the absence of lesbian and gay issues or existence in news periodicals, literature, academic texts, television, film,
and other media was a source of chronic cynical observation by lesbian
and gay people; right now it is unlikely that a day will go by in which
a lesbian- and gay-themed news story does not appear in, say, the *New
York Times*—and there is an excellent chance that it will appear on the
front page. The 1992 presidential race propelled lesbian and gay existence onto the front lines of campaign rhetoric and national discourse:
Pat Buchanan's speech at the Republican convention, Ross Perot's

declaration (later reconsidered) that he would not place lesbians or gays in Cabinet posts, and the candidate Bill Clinton's ill-fated promise to end the ban on lesbians and gays in the military all provoked massive pollster activity in which the opinions of "people in the street" and citizens randomly selected by telephone were relayed to a public deciding how to position itself. Lesbians and gays moved quite abruptly from the problems of "invisibility" to a dazzling and confusing new "visibility."

We are now in what many activists, lobbyists, journalists, and profiteers have enthusiastically dubbed the "gay nineties." Nineteen ninety-three was certainly a watershed year for visibility. The National March on Washington for Lesbian and Gay Rights, the largest civil rights march in history, was carried live for seven hours on C-SPAN and was picked up as a headline news item by virtually all major print and electronic media. Debates about lesbians and gays in the military involved the courts, the Cabinet, and the Congress, and brought gay activists to the White House for an unprecedented chat with the president. Lesbians were called "chic" for the first time in anyone's memory and graced the covers of magazines like *Newsweek, Vogue, New York,* and the "Style" section of the *New York Times;* even *Cosmopolitan* and *Redbook* scrambled to ride the trend.

At the same time, the issue of gays in the military devolved to the point where the mantra "Don't ask, don't tell" mandated the hypocrisy of silence as federal policy. "Chic" lesbians still grappled with unemployment discrimination, inadequate healthcare, violence, and loss of child custody (Acey 1993). And referenda appeared on ballots around the country in record numbers to ban the deployment of sexual orientation as a protected civil rights category. Some of these explicitly insisted that homosexuality be discouraged in school—including state-funded higher education—as perverse, abnormal, and wrong. Spurious nomenclature such as "community standards" and "traditional family values" was (unsurprisingly) invoked, as it has been in past incarnations of reaction to bending the rules of gender and sexuality, and groups gave themselves names such as "American Family Association" and "Oregon Citizens Alliance" (Goldberg 1993) to smooth a patina of warmth and populism over their efforts to ensure democratic, ratified bigotry. Thus, inevitably, while lesbian and gay existence did begin to pop up frequently in classroom discourse, it was still the contestedness of lesbians' and gays' claim to "rights" that primarily framed the discussion—not people's complex experience as citizen-subjects. As one gay student of mine commented ironically, "I love hearing the question of whether or not I should be allowed to exist tossed around in a 'lively debate.'"

In the writing class, the reduction of lesbian and gay existence to a polarized "rights" debate may be of interest to teachers who are longtime fans of capital punishment and abortion as topics for infinite argument. But for many others in the composition community, helping students find their place in the sphere of academic and public discourse has come to be seen as something far more complex than the liberal tradition of argument would allow. As the editors of a landmark anthology of essays on postmodern rhetoric put it, "Language is a way of contending, in all senses of that word, with the processes through which discourse shapes human thought and social relations in a context of change and struggle" (Harkin and Schilb 1991, 6). For this reason, questions about who our students are, about who we are as teachers of language, and about the diversity of variables involved in helping diverse people to write and learn have become important in composition. A prodigious literature has in fact emerged, the aim of which is to reshape our consciousness of how different groups of people make meaning in a multiliteracied environment.

Yet even within this new way of thinking about writing—one which knows the importance of recognizing students' gender, race, and class identities because they are the sites in which subjectivities (and, inescapably, knowledge) are produced—the complexities of sexual identity are rarely brought into the picture (except, perhaps, in those instances when one is reeling off a list of identity-markers that teachers ought to "consider"). In fact, while lesbian and gay studies curricula have proliferated in colleges around the country (and even, in rare cases, high schools), and lesbian and gay scholarship is now being published copiously across the disciplines, remarkably little critical examination of homophobia and lesbian and gay reality has penetrated the generally flexible borders of the self-consciously interdisciplinary field of rhetoric and composition. In the last few years, anecdotal accounts of pedagogical experiments have surfaced at conferences and in carefully selected "multicultural" anthologies. Yet our understanding of lesbian and gay subjectivities—and of the role of sexual identity in producing discourse generally—remains quite limited.

I am proposing, quite simply, that the field of composition find out about its lesbian and gay students. The wave of national publicity currently surrounding lesbian and gay people has done little to reduce them from the abstractions they have always been. In an essay about teaching a freshman composition class whose theme was AIDS, Peter Bowen (1993, 153) hilariously and poignantly captures many heterosexual students' distilled notions of gay people when he describes an assignment in which they were asked to imagine being gay for a few hours:

> [J]ust as some students strategically evaded the assignment, others
> completed it by identifying evasion as the modus operandi of homo-

sexuality. "It's easy to hide it," one student's narrative journey began, while another simply wished she "could just be open about who and what" she was. Devoid of any sense of pleasure, desire, or romance, these "gay" narratives construct their protagonists as guilty, shame-ridden fugitives, who, when they were not "looking over" their "shoulder" to avoid detection, were looking forward with dread and shame to the prospect of coming out to family and friends. So intensely did students connect homosexuality with concealment that at least two women came out as gay men in their journal entries. While such testimonials, which were often disqualified in the last line ("but thank God, I'm not gay"), frequently empathized with the repression of gay people, they also preserved that oppression through their spectacular reconstruction of the closet.

If this is a common conception of the back rooms of ordinary citizens, rich and famous lesbians and gays don't seem to round out the picture, either. Though superstars such as Martina Navratilova, k. d. lang, and Ian McKellen, for example, are now "out," the sheer factuality of their lesbian or gay existence is remarkably satisfying to a public habituated to consuming the detailed "meanings" of its idols' lives. The risks that artists and athletes (as well as virtually all other lesbians and gays in our society) take in coming out, the rewards that motivate and enable them to come out, the ways they calculate those risks and rewards, the factors that position them to negotiate that calculation, the ways they locate and define and propel themselves within the master narratives of hegemonic heterosexual culture, the communities and identities they form within and in opposition to that culture—all of these things produce particular sorts of relationships to the world that have everything to do with who they "are." These are the sorts of things that teachers of writing need to know about if they are to help their students "contend" with that world through language.

Creating an academic environment in which the complexities of lesbian and gay subjectivity can enter public discourse will, first of all, entail "outing" realms of experience, fear, feeling, and prejudice that have not been substantively dealt with in our classes and departments before. Of course, this won't be easy, or it would have been done already. Behind the media glitz and hype, most academic institutions and the communities that contain them are *still* homophobic enough to discourage teachers and students from coming out or even speaking out strongly for change. Many schools and colleges still lack policies against discrimination based on sexual orientation.[1] And social visibility and political progress produce backlash; gay youth who are "out" in school have long faced verbal abuse and physical violence, raising their truancy and dropout rates (Tracey 1990; Comstock 1991), and antilesbian and antigay violence continues to escalate. In *The Women's Review of Books*, Felice Yeskel (1992) described the "increasingly organized and vocal" backlash on her University of Massachusetts campus after organizations and services for lesbian, gay, and bisexual students were put in place: homophobic graffiti, harassment, and intimidation impeded efforts to deliver a gay-affirmative quality of education and campus life. Various attempts to curb lesbian and gay art and scholarship get launched periodically, such as Jesse Helms's war on funding criteria at the National Endowment for the Arts, the fracases that erupted around Robert Mapplethorpe's work at the Smithsonian and in Cincinnati, and mass ad hominem attacks like the Briggs Initiative, which a decade and a half ago tried to ban lesbians and gays from teaching in California schools. (It was defeated after a concerted statewide mobilization of the gay community.) Lesbian and gay scholarly work still has dubious cachet on a resume—outside of a cadre of avant-garde institutions and departments it can, in fact, render a job applicant unemployable in many cases[2]—and has only barely begun to be suggested as a category of proposal or submission for conferences, journals, or other professional publications in composition and rhetoric, even when their theme is "multiculturalism" or "diversity." On a broader scale, people don't speak out when it might mean coming out because, aside from jobs, they risk losing homes, children, and legal rights, as well as community, friendship, and respect. Many lesbians and gay men have been estranged and disowned by parents and siblings in what may strike some as primitive rites of ostracism which are yet frequently practiced in otherwise "close" and "liberal" families.

I have been involved with lesbian and gay activism, performance, and writing for more than fifteen years. Yet I am also a lesbian teacher who, until four years ago, hesitated to come out to my students en masse and to many of my colleagues—except in protected parts of the "ivory closet" (Escoffier 1990), such as women's studies programs. I did come out to individual students, usually those I perceived to be gay or progressive. I believed in the political importance of being out, because closeted gay people contribute to the conspiracy of lies that render the false impression that the species we call people is generically heterosexual. So I asked myself what I had to lose by coming out to my students. In my relationship to them, wasn't I the one with the greater amount of power? Of course, the worst scenarios I could imagine, should the students homophobically rebel, involved violence. Other retributive acts I envisioned were ones in which I was reported for obscenity in the classroom or otherwise harassed. I surmised that the New York City colleges in which I then taught part-time were less likely than some others to support the actions of students who did such things, though I had no clearly articulated bedrock of safety upon which to rest this hopeful conjecture. If these schools did have antidiscrimination policies including sexual orientation, they certainly had not been publicized adequately to allay my own fears or the fears of others—faculty or students—in the same position. But besides the fear of such concrete reprisals or even violence, I feared something else, and that was the loss of the warm, open, supportive relationship I liked to have with my students, even if it was shakily based on false premises.

I can hypothesize that the closeted gay students in my classes remain silent out of some of the same fears. Although a number of students have come out to me privately, or have implicitly come out to the class, only one student out of all of my mainstream classes has ever explicitly come out publicly (and that was done hesitantly, as a gesture of solidarity after *I* came out). However, many students have had occasion to make or giggle at homophobic remarks, and a few of them have chosen to write about their dislike of gay people. Those times when I have asked them to read and discuss a gay-themed article or essay, there have usually been at least some students who have either laughed, expressed hostility (such as, recently, "Gay people are getting too bold these days"), or, when challenged by an idea or a fact they hadn't known, become defiantly skeptical. This has happened even in classes that have talked and written about a variety of other social issues and oppressions—classes of students who have expressed their outrage about racism, sexism, ageism, anti-Semitism, and other isms, from rhetorical positions ranging from the political to the senti-mental. Usually, they will attempt to mitigate their own anger and derision by citing ostensibly liberal rationales: sexual orientation is "private," "nobody's business"; they don't mind what people do in their homes, they just don't like to see two men holding hands or kissing on the street or in the subway; they just don't like to see boys dressed or acting like girls; they have known a gay person at work, in school, or in the community, and "accepted" the person just like anyone else as long as the person kept quiet about his or her sex life. Some of them are anxious to make it clear that they are not "prejudiced," and fre-quently deflect attention away from their homophobic feelings about gay people in general by invoking images of transvestites, transsexuals, and pederasts. By overlaying the actual discussion with what in usual social terms is a hyperbolized one, they seem to feel that their negative reactions are justified, in that they target what are generally perceived as extreme cases of sickness and absurdity.[3] Others frankly acknow-ledge their antigay feelings and beliefs, secure that cultural precedent has rendered them understandable and acceptable.[4] A *New York Times* article on homophobia cited research which demonstrated that "[anti-gay] hostility is far more accepted among large numbers of Americans than is bias against other groups," and that "while teenagers surveyed were reluctant to advocate open bias against racial and ethnic groups, they were emphatic about disliking homosexual men and women.

They are perceived 'as legitimate targets which can be openly attacked'" (Goleman 1990). Within composition, David Bleich (1989) has written about the results of a writing assignment he gave that asked students to describe a conversation with someone about homosexuality. He provides excerpts from the student texts that illustrate the majority feeling—about 60 percent—that "homosexuality was disgusting and gross—the most frequently used adjectives—and many men who did not actually advocate either extermination or gay bashing felt it was excusable to either beat up gays or 'throw them out the window' if one of them made a sexual proposal to them." Bleich found, however, a strong correlation between sexist and heterosexist forms of domination and belief: only one woman said she would react violently to a proposed sexual encounter, and "no women advocated mass extermination, though one said that bisexuals (who spread AIDS) 'don't deserve to live'" (23). Clearly, this sentiment extends far beyond the classroom: lesbians and gays are virtually the only group left facing mass discrimination with no federally mandated civil rights protection, despite such a painfully obvious need for it. And as gay legal scholar Richard Mohr (1988) has pointed out, in the absence of that protection, complaining of discrimination can simply compound it, since the voicing of the problem publicly identifies the complainant as a stigmatized person and enlarges the sphere of vulnerability.

The focus on multicultural curricula has evolved in recent decades not as an abstract need to make education itself more diverse, but rather in the context of political developments and liberation movements in the nation and the world. Our society's gradual extrication from the mythical notion of itself as monocultural is probably more the result of the dialectic between academia and activism than of anything that has happened strictly in one or the other of those realms. As various groups have resisted social marginalization and disenfranchisement, they have also argued for the importance of representation in academic texts, syllabi, policies, and programmatic agendas. Divisiveness within the academic community about the appropriateness of such inclusion has largely emerged from divergent notions of the place of ideology itself in the classroom. In composition, the argument at its surface level has been about whether or not ideology belongs in a writing class; at a deeper level, it is about *which* ideology belongs in a writing class, since new historicists, deconstructionists, social constructionists, and liberatory and critical pedagogues have repeatedly shown that culture is never neutral, unmediated, or value-free. Academicians who resisted ideology just at that moment when it ceased to be white, male, and Western were really fighting not just academic, but vast social and political change.[5] By the same token, writing instructors who exclude lesbian and gay existence from the sphere of knowledge and inquiry drawn upon every semester are, consciously or not, enacting resistance to a form of social reconceptualization that threatens to erode yet another set of borders which have heretofore demarcated comfortingly recognizable zones of insiders and outsiders.

The Idea of a Lesbian and Gay Culture

Often, when lesbian and gay existence is discussed at all, it is consigned to the category of "personal identity." Yet given that a new constituency literally had to form and mobilize itself in order to challenge a society staunchly safeguarding homogenously heterosexual constructions of itself in its media, its government, its arts, its advertising, its military apparatus, its religious and educational institutions, and its notions of the family—with exceptions labeled "deviant"—to insist on interpreting that difference individualistically as a matter of "personal identity" promotes an amplified form of disempowerment. What is probably most notable about the late twentieth-century lesbian and gay liberation movement is that by creatively using the new "social space" afforded by contemporary work and domestic arrangements (D'Emilio 1983a, 1983b) and usurping the imperative silence of closetedness, it has made possible the emergence of what some would call a new "culture."

Much has been at stake for lesbian and gay people, not only in coming together and mobilizing as a group, but in promoting a sense of this group *as* a group to the society at large. In "Beyond Tolerance" (1965), Robert Paul Wolff argued that pluralistic democracy is limited by its tolerance only for established social groups that it *already* recognizes as coherent, even if somewhat odd, configurations; tolerance does not extend to idiosyncratic individuals. "One might expect," he reasoned, "that a society which urges its citizens to 'attend the church or synagogue of your choice' would be undismayed by an individual who chose to attend no religious service at all" (37). Similarly, "agnostic conscientious objectors are required to serve in the armed forces, while those who claim even the most bizarre religious basis for their refusal are treated with ritual tolerance and excused by the courts" (41). Society, he said, is willing to extend the tolerance of pluralism only to groups it can distinguish as legitimate because they already conform in some recognizable way to dominant social principles; those that are "beyond the pale" are "treated as crackpots, extremists, or foreign agents" (44). Pluralist theory grants every "genuine" social group a chance to partake in democratic decision making and to receive its rightful piece of the pie: "Any policy urged by a group in the system must be given respectful attention, no matter how bizarre." Yet "[b]y the same token, a policy or principle which lacks legitimate representation has no place in the society, no matter how reasonable or right it may be" (45). Almost uncannily foretelling what would happen when a lesbian and gay political constituency would manifest itself thirty years later, Wolff wrote, "With bewildering speed, an interest can move from 'outside' to 'inside' and its partisans, who have been scorned by the solid and established in the community, become presidential advisers and newspaper columnists" (44).

For lesbians and gays, then, as for other groups (such as, for example, deaf people or speakers of Black English), self-definition as a social community or "culture" has been instrumental in gaining access to recognition and entitlements. For instance, though virtually everyone agrees that a federal civil rights bill protecting lesbians and gays is a long way off, the sheer fact that as a group lesbians and gays are fighting prominently for such a bill locates them within the familiar tradition of other groups, such as women and African Americans, whose long struggles for equality are well known and oft recited within popular lore. It is this familiarity that engenders enough public sympathy to produce local gains such as custody victories, domestic partnership benefits, bereavement leave, survivor tenancy rights, lesbian and gay studies courses, and occasional spots on sitcoms.

Anthropologists have attempted in various ways to define culture, though they have never reached absolute consensus. Most contemporary definitions suggest that a culture is a repository of shared ideas, systems, and meanings that find expression in patterns of behavior and custom within a particular social group. It is the *ideational* component that defines the culture: what the people *learn* more than what they *do*, though it is quite probable that they will have in common certain things that they do insofar as they arise from their common knowledge. The linguist M. A. K. Halliday (1978) describes a culture as "an edifice of meanings—a semiotic construct" and maintains that "language *actively symbolizes* the social system, representing metaphorically in its patterns of variation the variation that characterizes human cultures" (2–3; emphasis his). Arthur C. Danto (1990, 33) describes the way cultures become conscious of themselves:

> A culture exists as a culture in the eyes of its members only when they perceive that their practices are seen as special in the eyes of other cultures. Until the encounter with the Other, those practices simply define the form of life the members of the culture live, without any particular consciousness that it is just one form of life among many.

Halliday's and Danto's constructs suggest ways of conceptualizing "lesbian and gay culture," and in fact, this conceptualization has taken on wide currency. Lesbians and gays in the twentieth century have lived with an acute sense of difference within, and definition by, the culture of the Other, and have shared meanings in some loose form at least since communities based on sexual orientation began forming in the U. S. in the 1940s (D'Emilio 1983a, 1983b). This sense of difference was for a long time based largely on exclusion and negative representation: existing outside familial, legal, and religious sanctions, popularly portrayed as immoral and predatory, homosexuals when they met at all constituted a largely underground "culture" prior to the Stonewall uprising of 1969 that marked the beginning of mass resistance and liberation. Since then, an extensive network of cultural machinery has proliferated: there are gay and lesbian bookstores, churches, periodicals, plays and theatre companies, comedy clubs, books and presses, film festivals, resorts and cruises, legal and medical practices, political groups, parties, caucuses, and openly gay candidates, social organizations, families, artificial insemination centers, marches, sporting events, and academic programs.

Problems with "Identity" and the Construction of "Community"

Although many cite this boom in the artifacts of lesbian and gay identity as evidence of a "culture"—or, as it is more widely called, "community"—we happen to be living in a time and place where the very notion of community based on shared identity is being heavily interrogated. The lesbian and gay community, along with the women's community, communities of color, and other communities of affinity is torn between those who posit a sense of group coherence based on one shared characteristic and those who deconstruct the premise of coherence, insisting that identity is multiple and fragmented and that "communities" predicated on identification alone are illusory, and thus fragile and doomed to implosion. They are fragile not only because the multiple threads of our identities intersect in exceedingly complex and unpredictable ways, and one single strand may very well be an unreliable basis upon which to forge sociopolitical alliances—but also because the meanings of even seemingly singular parts of our identities are unstable and evade consensus. For instance, when I asked several undergraduate students who call themselves lesbian or gay what they meant when they described themselves that way, some explained that it meant being *attracted to* the same gender, others that it meant *identifying with* the same gender, others that it meant a feeling of "Otherness" or difference from those who conformed to gender roles, and so on. In a graduate seminar populated mainly by lesbian and gay students, some said they felt their gayness was something they had been born with while others said it was something they had chosen; some chose it because of same-gender attraction, some because it felt more "natural," and others—particularly women—because they felt that heterosexuality was an oppressive institution; and some saw it as a lifelong state, while others saw it as an ephemeral or situational state. This variety of definitions seems to be fairly typical of the "lesbian and gay community" at large: people may share a word with which they define themselves, but the condition signified by that word does not seem to be shared.

These two ways of viewing "identity"—as something that can be a basis for community formation and liberatory social change, on the one hand, and on the other hand as a construction so particularized and idiosyncractically realized that the notion of a "group identity" becomes diminished to the level of a wistful fiction—have been weighed against each other recently—primarily in academic, but also in activist, spheres. The debate rages not only between opposing camps, but also intrapersonally. If, for example, we accept that the category "woman" doesn't really exist but has been first a patriarchal, and then a feminist, falsely unitary invention—as postmodern feminist theorists such as Judith Butler (1990), Julia Kristeva (1986), and Nancy Fraser, and Linda Nicholson (1990) contend—must we concomitantly accept forfeiting proactive strategies such as the fight for safe and legal abortion, birth control, and equal pay, and the fight against rape, sexual harassment, battering, and social inequity? If "woman" doesn't exist, can any feminist agenda exist? Similarly, what happens to the category "lesbian and gay"—a category in which membership has at various points throughout the twentieth century meant risking police raids and imprisonment, street violence, incarceration in mental institutions, expulsion from jobs, families, and religious institutions, loss of child custody, dishonorable discharge from (or prohibition from entering) the military, McCarthyite inquisitions, disqualification from employment in education or government, and general social pariahhood—when we attempt to dissolve it? What does it mean in 1994, when the lesbian and gay rights movement is experiencing unprecedented political power and the notion that the group is entitled to "rights" is being argued and even accepted to a far larger degree than ever before, to say that to call oneself a "lesbian" or a "gay man" is a totalizing and ultimately meaningless fiction? In other words, how can we destabilize a category without also abandoning our claim to material and social entitlement and our repudiation of marginalization and prejudice? Or, as feminist theorist Susan Bordo (1990, 153) has put it, "Most of our institutions have barely begun to absorb the message of modernist social criticism; surely, it is too soon to let them off the hook via postmodern heterogeneity and instability."

Yet on the other hand, what does it mean to cling to old, comfortable identity categories for certain pragmatic reasons when we have deconstructed them precisely *because* in crucial ways they really weren't working, even for the communities built upon them? The lesbian and gay "community" has experienced the contestation and disruption of the very "affirmative" meanings with which it attempted to usurp old, homophobic ones. For example, many lesbian feminists in the 1970s felt that lesbianism was a matter of political choice and commitment in which gender, rather than sexuality, was the fundamental unifying factor; many gay men in the 1970s felt that gayness was most aptly expressed by sexual liberation; and many lesbians in the 1980s and 1990s have likewise claimed same-sex attraction and freedom of sexual expression as definitive properties of lesbian existence, and depicted 1970s-style lesbian feminism as an antisex, repressive regime. People of color and members of other ethnic groups have said that white gays and lesbians built a false, solipsistic, and racist image of "community" based on a gay-versus-straight opposition that was reductionistic of their personal and political experience. Many gay civil rights activists and professionals have been called "assimilationists" by radicals, while radicals have been called "extremists" and "too confrontational," and have been accused of tarnishing an otherwise improved public image for lesbians and gays. Many gays yearn for the right to marry (mass weddings have been performed at each March on Washington, as spectators wept and applauded); others have found spiritual redemption in milieux of radical promiscuity. Separatists and nationalists have been criticized for promoting hatred and reverse bigotry, while they in turn have accused others of self-denigration, limited vision, and misguided fear of militance. Many have felt that the acceptance of lesbians and gays into the military would be an important political step, while others—particularly those affiliated with feminist and leftist politics—have disparaged that goal for its implicit endorsement of a reactionary institution. Some feel that the all-inclusive word "queer" accurately describes anyone, regardless of their sexual behavior, who wants to reject the norm of heterosexual conformity by claiming the appellation, while others feel it is politically essential to distinguish between those who are "lesbian or gay" and those who are "straight," or to register the unequal status of lesbians and gay men in a movement that has not eradicated male privilege. Bisexuals have claimed that their existence inherently problematizes such binaries and that insistence on polarization has left their needs and perspectives ignored, while gays and straights have respectively attempted to reinscribe bisexuals as "real" denizens of specific identity categories.

In short, these and countless other arguments have not only divided the "community," but have led to the production in the gay press, at rallies, in courses, and in social situations of ongoing metanarratives about the community's fragmentation. When queer theorist Ed Cohen (1991, 71–72) began his title of a rumination on gay identity and community with the question "Who Are 'We'?" he was voicing an undercurrent of unease with absolute definitions that by the late 1980s ran like a fault line beneath much "community" work and activity. He writes in his first paragraph:

> I often leave [gay and lesbian studies] meetings wondering how these people ended up in the same room with each other, thinking it's a miracle that any mutual understanding exists, and trying to figure out what in the world we have in common. . . . I mean, I'd like to have the feeling—as one reading group participant recently characterized his feeling about gay bars in the 1970s—that gay and lesbian studies was a place where we didn't have to explain to anyone "who we are." However my visceral response belies this characterization: the more often I find myself at these collocations, the more often the nausea in my stomach seems to tell me that "I" have no idea "who 'we' are."

Writing this book from 1993 to 1994, I too have lost the certainty about "who 'we' are" that at one point galvanized my choice of a dissertation topic. Originally, I conceived this theme rather simply: lesbians and gays were a group still neglected in academia's movement toward inclusiveness of diverse social groups and particularly in composition's interest in "multiculturalism." I believed that an argument pointing out this exclusion and its debilitating effects on students would lead to the filling in of a gap. Today, I still partly believe that, only my concept of what I started out calling "lesbian and gay reality" has shifted away from something pertaining to a collection of identifiable bodies with clearly marked and recognizable ways of knowing and experiencing. Instead, I imagine a more amorphous condition that anyone might have, and that might be had or interpreted in myriad ways—though some do seem to feel that they experience it in ways that are shared by others. Partly because of this new way of thinking about who "we" are and partly for other reasons which I will discuss later, the meaning of "inclusion" as a goal has been thrown into question.

My conceptual shift probably started when I began to read about essentialism and became convinced that much of my political development—which was heavily rooted in identity politics—had been based on assumptions that one must be able to effectively generalize about a group in order to make meaning and bring about change regarding its members' experience and conditions. I can, in fact, remember many times when, faced with the contradictions of feminism (which was my generative political experience), I groped in a panic for resolving explanations, rather than admit—let alone embrace—the fact that there

were significant "truths" to be learned from the contradictions themselves. For instance, when someone would sincerely ask me to explain
what "feminism" actually was, I would feel overwhelmed at my perceived task of amalgamating the many feminist perspectives I knew
into a coherent statement which suggested a clear common denominator. The task was especially difficult since I was alternately around
feminists who refuted Freud's idea that biology is destiny; feminists
who maintained that women's gentle and antiviolent "nature" was
superior to men's natural aggression; feminists who thought that gender differences were entirely the result of cultural constructs; feminists
who thought that gender differences were the most organic, significant,
and intractable feature of civilization; feminists who wanted social
parity with men; feminists who wanted total separation from men;
feminists who saw economics as the root of women's oppression;
feminists who saw reproduction as the root of women's oppression—et
cetera. Yet it never occurred to me in those days to simply say that
"feminism" was not just one thing, but a plethora of things, all of which
had to do with ways of rethinking meanings of gender—even though
I had to rack my brains, and always unsuccessfully, to find a way
around that simple and, one would think, obvious fact.

I remember a time in the summer of 1980 when my family visited
me at the country house where I lived while I was in a creative writing
program. We were going out for a walk and it had gotten chilly; my
stepfather had not brought a jacket, so I offered to lend him a sweater.
My mother instantly became anxious at the idea of him wearing what
she felt was a "woman's" sweater, but knowing of my feminism and
anticipating a polemical reaction, she defended herself by remarking
sardonically, "I suppose you're going to say there's really no difference
between men and women." "Actually," I answered, "I think there are
enormous differences between men and women. I just don't think
there are big differences between sweaters." I thought it was a clever
answer that undercut what I perceived as her "conventional" anxiety
about maintaining proper gendered order and her lampooning of my
feminism. Yet what I think actually happened was that, calculating that
I couldn't possibly dent her bipolar notions of gender, I automatically
relocated my defense to another "feminism" which I presented as a
sort of "bottom line." In other words, she made her move based on
her belief that "feminism" was one thing; I made my countermove by
conveying the assumption that it was another thing altogether, and in
such a way as if to say, "Where did you ever get that idea?" Yet in
truth, both of our notions of "feminism" came from prominent discourses of the time, and I just as easily could have argued from hers if
it had promised to be effective. Nevertheless, even beyond the parameters of our argument I blotted out consciousness of the multiplicity of

meanings that were clearly contained under that umbrella heading "feminism," as if surrendering the certainty of a singular position would leave me—us, feminists—desperately vulnerable, unpositioned and unequipped to answer what felt like (but, in fact, wasn't) the singular force of patriarchal oppression.

Just as "feminism" seemed to need to be reduced to a single unifying principle (though that principle shifted remarkably often) in order to feel useful, so did the category "woman." I remember many maxims from my early feminist days: the feminist teacher who iterated that "women always apologize" (yet seemed uncomfortable when I or other female students expressed our views assertively); the ecofeminists who said that "men rape the earth" while "women nurture"; my straight feminist friends who reported their relationships problematic because men were "simple" while women were "complex"; and those amazingly opposite insights into gender roles in conversation: "men dominate conversations, women listen" and "men don't know how to talk, they're so taciturn, while women take all the responsibility for communicating." What is interesting to me, looking back at that time, is not just the fact that those generalizations painfully oversimplified, and only held up by simply bracketing out any information that threatened to puncture them, but moreover the fact that we so badly *needed* to generalize in the first place.

Generalizing was critically important; it was, for instance, key in the process known as "consciousness raising." Consciousness raising required each woman in a group to tell her story of a particular kind of experience—for example, her experience of sexuality, of violence, of having been raised and schooled as a female. What was discovered in consciousness-raising groups of the sixties and seventies was that experiences previously believed to be "unique" or fundamentally "personal" because they had been privatized were in fact widespread—and thus "political" or "social"—phenomena. If, for example, virtually every woman in the room reported that she had at some time in her life been sexually molested or that such an attempt had been made, one could make the highly useful generalization that sexual assault was not a story of an occasional lone "pervert" and an unlucky "victim," but rather of an event endemic to our society that was in some veiled way inscribed upon its notion of normal—rather than deviant—social conduct. Similarly, as each woman reported her frustration at having sole or primary responsibility for domestic work, even if she worked as many hours as her male partner did, that frustration ceased to be characterized as the mark of eccentricity or personal anomie and was recast as a systemic, and therefore political, problem. Thus, "the personal is political" meant that personal experience is *not* only particular and individual; it is symptomatic and illustrative of social beliefs, practices, and discourses. In this sense, generalizing enabled the formation of analyses, alliances, public discourses, and mass actions that produced liberating social change.

Yet a generalization outlives its usefulness at the point at which it reifies itself by ignoring the disruptive voices at its margins. Those voices don't only threaten to disrupt it; they are also disrupted *by* it, which is usually why they have gotten noisy to begin with. A classic example of such a voice at the margin is Sojourner Truth, the abolitionist and former slave who in her famous 1851 speech at a women's rights convention in Akron, Ohio, overcame white feminists' attempts to silence her rebuttal to an antisuffrage remark by a clergyman. He had claimed that women shouldn't have the vote because they were essentially weak and helpless—"women" in this case obviously meaning "white women" to all concerned—and Sojourner Truth interjected the following:

> The man over there says women need to be helped into carriages and lifted over ditches, and to have the best place everywhere. Nobody ever helps me into carriages or over puddles, or gives me the best place—and ain't I a woman? Look at my arm! I have ploughed and planted and gathered into barns, and no man could head me—and ain't I a woman? I could work as much and eat as much as a man—when I could get it—and bear the lash as well! And ain't I a woman? I have born thirteen children, and seen most of 'em sold into slavery, and when I cried out with my mother's grief, none but Jesus heard me—and ain't I a woman? (Flexner [1959] 1975, 91–92)

Almost a century and a half ago, Sojourner Truth in effect deconstructed the category "woman," and in the process of forcing its reconfiguration to include those arbitrarily consigned to its outskirts she ineluctably altered what was possible for those embraced—or locked—within it. Her articulation of her experience made possible the revision of "We believe women aren't so fragile that we need to be helped into carriages and lifted over ditches; in a better world you would see that we are competent enough to vote" to read instead, "Women have *already* proved—have, in fact, been forced to show—that we can work as competently as men, and therefore obviously deserve the vote." White women generalized about their condition, and mobilized to change it; a Black woman punctured their "we" with her "I," rendering their generalization obsolete and propelling the movement beyond its limiting parameters.

In 1984 Adrienne Rich (1986) wrote an essay called "Notes Toward a Politics of Location" in which she took a critical and revisionist stance toward her own former reliance on generalizing as a tool of political analysis and praxis. Here are some excerpts from that text:

I wrote a sentence just now and x'd it out. In it I said that women have always understood the struggle against free-floating abstraction even when they were intimidated by abstract ideas. I don't want to write that kind of sentence now, the sentence that begins "Women have always. . . ." We started by rejecting the sentences that began "Women have always had an instinct for mothering" or "Women have always and everywhere been in subjugation to men." If we have learned anything in these years of late twentieth-century feminism, it's that that "always" blots out what we really need to know: When, where, and under what conditions has the statement been true? (214)

Perhaps we need a moratorium on saying "the body." For it's also possible to abstract "the" body. When I write "the body," I see nothing in particular. To write "my body" plunges me into lived experience, particularity: I see scars, disfigurements, discolorations, damages, losses, as well as what pleases me. Bones well nourished from the placenta; the teeth of a middle-class person seen by the dentist twice a year from childhood. White skin, marked and scarred by three pregnancies, an elected sterilization, progressive arthritis, four joint operations, calcium deposits, no rapes, no abortions, long hours at a typewriter— my own, not in a typing pool—and so forth. To say "the body" lifts me away from what has given me a primary perspective. To say "my body" reduces the temptation to grandiose assertions. (215)

The difficulty of saying I—a phrase from the East German novelist Christa Wolf. But once having said it, as we realize the necessity to go further, isn't there a difficulty of saying "we"? *You cannot speak for me. I cannot speak for us.* Two thoughts: there is no liberation that only knows how to say "I"; there is no collective moment that speaks for each of us all the way through.

And so even ordinary pronouns become a political problem. (224)

I quote at length from Rich because I feel that in this essay she very eloquently articulates a shift that has been felt by many people involved in identity politics. "Location" is a concept whose metaphoric value hinges on a literal truth: our epistemological location can be charted, to an overwhelming extent, according to the specific juncture at which the various axes along which we are positioned in the world converge. If I am a "lesbian," its meaning for me must certainly have something to do with the fact that I am Jewish, a New Yorker, forty years old in 1994, highly educated, middle-class, with a history of political activism, with friends who have died of AIDS and friends who are now HIV positive, from a socially and politically conservative family, etc. I know, from extensive reading, how different it would have been to have been that ostensibly same thing—a "lesbian"—in Nazi Germany, in the U. S. during the McCarthy years, in Natalie Barney's salon in early twentieth-century Paris, as a poor small-town girl counting on the military as the only way out, as a Native American growing up on a reservation, as a working-class bar dyke, as a Salvadoran immigrant, as an elementary-school teacher in the Bible Belt, as a nun. And I know that in prior eras some of the feelings that I now call "lesbian" would have been instead attributed to "inversion," "romantic friendship," or perhaps to nothing at all; there might have been no words to describe this experience, and perhaps, as a result, no experience that I could mentally formulate (Foucault 1990; D'Emilio 1983a, 1983b; Faderman 1981).

Lesbian/Gay Identity and Composition

If my sense of what it means to be a "lesbian," then, is so bound up with these specific features of my own life, what does it mean to suggest that composition consciously address itself to, and in some ways reconfigure itself around, the needs and interests of "lesbian and gay" students? In other words, who are these people? What needs and interests might they have in common? On behalf of whom, and within what framework, am I advocating curricular change? These questions leave me feeling that I am tumbling down the slippery slope of social construction theory in a way that Carole Vance described in her keynote address at the 1987 "Homosexuality, Which Homosexuality?" conference in Amsterdam (1989, 21–22):

> [T]o the extent that social construction theory grants that sexual acts, identities and even desire are mediated by cultural and historical factors, the object of study—sexuality—becomes evanescent and threatens to disappear. If sexuality is constructed differently at each time and place, can we use the term in a comparatively meaningful way? More to the point in lesbian and gay history, have constructionists undermined their own categories? Is there an "it" to study?

Amazingly to me now, it hardly occurred to me to wonder about these questions when I proposed two courses in two different New York City colleges, one called Writing About Lesbian and Gay Experience and the other called Writing About Lesbian and Gay Issues,[6] both of which ran in the spring of 1992. At the end of those courses, I recruited students to be interviewed for this study, and it was only after interviewing them and closely reviewing their responses and the texts they had produced that I realized the extent to which (1) I had created generalizations in my mind about the issues lesbian and gay students faced in mainstream writing classes, and (2) I had *needed* to believe in "general rules" about lesbian and gay students, so that they could be presented wholesale to an academy that would have a clear mandate to change its policies and assumptions.

What all of my students did have in common was the awareness that they lived in a homophobic world, and that homophobia affected them in some way. However, the ways in which they seemed to be affected, as well as the ways they manifested responses to that homophobia in their writing acts, varied greatly. For some, homophobia had had a silencing effect on their writing, whereas others drew what they characterized as a perverse sort of inspiration from homophobia and eagerly rose to the challenge of writing *against* an oppressive social discourse. Some, after years of frustration with schools that obliterated lesbian and gay existence from the sphere of knowledge, wanted to write about nothing *but* being gay; others had become convinced that gay life was not appropriate academic material and that to write about it was "selfish" or "self-indulgent"; while still others saw their experience with homophobia as a useful conduit to apprehending other forms of social disenfranchisement, such as racism or sexism. Some saw our class as a way to "come out," or to come out in a new way—perhaps in an academic way, or a more deeply theorized way; some used it to find courage or language to come out to their families, to come out in their artistic work (often in the context of theatre), or literally to come out of a purely privatized experience of sexuality and into the realm of political activism and public discourse; others said they had never had a problem with being out; one student said that the class had, ironically, helped him to come out as a Hispanic, which he had experienced as a more denigrated part of his identity and which he had kept more hidden than his gayness; and one student, inadvertently "outed" to his father and thrown out of his house in midterm, was so numbed that he withdrew officially from the course but continued to sit in on it as—as he put it—the only "therapeutic" environment he knew.

Predictably, age, gender, race, and class locations of students positioned them differently regarding the ways they interpreted lesbian and gay experience as well as specific texts about that experience. Several heterosexual students probed the meanings of their heterosexuality in new ways, writing analytical papers which decentered an identity whose constructedness and power relationship vis-à-vis other identities they had never before considered. The heterosexual students also brought varied experiences to the class: one decided during the course that she was bisexual, and after the course began to call herself a lesbian; one, the child of divorced parents, had been alternately raised by her lesbian mother in an interracial household in New York and her father in a Klan stronghold in the South, and wrote about "the gay family" from an unusual standpoint; the daughter of a liberal Jewish family used course material about gays in the Holocaust to reread years of Hebrew school training and family discussions, wondering why the story of Nazi Germany had always been portrayed as a singularly anti-Jewish event.

Ultimately, sexual identity emerged—in some sense, for all the students, though usually most urgently for the lesbian and gay students—as an important epistemological context and social location in which writing acts were situated. Though the students' experiences and even the bases of their self-definitions were quite diverse, the totality of them resisting neat encapsulization, they were no more and no less so than than one would expect the experience and definition of any other identity component to be. In fact, the complexity and centrality of sexual identity in their meaning-making processes appeared so much to resemble those of other features of identity that the dearth of attention given it in writing classes struck me anew as an egregious omission. The students, for their part, in their interviews and in texts that they wrote in class expressed this view virtually unanimously.

Yet the reason for this omission was a mystery to no one. Leaving sexual identity out of the classroom is not an accident; it is an expression of institutionalized homophobia, enacted in classrooms not randomly but systematically, with legal and religious precedents to bolster it and intimidate both teachers and students. Consider, for example, the first paragraph of a recent memorandum written by a tenured, full professor of English at Cosmopolitan University,[7] one of the sites of my study, in response to a letter arguing for domestic partner benefits for university employees:

> I and other members of the Faculty Council have received a letter from Professor S., a member of the Association of Lesbian and Gay Faculty, Administration, and Staff, complaining that the absence of provisions for domestic partner benefits for either same or opposite sex couples is a serious failing. I do not believe that serious attention should be given to this complaint. Such liaisons have no standing in law or religion. If they are sexual relationships, they are widely regarded as immoral, they may be illegal in many states, and they will be thought offensive by the vast majority of faculty, staff, students, and their parents. In my view Cosmopolitan University should not appear to condone or endorse such relationships by providing special benefits to them. (Memo to Faculty Council Benefits Committee, November 25, 1992)

If, as this professor contends, homosexual relationships are "thought offensive by the vast majority of faculty, staff, students, and their parents," what does it mean for lesbian or gay students to approach writing assignments that ask them to do such things as to reflect upon the "self," to narrate personal events, to interpret texts in ways that reveal the subjectivity of the writer, and to write research papers on topics that are "of interest to them"? Think of how they are told to be aware of issues of audience, subject, and purpose, and to claim textual authority. Then consider the convoluted dimensions these rhetorical issues take on when lesbian and gay writers inevitably have to choose between risking a stance from an outlaw discourse or entering into the familiarly dominant discourses of heterosexuality.

Sexual identity is a component of personal and social identity highlighted for lesbians and gay men because homophobia in the culture makes it problematic. Because lesbians and gay men must constantly assess the consequences of being out and negotiate the terms of disclosure, often necessitating elaborate monitoring of what is said and even thought ("internalized homophobia"), a particular complication is woven into their processes of construing and constructing knowledge. Even for those who are most out, acts of making meaning involve constant confrontations with many of the premises and mandates of the dominant culture—creating an epistemological condition roughly equivalent to what W. E. B. Du Bois ([1953] 1961) called "double consciousness." Lesbian and gay writers do not have to be familiar with reader-response theory to know that in a homophobic society, the transaction between a heterosexual reader and a homosexual text can yield explosive meanings.

Sexual identity informs heterosexuals' epistemologies, too, though in ways that may be less immediately apparent to them—just as most socially dominant or validated identities are more dimly perceived as players in people's meaning-making operations than are the identities of Others. Heterosexuals, like white people, insofar as that part of their identity is not regularly challenged or scrutinized, are free to not regard it as a significant fact demarcating their selfhood; it is possible for them to experience it instead as part of a seamless garment of "human-ness"—which is to say, they frequently do not "view" or "see" it until it is touched by the discourse of the Other. Yet, as a number of queer theorists have pointed out, the homo-hetero opposition is firmly entrenched in Western dualistic thought, and although homosexuality is popularly viewed as a transgression against the norm of heterosexuality, it can perhaps more accurately be seen as a corequisite for it, without which there would be no pairing and "heterosexuality" as an identity could not exist. The fact that heterosexuality, as a culturally normative position, usually sidesteps metadiscourse and self-realization in a way that homosexuality does not doesn't mean that it is not a solid fixture in the interpretive and expressive processes of hetero-sexual student writers.

Tugging against the legacy of academy-endorsed homophobia is the precedent of CCCC, which for its 1993 convention included the category "Gay and Lesbian Concerns in the Profession" for the first time as an "area to be emphasized" in its program proposal form. This inclusion should in fact not be surprising, since the field of composition has increasingly come to recognize and research the vast significance that writers' locations within particular communities and social conditions have for their writing acts. One section of the proposal form read as follows:

> We have . . . acknowledged that merely studying writers and writ-ing—stripped from their personal, social, and political contexts—is insufficient as a way of coming to know the things that are important to us. Recent conventions with themes such as "Strengthening Com-munity through Diversity" and "Contexts, Communities, and Con-straints: Sites of Composing and Communicating" have highlighted the growing pains that any cross-disciplinary group endures. We are in search of what Adrienne Rich called "a dream of a common lan-guage," while at the same time we are trying to allow room for new ideas, growth, and change—the essential characteristics that make us cross-disciplinary in the first place. (Lillian Bridwell-Bowles, 1993 Program Chair)

This statement of an organization's thinking-in-progress illustrates that multicultural awareness has come to be regarded by rhetoricians not simply as an ideal of fairness, but as a fundamental attribute of effective pedagogy. Sites of identity and affinity are undergoing rigorous scru-tiny as shapers of students' epistemologies, language, and semiotic constructions. The spheres of most frequent analysis are those involved in racial-, gender-, and class-identity formation. I am arguing that sexual identity is inscribed in discursive acts in ways that both parallel and overlap with the effects of these other identities, and that including sexual identity in our consideration of diverse identities is a necessary component of legitimate composition research and practice. The fact that "lesbian and gay" may be an amorphous category and its meaning indeterminate is no reason to drop the whole enterprise, since genders, races, and classes are equally amorphous when probed beyond their surface coherence.

My primary purpose in this book is to illustrate some of the complex dimensions of lesbian and gay experience in composition classes. This involves exploring the forces at work for lesbian and gay student writers in the social act of writing, which will hopefully suggest the need for the recognition of lesbian and gay discourses among the multiple discourses that composition theory sees as the site of its work. Composition is a field whose structures have begun to reflect the premise that the social roles of writers are inscribed upon their writing acts. Given that composition is rapidly evolving within a social constructionist theoretical framework, it would appear inappropriate for composition to ignore the way that sexual identity—like race, gender, and class—is constructed through language.

In addition to social construction theory, my work is informed by related work that has been done on liberatory, or critical, pedagogy. Critical pedagogy has had wide applications in writing classes. Critical pedagogy asks students to analyze conditions in their lives not only to cultivate academic forms of expression and interpretation, but also to promote consciousness of the world outside the classroom, the ways ordinary people are actors in history, and a sense of language as a socially constitutive and transformative force. Critical pedagogy sees education as a key agent of social change, rather than as simply a route to personal improvement or mobility. It posits itself as emancipatory rather than assimilationist in that it asks students to read against hegemonic social discourses rather than with or into them. As lesbian and gay students *must* read against the hegemonic discourse of homophobia in order to come out—personally, academically, politically, publicly—critical pedagogy seems like an inevitable component of any gay-affirmative classroom practice.

Narratives by and about lesbian and gay students who have taken one or the other of my gay-themed writing classes, along with samples and analyses of their work, are at the heart of this book. I have included excerpts from my interviews with them, texts they produced in my class, in some cases texts they produced in prior writing classes, and reflective pieces that they wrote in my class. By illustrating what can happen to lesbian and gay student writers in a queercentric environment, I hope to expose some of the ways that composition might better serve lesbian and gay student writers and overcome some of its heterosexist premises. I also hope to demonstrate that homophobia in the classroom actually undermines composition's broader intentions, and that incorporating lesbian and gay studies into the framework of its thinking will benefit the field as a whole. I hope that my work will impel composition theorists and practitioners to reconsider some of the shape and substance and application of our discipline—that which at the least may be seen as adversely affecting a signficant group of our students, and which in a broader view has deleterious effects upon our whole society. Such reflection should have additional benefits to composition, in that it may provoke the imagining of new structures relevant to other communities whose Otherness also refuses conventional wisdom about the act of writing.

A Few Words About Classification and Definition

Of course, my language reaffirms the very polarity that I at least half-regard as fictive. If I acknowledge that the homo-hetero opposition is the product of dualistic thinking, and if I wish to puncture the rigid taxonomies and prejudices that have produced homophobia, it seems paradoxical that I nevertheless divide the students in my field of vision into "homosexuals" and "heterosexuals." Furthermore, such a division seems to beg the question of how people qualify for these categories in the first place. What *is* a "homosexual," anyway? Is it someone who *has sexual relations with* same-sex partners? Someone who *desires* same-sex partners? What if someone has sexual relations with the opposite sex but desires same-sex pairing? What if someone has sexual relations with members of the same sex, rejecting sexual desire for the opposite sex as not to be acted on (as was the case with some 1970s lesbian feminists)? What if someone has sexual relations with/desires both sexes? Or switches sexual object-choice in midlife? To what extent does the definition have to do with gender-appropriateness as determined by cultural norms? To what extent does it have to do with self-definition, for whatever reason? What if we are all really, as Freud claimed, polymorphously perverse?

I believe that each of these criteria has some claim to definition. However, I am going to fall back on the very schism that many in the field of gender studies are seeking to dismantle, *not* because I feel it reflects any underlying "truth" about human identity, but rather because I *do* feel it reflects a "truth" about our culture. Recognizing that the categories we exist within (and in fact our entire sense of "self") are social constructions should not lead us to a perception of these things as somehow lesser in their effects than we would have them be if we viewed them as springing from some essential source. However constructed, the products of our collective social imagination receive particular rewards, punishments, license, restrictions, affirmations, and violations in the social world. For present purposes, suffice it to say that many people indeed experience their sexuality in fluid or inconsistent ways, yet are likely to claim (or be assigned) particular sexual identities because our society in the twentieth century is disposed to file people in such ways in order to make sense of them. Because this system of classification has a significant impact on how people see themselves, and how people see themselves has a lot to do with how they behave and negotiate social meanings and how and what they write, I will use the categories "lesbian/gay" and "heterosexual" in my investigation. My only criteria for inclusion in each category are people's self-descriptions (or self-perceptions). (By "people" I refer to both specific subjects in my study and to hypothetical students I may theorize about—i.e., when I use the term "lesbian student" I mean a student who feels that that term describes her.) I will include bisexuals in the category "lesbian/gay" for lack of a more all-inclusive term, and because the two bisexual women I interviewed felt that the category "lesbian/gay" was suitable for them, if less precise than "bisexual."

The contemporary term "queer," used mostly by younger activists and artists, conveys in popular jargon the basic idea of a broad category embracing a spectrum of those who deviate from the heterosexual norm. I will occasionally use that term because, though colloquial at this time, it is more inclusive, and thus often more accurate, than any term currently in our formal language. In addition, the prodigious body of theoretical work in lesbian and gay studies now emerging from academic presses has broadly come to be known as "queer theory," and it is from that new canon of information that much of my own thinking has developed.[8]

I have encountered a problem similar to that which I have had with "lesbian and gay" with the word "community." At times in this book I use the multiple form "communities" to suggest that "the lesbian and gay community" is in fact not monolithic, but is comprised of numerous groupings that identify themselves, and whose members identify themselves, in various ways. At other times I employ the singular term "lesbian and gay community" for lack of a less awkward alternative and in order not to divert my discussion to a self-conscious explication of what I "really" mean. However, because a large part of the problem that has emerged from contemporary discussions of "community" is that we don't know what we "really" mean by it, I want to clearly establish that I am taking the liberty of using it as a deliberately imprecise abstraction which will suggest the many ways it is being interrogated and understood. In other words, I am not trying to signify a "real" community possessed of genuine shared consciousness; I am trying to signify loose configurations whose members have believed in certain ways at certain times that they were in some manner connected by shared knowledge or experience.

I began this work with the premise that homophobia and the silencing of lesbian and gay discourse *do* have a significant impact on students who do not define themselves as lesbian or gay, insofar as the silencing of any social group creates cognitive gaps for the whole community. Furthermore, any taboo wields an imperative for all members of a society to consciously position themselves outside the sphere of culpability; in doing this, they are complicit in reaffirming the taboo and frozen in their assigned social locations. As Diana Fuss (1991, 3) has written:

> To protect against the recognition of the lack within the self, the self erects and defends its borders against an other which is made to

represent or to become that selfsame lack. But borders are notoriously unstable, and sexual identities rarely secure. Heterosexuality can never fully ignore the close psychical proximity of its terrifying (homo)sexual other, any more than homosexuality can entirely escape the equally insistent social pressures of (hetero)sexual conformity. Each is haunted by the other. . . .

The defenses employed in self-definition aren't unique to the realm of sexual identity. They work similarly to enforce racial demarcations, for example, as described by Toni Morrison (1992):

> [I]t may be possible to discover, through a close look at literary "blackness," the nature—even the cause—of literary "whiteness." What is it *for?* What parts do the invention and development of whiteness play in the construction of what is loosely described as "American"? . . . Black slavery enriched the country's creative possibilities. For in that construction of blackness *and* enslavement could be found not only the not-free but also, with the dramatic polarity created by skin color, the projection of the not-me. (9, 38)

The presence of lesbian and gay discourses in the classroom, then, contributes significantly to our understanding of the ways that seemingly remote, autonomous identities are in fact deeply implicated in one another's existence—and of the ways that in writing we produce ourselves through our production of the other. Such notions suggest, too, that identity is not immutable and static, but rather may be reconstructed, repositioned, or redefined. The absence of a particular discourse may itself be a message. Michel Foucault ([1978] 1990, 27) has written:

> Silence itself—the things one declines to say, or is forbidden to name, the discretion that is required between different speakers—is less the absolute limit of discourse, the other side from which it is separated by a strict boundary, than an element that functions alongside the things said, with them and in relation to them within overall strategies.

No one in Western culture exists outside the complex web of signification forged by homophobic discourse and silence about sexual difference. Eve Kosofsky Sedgwick (1990, 185–86) has used the term "homosexual panic" to describe the condition, beginning in the nineteenth century, of so-called heterosexual men who define themselves *"as against* the homosexual" in societies where the prescribed condition of intimate homosocial male bonding (as in, for instance, the armed forces or sports teams) and the prohibited reality of homosexuality so startlingly resemble one another—where privilege and pariahhood thus exist so perilously close to one another—that men are in a constant state of paranoia and manipulability. If we conceive of sexuality as a sharply partitioned dichotomy, then knowing about the "self"—something students are invariably asked to do in writing classes, in some form—certainly involves problematizing the schema wherein we achieve self-definition through vacancies created by others having taken up particular positions on the psychosexual map. Alternatively, Adrienne Rich (1982, 20) has written of a "lesbian continuum" which includes "a range—through each woman's life and throughout history—of woman-identified experience; not simply the fact that a woman has had or consciously desired genital sexual experience with another woman." If we conceive of sexual identity as existing along such a continuum, then we are all located on it—and writing about the "self" involves other forms of social knowledge. Whatever taxonomy of sexual identity we might choose to employ, the subject of queerness is not the province of some faceless Other, but rather has social and epistemological relevance for everyone.

Notes

1. Such policies are increasingly being proposed and adopted, but they remain heavily contested. According to an article in the *Chronicle of Higher Education*, the National Gay and Lesbian Task Force reported that by early 1992, "at least 150 institutions and multicampus university systems had such policies." The article goes on to state that on some campuses, "proposals to add language on sexual orientation have led to heated debate" (Mooney 1992, A18).

2. Twenty-four states in the country and the District of Columbia still have sodomy laws on the books, their presence more acutely felt since the U. S. Supreme Court's *Bowers v. Hardwick* decision in 1986 upheld Georgia's sodomy law. Challenges to other states' statutes have subsequently been struck down, citing *Bowers* as a precedent. There is no national lesbian and gay civil rights law, and only a few states and a scattering of progressive municipalities have ordinances protecting the civil liberties of lesbians and gays. Thus, in most areas of the country there is no protection for lesbians and gays from discrimination in either public or private employment. In 1992 the state of Colorado adopted strict legislation in the form of Amendment 2, designed to preempt any such protection and override local ordinances within the state. The amendment states: "Neither the State of Colorado, through any of its branches or departments, nor any of its agencies, political subdivisions, municipalities or school districts, shall enact, adopt or enforce any statute, regulation, ordinance or policy whereby homosexual, lesbian or bisexual orientation, conduct, practices or relationships shall constitute or otherwise be the basis of, or entitle any person or class of persons to have or claim any minority status, quota preferences, protected status or claim of discrimination." At the time of this writing, the constitutionality of the measure is being debated up the hierarchy of the courts. An even more virulently antigay measure was voted down at the same time in Oregon after a nationwide mobilization to defeat it. In 1993, nineteen antigay rights initiatives were proposed—and ultimately approved—at the local level around the country, and antigay groups composed primarily of funda-

mentalist Christians are attempting to place initiatives limiting the rights of lesbians and gays on the ballot in eight states in 1994. The two state initiatives in 1992 previously constituted the record number of antigay rights initiatives in one year. Ultimately, then, there are no grounds for legally contesting religious or "moral" rationales for screening homosexuals from employment as teachers in most parts of the United States; it remains legal to fire a homosexual in all but seven states. (Mohr, 49; Goldstein, 24; Holmes, A17. Data on state laws furnished by National Lesbian and Gay Task Force. Text of Amendment 2 furnished by the Equal Protection Campaign of Colorado.)

3. For an illuminating discussion of "the sex hierarchy"—the vertical scale of social acceptability on which forms of sexuality are measured—see Rubin (1989).

4. Almost always, these responses change when I come out to a class. I am not suggesting that my students find me so engaging that this new knowledge wipes away all their homophobia, but rather that a visible and audible lesbian "I" in the classroom alters the players in, and thus the terms of, the discourse. Students' panicked need to demonstrate what they are "not" diminishes markedly when I am available to be that "not" for them. At that point, they generally perform their heterosexual identities through friendly "interest," "curiosity," "support," or at worst, polite dissention ("Because of my religion, I can't approve of the gay life-style, but. . . .").

5. A prime spokesperson for such academicians is Maxine Hairston. See, for example, her article "Diversity, Ideology, and Teaching Writing." Also see James D. Williams's review essay "Politicizing Literacy."

6. "Experience" was amended to "Issues" in the second course title at the suggestion of the department chair.

7. The name "Cosmopolitan University" is pseudonymous, as is the name of the other college in which I gathered data for this study.

8. "Queer" remains an emotionally contested word, not only because the borders of its meaning are in an ongoing process of negotiation, but because it evokes, particularly for older lesbians and gay men, vivid associations with humiliation and violence. A recent *New York Times* article compared the current reappropriation of "queer" by young radicals to young African Americans' use of the word "nigger," calling it "a defiant slap at an old slur" aimed to "demystify" and "strip" the word of its pejorative meaning (Marriott). In both cases, the generational splits on the acceptability of the linguistic appropriation seem deeply etched in divergent experiences. Those who recall being called "queer" or "nigger" at the time of an assault understandably find it impossible to cultivate the word as a term of empowerment. Those, on the other hand, for whom the word has symbolic or historical rather than personally experiential significance find it much easier to connotatively flip it and employ it without severe emotional distress.

Part Two

Ways of Teaching

Chapter Two

"Truth" or Consequences

The Lesbian or Gay Student in the Mainstream Writing Class

In current-traditional homophobic culture—that is, the vast so-called "mainstream" space occupied by those who haven't evacuated to hip, queer-friendly enclaves—some age-old problems remain in force for the lesbian or gay student writer. At the heart of them is a peculiar clash of pedagogical imperatives: to depict observation and experience "truthfully" (as encouraged by the romantic pedagogical tradition) and at the same time to depict them "falsely" (that is, to grasp at an adopted subject position so tenaciously that one becomes quite unmoored from the matrices that yield one's own—as demanded by homophobic society). A fairly typical example of the dilemma can be found by analyzing a writing prompt that was used for the entrance essay in a small college program for adult workers where I taught for several years:

> Select an episode in your life that you now see was important in giving you a sense of direction about something specific—for example, deciding to stand up for an unpopular cause, whether or not to go to college, to get engaged, to register for the draft.
>
> Write 3–6 paragraphs describing that moment or episode, giving your readers a vivid picture of the buildup of feelings and ideas that led to your decision.

Each of the examples furnished by the question suggests that the writer think about some decision to *act;* the action would have, clearly, significant consequences. But the significance of the action seems to be twofold in each case: first, it would seem that a sort of passage would

35

result from the action, that the protagonist of the narrative would be relocated socially regarding such things as status, responsibility, vulnerability to danger; and second, that this social relocation would force the protagonist into some new discursive space. In fact, there seems to be implicit in such questions ("Write about an experience . . ."; "Think of a time when . . .") the idea that shifts in social positions breed discursive shifts, or shifts in the subject's rhetorical stance toward the world.

The writer is asked in this case to select an episode that opened the door, essentially, to a discourse that endured to some extent ("that you now see was important in giving you a sense of direction"). For the lesbian or gay student, the experience of coming out may have been (or may be right now, or may be contemplated as) the most profound social and discursive repositioning of her/his life. Coming out has variously been described as a movement toward psychological health (Dunker 1987); as an emergence from confinement (Zitter 1987); as a structured transition during which an individual puts the entire social mythology about the immutability of kinship ties to its ultimate test (Weston 1991); and as a performative speech act that "can bring about the revelation of a powerful unknowing *as* knowing, not as a vacuum or as the blank it can pretend to be but as a weighty and occupied and consequential epistemological space" (Sedgwick 1990, 77). It has also been described as a highly charged and ambiguous enterprise, moving one simultaneously "out" into the vulnerability of devalued space that is exterior to a prestigious center and "out" from silence and obscurity into a brightly illuminated world of speech and cultural visibility (Fuss 1991). As Diana Fuss has put it, "to be out is really to be in—inside the realm of the visible, the speakable, the culturally intelligible" (4). The magnitude and tumult of coming out have been described in the psychological literature as "akin to the adolescent period of exploring and experimenting" (Coleman 1985, 35) though it often occurs much later than adolescence—even at midlife or later in many cases (Dunker 1987). (Its magnitude and tumult are, in fact, a creation of its prohibition; it is only in a society that forbids homosexuality that the tensions, both creative and destructive, of coming out can be experienced at all.)

However, unlike adolescence, which has received copious treatment in the humanistic, social science, and natural science literatures, and unlike religious, educational, military, matrimonial, reproductive, and other celebrated commencements, coming out remains an unhonored, unblessed, and confusingly unstructured passage in mainstream culture. Thus, although we have the statistical information that a good number of our students have been involved in such a momentous rite of passage—one whose purpose is to create a new "sense of direction" for the person's entire life, not the least of which is the kind of social adjustment she will achieve—within the predominant discourse of homophobia, the student will most likely reject this experience as a content-source of her college entrance essay. And whether the readers of the exam are concerned with "authentic voice," "sense of audience," David Bartholomae's preference that the writer "mimic the language and interpretive systems of the privileged community" (1985, 157), or virtually any other contemporary criteria of writing assessment, this elimination will cost the writer an opportunity to be evaluated on work springing from what may have been her most secure rhetorical footing.

In an essay called "Literacy and the Lesbian/Gay Learner," Ellen Louise Hart (1988) looks at some of the problems lesbian and gay students encounter within the current theory and practice of writing pedagogy. She points out, for example, that Peter Elbow's description in *Writing Without Teachers* (1973) of the uninhibitedness that freewriting permits—"Even if someone reads it, it doesn't send any ripples"—fails to imagine the predicament of the lesbian or gay Other in the classroom of a homophobic culture:

> [A] student who is lesbian or gay may not feel that she can express herself freely and honestly and she will therefore censor herself. She may fear "ripples" from the teacher or even more from her peers in the class. And so she will divert her first and best, her most vital idea, and the work of getting better at using language is getting undone. (32–33)

Hart's argument focuses on the ways popular techniques like freewriting can sell lesbian and gay writers short and on the environmental constraints that could be lifted to benefit these writers. Several years later, in a description of a lesbian- and gay-inclusive course that she teaches at the University of California at Santa Cruz, Hart reaffirmed her commitment to a pedagogy that "values personal experience writing and provides an environment where it is safe for all students to write *authentically*" (1992, 155, emphasis added). Hart's language suggests a fundamental alignment with the Elbowian belief in an inner authenticity which, whether contained or released, has a pure character of its own; her problem with freewriting has only to do with the politics of its application in a homophobic classroom. Yet her objection to Elbow has implications that extend beyond the singular experience of lesbian and gay students if we consider the ways that these students are flagrantly emblematic of, rather than different from, other individuals whose natural expression is also circumscribed by a judgmental, retributive world operating according to strict social rules.

Elbow's expressionistic rhetoric has been criticized by James Berlin

(1988), Andrea Lunsford (1991), and others for its idealization of the unique, stable "self" which is capable of achieving a sense of power through the control of language. These critics have pointed out that Elbow's view of the writer is of one disengaged from a social world, looking inward to discover some private "truth" that is "uniquely" his.[1] For lesbian and gay writers, the notion that identity and perception are individualistic matters of "private truth" has manifested itself poignantly in the historically disabling—yet popular—reification of the essential homosexual "self" somehow trapped and secretly sealed within a hostile and uncomprehending social environment that rages outside. A construct that posits lesbian and gay identity as outside the realm of the social also places it inevitably outside the realm of language and public discourse; therefore, significantly, one objective of the lesbian/gay liberation movement has been to disturb the seeming intransigence of the "public/private" dichotomy—as it is encapsulated in such aphorisms as "Who I go to bed with is nobody's business but mine" and "I don't care who you sleep with." Yet an Elbowian approach to writing insists not only on preserving the dichotomy, but on affixing values relevant to writing to each part of it: the public, social world of clashing ideologies and perspectives is the one where it is constantly, frustratingly necessary to edit one's thoughts—and is thus an environment which inhibits the natural flow of ideas; the private world of interior consciousness is a permissive "vacuum" free of judgment—thus an environment where hesitation and self-censorship are unnecessary, into which natural qualities of "voice, force, and connectedness" can freely creep (3–7). Elbow's solution is to create texts in this interior world, and then, after some polishing, thrust the best of what gets produced there out into the social world. Yet although Elbow acknowledges that "it's not just 'mistakes' or 'bad writing' we edit as we write. We also edit unacceptable thoughts and feelings, as we do in speaking" (5), he rather glibly elides the whole question of how the material of this inner world, ostensibly so unpunctured by social complications, can ever *be* unacceptable, as well as how it can be transferred to the outer sphere without dire consequences for the writer. Obviously, this paradox holds for all writers attempting this scheme, just as the notion that consciousness is asocial or monologic is rapidly losing credence among rhetorical theorists and throughout the academic world. At the same time, I would hold that lesbians and gay men experience the paradox in extremity, as they remain a group positioned in extreme vulnerability in our culture, vilified in religious, familial, military, medical, and juridical discourses without recourse to protection or compensation. Given the ways that lesbians and gay men function as social signifiers and the complex systems of "editing" that are involved as they insert themselves into public discourse, their dilemmas are instructive, emerging as flagship cases signalling the underlying hazards and concomitant limits in the usefulness of Elbowian writing pedagogy for all students.

Yet Elbow is hardly an isolated example of a strategy manufacturer who never thought to safety-test his device in situations where "having something to say" can mean risking vilification. Many contemporary writing theorists—and I include a range from Elbow's fellow romantic expressionists Donald Murray and Ken Macrorie to some of the innovators who have most helped to restructure the mechanics of writing classes to tap their strength as social, dialogical systems[2]—offer little more tangible comfort to lesbian and gay writers, who will often choose, consciously or not, to subvert their own most potentially exciting experiments with writing in the absence of an antihomophobic discourse. And although I, like countless writing teachers, have made extensive use of the strategies that these innovators have suggested and found them valuable, I can't help but think of who or what falls through the cracks as we attempt to ubiquitously apply them. Perhaps, conceived for generic students, those strategies are selectively employed by students to write about subjects that feel to them safely generic. Rarely will the student who is constructing a writing portfolio to be read and evaluated by an unknown faculty member choose to include a gay-themed text. And rarely will a student bring such a text into a peer response group. In fact, it is common in my experience for a writer who is working with material she perceives to be dangerous in any way to beg out of the usual public channels of review and ask that the work be read only by me, the instructor.

Which of our theories of writing *don't* explode when we consider their ramifications for lesbian and gay writers? Linda Flower and John Hayes (1988, 102) tell us, "If we can teach students to explore and define their own problems, even within the constraints of an assignment, we can help them to create inspiration instead of waiting for it." David Bartholomae and Anthony Petrosky (1986, 8) write about their innovative basic reading and writing course at the University of Pittsburgh: "The subject of our students' study . . . is their own discourse—their representations of the class's common material, the key terms and structures of their discussion and essays, the context they represent and imagine." C. H. Knoblauch and Lil Brannon (1984, 109) estimate that "the school setting . . . is a particularly rich, if not the richest, context for writing. . . . In short, the writing workshop becomes a microcosm of the intellectual community that 'school' is supposed to represent." Kenneth Bruffee (1980, xvi) says that his *Short Course in Writing* "is flexible because it begins where writing students of any age, experience, or competence can—and in fact should—begin: generating ideas out of personal experience, perceiving issues implicit in those experiences, and generalizing on those issues." James Sosnoski (1991, 202), responding to a series of texts collected in *Contending with Words: Composition and Rhetoric in a Postmodern Age*, observes that "students become the subjects they study." Marilyn Cooper and Michael Holzman (1989, x) see writing as a social activity in that it "is located in the social world and, thus, is fundamentally structured by the shape of that environment." Shirley Brice Heath (1983) urges that teachers and students become ethnographers of local communities. Ira Shor's (1980, 109) liberatory classroom aims to "challenge the ego-damaged characters of the students" in order for them to experience themselves as subjects; he feels that "integrative study formats offer peer-group validation" to combat alienation and foster community. "Composing means identifying the parts and bundling them; in the composing process we recreate wholes by establishing relationships between the parts," says Ann Berthoff (1981, 77).

And on it goes. Even the theories that offer the most promise of connecting writing to radical social change fail to imagine the perils at which outlaw sexual identity is articulated in homophobic culture—in which school is a primary site of violence. If homosexuality is indeed "the love that dare not speak its name," what are the conditions that seal it from—and what are the conditions that might bring it into—the realm of the discursive? As teachers of writing, we might well ask ourselves: What must happen in order for lesbian and gay students to become viable writers within these theoretical constructs, which span the breadth of contemporary rhetorical perspectives? Is it possible to reconstitute the writing class as an explicitly queer-safe place—one in which the calculated risks of articulating one's "own discourse" and one's "subjectivity" are markedly diminished?

To even conceive of reconstituting writing classes as "safe" places for lesbian and gay students is not simple. Asking students to write and read on gay-themed topics may represent a sincere but inadequate effort to correct the situation if there is no recognition that school has traditionally been used—and is still carefully guarded—as a principal site from which to enforce the reproduction of heterosexuality. Simon Watney's essay "School's Out" (1991) suggests that the institutionalization of homophobia in education serves a social purpose similar to that of schooling's maintenance of race, gender, and class hierarchies: to replicate the social order and the status quo which it was created to serve. Watney shows how antigay culture constructs childhood as a separate world of innocence and sexual nonidentification and the school as the site where homosexuality threatens to be "promoted." At counterpoint are a society insistent on believing that "homosexuality can only exist as a result of the seduction of minors by predatory older perverts" (392) who are "especially dangerous because they cannot necessarily be readily identified" (394) and an emergent gay politics that reveals the "ordinary human features" (400) on lesbians and gay men. But in any case, school *is* an erotic place, says Watney, despite its mission to restrict sexuality and produce heterosexual identities. It enacts this mission by lying to kids—convincing them that they don't have choices and erasing the existence of gays and lesbians from history and culture. Watney says that we should "invert the usual question of what children supposedly want and need from education, and ask what it is that adults want or need of children in the name of 'education'" (398). Clearly, it is the reproduction of heterosexuality through the school curriculum.

This certainly helps to explain why the contexts of literacy are so heavily policed. Countless print and graphic artifacts have been created within lesbian and gay communities, helping these communities to reflect upon and interpret their own experience and cultivating a sense—as simultaneously fragile and important as that of any other community—of connectedness, agency, and shared culture through language. Yet when lesbian and gay people enter the officially sanctioned headquarters of literacy training—i.e., the school—they are implicitly asked to check the literacy they have acquired in the lesbian/gay community at the door. Even in those rare instances when they are not overtly censored—and those instances are indeed far rarer than well-meaning liberals can imagine—it is enormously difficult for scholars and writers in development to insert a discourse from a domain in which they are supported and their experiences articulated into a domain in which their lives are simply not discussed, and in which they must always anticipate opposition should they initiate that discussion.

What, then, happens to them in a writing class? As composition theorists widely disseminate a view of writing as a social act, writing classes are increasingly being structured as sites of collaborative activity. Karen Burke LeFevre writes in *Invention as a Social Act* (1987, 2), "Invention often occurs through the socially learned process of internal dialogue with an imagined other, and the invention process is enabled by an internal social construct of audience which supplies premises and structures of beliefs that guide the writer." She contends that an unmediated "flow" of ideas is inconceivable for writers in a social world, and examines some ways that students get caught in the competing discourses and purposes of the various social collectives to which they belong. She raises the example of a student writing for a hospital newsletter who must suppress her data about the hospital's system of storing X-rays because her article must be approved by a public relations director who does not want the system to appear inefficient (133). "Given such situations, what is a writing teacher or tutor to do?"

LeFevre asks, dismissing the usual techniques designed to "open up" the writer and "unleash ideas" as beside the point. Her answer seems to me to be instructive for those of us who would like to help lesbian and gay writers negotiate the very real distance and dissonance between themselves and the heterosexist assumptions that are certain to exist among much of the audience they can assume in an academic setting. Rather than relying on the romantic idea that all students are free to draw upon a "voice within," LeFevre suggests that

> we can help writers articulate their concerns and their perceptions of the constraints they face. We can talk about ways they might test the accuracy of their perceptions, or work around their constraints, or discuss problems with those responsible for creating and enforcing certain rules and policies. The writers and their supervisors [read: peers, professors] may or may not try to change the status quo. What we cannot do is act as if these problems do not exist, as if people's jobs [read: lives, mental health, social existences] are not at stake, as if invention means asking the journalist's five W's and an H without taking into account the very real implications that these choices have for writers in their social contexts. (134)

When students write about lesbian and gay issues and experiences, the context of homophobia multiplies the rhetorical acrobatics that any writer must perform given the indeterminacy of the epistemological positions of real and imagined audiences. Following LeFevre's example, writing teachers need to be able to help students clarify the complex intentions, possible interpretations and reader-responses, and consequences that they will have to negotiate. Without a clearly established counterhomophobic discourse in the classroom, it is unlikely that such an enterprise could even be considered.

Ultimately, giving lesbian and gay discourse play in a composition class will be fraught with significance for heterosexual students as well, since all people are players in the large social drama in which sexuality is constructed, just as we collectively construct social dramas regarding race, gender, and class. The inclusion of lesbian and gay discourse activates, in a new and particularly charged way, a consciousness of how multiple discourses within a composition class are both contiguous and overlapping. Exploring the social realities of lesbians and gay men—something virtually everyone in our culture has feelings about—invites students to confront some of their own particularly charged processes of symbol making and the linguistic constructions that enable these processes; understanding that they construct reality is also key to recognizing their singular ability as human thinkers to reconstruct it. Ironically, it is very possible that a sustained examination of "lesbian and gay realities" will lead to the deconstruction and evaporation of the very notion and term, as students begin to question the genesis of the borders which bound supposedly discrete and autonomous identities. As Bakhtin (1981, 293) has said, "[L]anguage . . . lies on the borderline between oneself and the other. The word in language is half someone else's." A composition class is a particularly fit site in which to discover that the word of the Other subtly colludes with, melds with—indeed, is embedded within—one's own.

The burgeoning field of lesbian and gay studies offers much to facilitate such explorations. Eve Kosofsky Sedgwick (1990, 1991), Judith Butler (1990, 1991), Diana Fuss (1989, 1991), Carole Vance (1983, 1989), and numerous other theorists of sexuality have challenged the systems of classification by which identities become inscribed, predominantly the dualistic thinking that has produced the homo-hetero opposition. Given that some form of asking students to examine the self is a popular assignment in composition classes, this opposition may provide a fertile field for analysis. In the popular imagination, homosexuals are made—by overbearing mothers and withdrawn fathers, by prolonged immature attachment to the mother, by hormone imbalances, by small hypothalamuses—while heterosexuals just naturally exist in nature. Much of the writing that has come out of lesbian and gay studies—influenced as it is by postmodern theory—challenges this dichotomy by demonstrating how *all* identities are constructed by historical time, place, and circumstance (Adam 1987; Butler 1990, 1991; D'Emilio 1983a, 1983b; Kennedy and Davis 1994; Duberman, Vicinus, and Chauncey 1990; Faderman 1981, 1991; Patton 1990; Vance 1983, 1989).

Lesbian and gay studies has much to offer enlightened writing programs because it exposes in unexpected ways our modes of making meaning and the ways systems of signification structure our thinking. It pushes us, too, to negotiate more self-consciously our relationship to a real or imagined audience. Just as multiple discourses of culture and identity have remapped the geography of academic disciplines in the last three decades, perhaps the nineties will be a time when it is recognized that two emerging interdisciplinary fields—rhetoric and composition on the one hand, lesbian and gay studies on the other—considerably illuminate each other.

Notes

1. The attack on Elbow's expressivism has been countercriticized recently by Stephen Fishman and Lucille McCarthy (1992). Fishman and McCarthy's alternative and affirmative reading of Elbow, in my view, involves a misreading of his critics. While Fishman and McCarthy defend Elbow as a theorist

concerned with the social *purpose* of writing—a point that, to my knowledge, hasn't been particularly debated by his detractors—they neglect to address Elbow's view of writing as an asocial *process.* When Fishman quotes Elbow— "Writing is a string you send out to connect yourself with other consciousnesses" (651)—he seems to miss the subtext I see, which is, "*Until* then, you 'yourself' as writer are *dis*connected from those other consciousnesses." In other words, Fishman seems to be underscoring the notion that the writing act *does* happen in isolation, moving you *toward* others without being already informed *by* others.

2. I think of Karen Spear (1988) and Kenneth Bruffee (1980, 1983) and their collaborative group paradigms; Ann Berthoff (1982) and her dialectical notebooks; Toby Fulwiler (1987) and his journals across the curriculum; Pat Belanoff (Belanoff and Dickson 1991) and her writing portfolios.

Chapter Three

Lesbian and Gay Studies
Landscape of an (Inter)Discipline

Like many socially oppressed groups eager to redress the injustices they confront daily, the lesbian and gay community has often felt pressured to subordinate some of the complexity of what it knows about itself to the exigencies of political utility. In the past decade, however, a new generation of scholars and theorists has leapt over immediately practical considerations of what will be good for the community and how it can achieve that good to question some of the very premises strategists work with. For them, social change is not just a matter of ensuring lesbians and gays a place in the recognized social order by inserting themselves visibly into existing public policy, but rather involves massive reconceptualization and reconfiguration of the social order. Whereas a lesbian/gay activist agenda might tend to be predicated on neo-Enlightenment democratic ideals and thus privilege the achievement of equal rights as a goal, postmodern theorists are more apt to ask, "What is a 'right'? Who gives it? Who imagines it in the first place? What makes any right 'inalienable'? What beliefs have shaped our sense of 'entitlement' and designated the categories of people who are 'entitled'?" And although many gays and lesbians have argued for the adoption of the term "sexual orientation" over "sexual preference" because no one can try to persuade them to abandon a condition they haven't chosen, many of the theorists are quick to illustrate the ways that sexual identities are social, historical, and ideological products, created by consciousness rather than perceived by it.[1]

If there is any "big bang" at the center of the explosion of lesbian and gay studies, it is certainly the notion of identity itself, and the shattering of old assumptions that identity is stable, coherent, and identifiable. Although romantic notions of an integrated self trudging through a linear existence have been extensively quashed throughout the many branches and applied sectors of postmodern theory, the indeterminacy of sexual identity in particular was an idea that fueled a debate among queer scholars which raged throughout the eighties. In this debate, the concept of sexual essentialism (a model in which sexual identity is regarded as an eternal, biological state that inheres naturally in a person, has universal meaning, and transcends historical circumstance) was pitted against a constructionist interpretation (through which sexual identity is understood as a product of particular socio-economic forces and the production of homosexual identities is viewed as a relatively recent phenomenon). During that time, methods of interpreting lesbian and gay experience and the sexual past changed as poststructuralist thought reconfigured the way we configure.

Some of the terms of the essentialist/constructionist debate might be roughly summarized by two representative sample theorists, one from each ostensible side of the divide. I use the word "ostensible" because, as they both suggest, there has been little consensus about the precise nature of the division between them. According to historian John Boswell (1990), who has been widely tagged as an essentialist, the concept of "debate" itself is specious here, since within academia, the "constructionist" majority has designated certain people "essential-ists" who don't self-identify as such. Thus the controversy is not, in fact, "a dialogue between two schools of thought, but . . . a critique by revisionists of assumptions believed to underlie traditional historiogra-phy" (67). That said, he explains that the "fundamental assumption of 'essentialists'" is "that humans are differentiated at an individual level in terms of erotic attraction, so that some are more attracted sexually to their own gender, some to the opposite gender, and some to both, in all cultures" (68). Boswell also gives his account of the fractured constructionist position:

> Some constructionists argue that a "homosexual identity" did not exist before a certain date (often the second half of the nineteenth century); others that "homosexuality" was not found before such a date; others that although "homosexuality" was known throughout history, "gay people" did not exist until relatively recently. Some writers argue generally that "sexuality" is not a constant; others posit more specifically that social constructs of sexuality are not constant. A more sweeping and profound version of these views is that there is no aspect of sexuality that is not socially constructed. (68)

Although Boswell claims that his own classification as an essentialist originated in accusations by constructionists, he does maintain (Mass 1990, 209), "I'm not a constructionist, and I think there were people with sensibilities much like those of modern gay people in almost every pre-modern society," and says definitively, "Those whose eroticism is primarily directed toward their own gender I'd call 'gay'" (222–23).

Speaking from the other "side," self-professed social constructionist anthropologist Carole Vance (1989, 14) maintains that essentialism is also a fractured perspective, and a far more entrenched one in our society, as "we have all been brought up to think about sexuality in essentialist ways":

> Essentialism can take several forms in the study of sexuality: a belief that human behavior is "natural," predetermined by genetic, biological, or physiological mechanisms and thus not subject to change; or the notion that human behaviors which show some similarity in form are the same, an expression of an underlying human drive or tendency. Behaviors that share an outward similarity can be assumed to share an underlying essence and meaning. . . . Gender and sexuality have been the very last domains to have their natural biologized status called into question.

Vance explains that essentialist premises permeated some of the first studies of lesbian and gay history:

> Early work in lesbian and gay history attempted to retrieve and revive documents (and lives) which had been lost or been made invisible. These lives were first conceived of as lesbian or gay, and the enterprise akin to a search for historical roots, an attempt to document the existence of gay people and experience. This was history against the grain, against the heterosexist narrative: in short, activist history and history as political work. (20)

Vance's view of historical work echoes that of social constructionist historian John D'Emilio (1983a, 101), who contends that "[I]n building a movement without a knowledge of our history, we instead invented a mythology. This mythical history drew on personal experience, which we read backward in time." The myth was predicated on the politically optimistic notion that "gay men and lesbians always were and always will be. We are everywhere; not just now, but throughout history, in all societies and all periods." By contrast, Vance's description of a social constructionist interpretation of lesbian and gay identity foregrounds *dis*continuity across time and culture:

> At minimum, all social construction approaches adopt the view that physically identical sexual acts may have varying social significance and subjective meaning depending on how they are defined and understood in different cultures and historical periods. Because a sexual act does not carry with it a universal social meaning, it follows that the relationship between sexual acts and sexual identities is not a fixed one, and it is projected from the observer's time and place to

others at great peril. Cultures provide widely different categories, schemata, and labels for framing sexual and affective experiences. The relationship of sexual act and identity to sexual community is equally variable and complex. These distinctions, then, between sexual acts, identities, and communities are widely employed by constructionist writers. . . . A further step in social construction theory posits that even the direction [of] sexual desire itself, for example, object choice or hetero/homosexuality, is not intrinsic or inherent in the individual but is constructed. Not all constructionists take this step. . . . (18)

The last contention of social constructionists described by Vance has been difficult for many newcomers to the concept to swallow, and might best be amplified by an analogy created by anthropologist Gayle Rubin (1989, 276) to explain the limits of purely biological accounts of human preferences. Just as "[t]he belly's hunger gives no clues as to the complexities of cuisine," says Rubin, biology is a prerequisite for human sexuality yet cannot "determine its content, its experiences, or its institutional norms." In other words, the sex drive is biologically ordained; a preference for leather is not.

Historians have played a pivotal role in the widespread acceptance of the social constructionist position. Although an early compilation of documentary work by Jonathan Katz called *Gay American History* (1976) was cherished for its rare accounts offering "evidence" of a gay past— such as accounts of women who passed as men well enough to join the army and marry other women, homosexual witch-hunts in Boise, Idaho, and George Washington's announcement of the court-martial of a lieutenant for sodomy—this sort of objectivist perspective later came to be criticized (by Katz himself, as well as by others) for its essentialist, transhistorical conceptualization of what "gay" meant; that is, it never questioned the validity of interpreting behaviors acted out in prior eras within contemporary semiotic frameworks. For example, until the late nineteenth century sodomy was regarded as an act anyone could be guilty of *committing* rather than an indicator of a pervasive pathological condition one *had* or who one fundamentally *was;* the "sodomite" then was different from, for instance, the "homosexual" whose identity has been the object of military scrutiny and regulation since World War II. In that vein, Lillian Faderman's *Surpassing the Love of Men* (1981), which followed a perceived continuum of romantic friendships between women from the Renaissance to the present, was criticized for its elision of the distinctions between erotic and nonerotic affectional love; yet in doing so it implicitly interrogated the nature of the category "lesbian" and illuminated the ways that its meanings are situated in historical context. For example, Faderman recounts the 1811 libel suit brought by Marianne Woods and Jane Pirie, the real-life antecedents of Lillian Hellman's boarding-school mistresses in her play *The Children's Hour,* against the grandmother of one of their pupils whose charges of lesbianism led them to lose their life savings when all the other parents subsequently removed their children from the school. Faderman writes of their successful case:

> The lawyers for Woods and Pirie felt it crucial to establish their characters as unimpeachable, and therefore attributed to them all the important moral values of their day: The women were Christian, they were sober and industrious, and, most of all, they were capable of enduring and self-sacrificing friendship. To be willing to involve one-self in totally committed female friendship was an indication of the seriousness of one's moral character. Paradoxical as it seems to us today, it would have been self-defeating for the women's lawyers to argue that Miss Woods and Miss Pirie had only a cold business rela-tionship. They sought to establish that the women loved each other with great, unquestioning intensity, knowing that the judges would agree that such overwhelming love (which was ennobling) would not permit the demon of sex (which was debasing) to wend its way in. The lawyers offered as evidence of the "purity" of these women a letter which, in the twentieth century, might well have been used by Dame Gordon's lawyers as proof that the two women were in love and hence probably lovers. . . . A twentieth-century judge could never declare as Lord Justice-Clerk Hope did in the early nineteenth cen-tury, "according to the known habits of women in this country, there is no indecency in one woman going to bed with another." (151–52)

Michel Foucault's *The History of Sexuality* ([1978] 1990) is the work that has probably had the most monumental influence on contempo-rary framings of the sexual past. Foucault rejects what he calls the "repressive hypothesis," or the view that prohibition of biological drives has been the primary historical fact about sex, in favor of examining the ways that social institutions have "put [sex] into discourse" (10–11). He examines the ways that the church, medicine, psychiatry, and the criminal justice system have all produced discourses about sex, often structured around forms of confession—to priest, doctor, analyst, jurist—variously promising to reward the speaker with absolution, health, relief, or reprieve. It was within this context in the Freudian nineteenth century, says Foucault, that "the . . . homosexual became a personage, a past, a case history, and a childhood, in addition to being a type of life, a life form, and a morphology, with an indiscreet anatomy and possibly a mysterious physiology . . . the homosexual was now a species" (43). John D'Emilio has further illustrated from a socialist perspective how the concept of homosexual identity—as opposed to homosexual *behavior* or *acts*—first began to emerge in the late nine-teenth century. In an essay called "Capitalism and Gay Identity" (1983a, 103–110), he traces the shifting significance of the nuclear family under capitalist expansion from a site of economic stability to "an affective unit, an institution that produced not goods but emotional satisfaction and happiness." As individuals became wage earners outside the home and were released from dependence on a self-sufficient household economy, it became "possible for homosexual desire to coalesce into a personal identity—an identity based on the ability to remain outside the heterosexual family and to construct a personal life based on attraction to one's own sex." Contradictorily, though, capitalism "push[es] men and women into families, at least long enough to reproduce the next generation of workers. The elevation of the family to ideological preeminence guarantees that capitalist society will reproduce not just children, but heterosexism and homophobia."

Social histories by D'Emilio (1983b), Barry Adam (1987), Toby Marotta (1981), Andrea Weiss and Greta Schiller (1988), Allan Bérubé (1991), and Martin Duberman (1993) delineate the formation in the decades before Stonewall of gay and lesbian communities in urban centers, whose incipient power was in place and capable of erupting virtually overnight into a mass liberation movement when triggered by a straw-that-broke-the-camel's-back police raid of a Greenwich Village gay bar on June 27, 1969. During the post–World War II era, in the midst of a virulent McCarthyism whose witches were homosexuals as well as communists, the first attempts at gay emancipation were initiated by members of the political left. The first members of the Mattachine Society, founded by Harry Hay in Los Angeles in 1951, were gay Marxists who sought to develop an analysis of homosexual oppression as deeply rooted in social structures, and internalized homophobia as the product of false consciousness which erroneously transposed societal ills into individual aberrations. They also sought to inculcate in homosexuals the idea that they were a distinct minority culture, and thus a group capable of organizing to fight for its own interests (D'Emilio 1983b, 66, 77). Later, these goals were dealt a crippling blow when accommodationists came to dominate the organization, insisting on the privatization of sexuality and the essential "sameness" of gay and straight people—an approach that Adam describes as "founded on an implicit contract with the larger society wherein gay identity, culture, and values would be disavowed (or at least concealed) in return for the *promise* of equal treatment" (64). The first lesbian organization, the Daughters of Bilitis, was created in 1955 out of the same assimilationist ideology. In the 1960s, political leaders like Barbara Gittings and Frank Kameny spearheaded a tendency back toward militant action and radical analysis. Gittings, as editor of DOB's journal *The Ladder,* insisted that it take an "antisick" stance and openly challenged the membership's debilitating dependence on the wisdom of the medical profession (Adam, 71; D'Emilio

1983b, 170). Kameny also vehemently dismissed the movement's veneration of professionals, identifying the Black civil rights struggle as a model for gay liberation and countering questions of etiology and arguments that homosexuals should "change" with pointed analogies:

> I do not see the NAACP and CORE worrying about which chromosome and gene produced a black skin, or about the possibility of bleaching the Negro. . . . I do not see any great interest on the part of the B'nai Brith Anti-Defamation League in the possibility of solving problems of anti-Semitism by converting Jews to Christians. . . . We are interested in obtaining rights for our respective minorities AS Negroes, AS Jews, and AS HOMOSEXUALS. Why we are Negroes, Jews, or Homosexuals is totally irrelevant, and whether we can be changed to Whites, Christians, or heterosexuals is equally irrelevant. (Quoted in D'Emilio 1983b, 153)

In San Francisco, the emergence of the Beat Generation—which included a number of gay writers, such as Allen Ginsberg—created a cultural base for a counterdiscourse about sexuality and the nuclear family. The Beat artists' rejection of middle-class norms and values offered an alternative construction of outsiderhood; suddenly gays could indict the institutions that had crushed them in a language popularly understood as hip and nonconformist, and which had the dignity of social protest (D'Emilio 1983b, 177–82).

In a sense, the cultural production of the Beats and the cultural and scholarly publications of the homophile societies—such as *The Ladder* and Mattachine's *ONE* magazine and *Homophile Studies*—were early incarnations of what would in later decades evolve as the institutional discipline of lesbian and gay studies.[2] For lesbian and gay people, as for other marginalized groups, the impetus toward the creation of a discipline about themselves has had at least two roots. The first has been the desire to create a discourse about themselves *for* themselves by generating knowledge of their own history and culture. The second is the desire to enter a larger societal discourse by making their reality operant within scholarly inquiries into what is broadly (and homogenizingly) known as "humanity." The work of the fifties and sixties, conducted entirely outside formal educational institutions and under the continuous threat of police raids, job loss, and harassment, represented a determined attempt to achieve the former objective. The latter remains a challenge for the nineties.

In the seventies, the first decade after Stonewall, the "and" in "lesbian and gay studies" (the academic reality of the larger term being itself yet a shimmering phantasm on the horizon rather than an actual presence) denoted separation rather than linkage. Despite the issue of several volumes in the Stonewall spirit of "pride" infused with the notion that "we are everywhere"—such as *Out of the Closets: Voices of Gay Liberation* ([1972] 1992) and *Lavender Culture* (1978), collaboratively edited by Karla Jay and Allen Young, and *Word is Out* (Adair and Adair 1978), based on a documentary film—gay men and lesbians tended to frequent different bookstores or, at least, peruse distinctly separate sections. Most of the scholarly and literary work of that time was produced *outside* formal academic channels (Escoffier 1990). That which came out of lesbian liberation was frequently gender-separatist and politicized in a feminist context, while gay male work reflected the celebratory nature of a sexual revolution. Lesbian feminists were further subdivided by ideology—socialist lesbian feminists generated a materialist critique of capitalist patriarchy, lesbians of color perceived multiple fronts of oppression, while mainly white radical lesbian feminists believed that women and men were endowed with fundamentally different natures, and opposed "the patriarchy" by attempting to create a separate women's culture, politics, spirituality, and economic sphere. Writers like philosopher Mary Daly (1973, 1978), theorists Charlotte Bunch (1975) and Ti-Grace Atkinson (1973), theorist/novelist Rita Mae Brown (1975a, 1975b), and poet/essayist Adrienne Rich (1978, 1979, 1982) delineated female universes which were epistemologically, ontologically, and linguistically lesbian. The Radicalesbians in New York City produced a paper called "The Woman-Identified Woman" in 1970 that defined lesbianism in terms that were taken up by others for the rest of the decade and beyond:

> What is a lesbian? A lesbian is the rage of all women condensed to the point of explosion. . . . It is the primacy of women relating to women, of women creating a new consciousness of and with each other which is at the heart of women's liberation and the basis for the cultural revolution. (Quoted in Bunch 1987, 185 and Brown 1975a, 63).

Bonding with women was seen as a source of power. "[A] Lesbian is a woman whose sense of self and energies, including sexual energies, center around women—she is woman-identified," wrote Bunch (1975, 30). Rich added to the definition in 1976, "It was a sense of desiring oneself; above all, of choosing oneself; it was also a primary intensity between women, an intensity which in the world at large was trivialized, caricatured, or invested with evil" (1979, 200). When literary critic Barbara Smith published "Toward a Black Feminist Criticism" in the lesbian/feminist journal *Conditions* in 1977, she wrote that she wanted to "try to understand what the existence or non-existence of Black lesbian writing reveals about the state of Black women's culture and the intensity of *all* Black women's oppression" (26).

Poet/essayist Audre Lorde, who consistently pointed out the diverse threads that comprised identity and advocated a politics of difference, was a notable exception in that era. Her essays and speeches written in the 1970s (collected in *Sister Outsider* 1984) prefigured the burst of theory by women of color and others starting in the early 1980s that generated new paradigms for the making of feminist (and lesbian) meanings, and spawned networks of critical metadialogues on the inclusivity, accountability, accessibility, and validity of feminist (and lesbian) discourse (e.g., hooks 1981, 1984, 1990; Anzaldúa 1987, 1990a, 1990b; Moraga 1983; Christian 1990; Alarcón 1990). The "Combahee River Collective Statement" (1983), written by a Black feminist group in Boston, was a political manifesto also "embodied in the concept of identity politics"; it asserted that its authors were "actively committed to struggling against racial, sexual, heterosexual, and class oppression," and saw as its task "the development of integrated analysis and practice based upon the fact that the major systems of oppression are interlocking" (275, 272). By the early 1980s, "identity"-based anthologies also appeared from women's presses, such as *Nice Jewish Girls: A Lesbian Anthology* and *But Some of Us Are Brave: Black Women's Studies* in 1982, and work from Kitchen Table/Women of Color Press including *Home Girls: A Black Feminist Anthology* (1983), *Cuentos: Stories by Latinas* (1983), and the hugely popular *This Bridge Called My Back: Writings by Radical Women of Color* (1981)—all of which were either solely or in part edited by lesbians and contained a large amount of lesbian work. A substantial amount of the work in these volumes was written by nonacademically affiliated women; at the same time, these texts took a central place in many women's studies programs. Much of the work in these collections theorized the meanings of composite identity—particularly, the complex social and epistemological experiences produced by the intersections of gender, race, class, and sexual identities within individuals and within communities. "Margins," "centers," "borderlands," and "mestiza consciousness" were some of the metaphors frequently employed to delineate the complexities of location for lesbians of color. As lesbian poet Donna Kate Rushin (1983, xxi) wrote in the epigraphic poem for *This Bridge Called My Back:*

> *I've had enough*
> *I'm sick of seeing and touching*
> *Both sides of things*
> *Sick of being the damn bridge for everybody*
>
> *Nobody*
> *Can talk to anybody*
> *Without me*
> *Right?*

I explain my mother to my father my father to my little sister
My little sister to my brother my brother to the white feminists
The white feminists to the Black church folks the Black church folks
To the ex-hippies the ex-hippies to the Black separatists the
Black separatists to the artists the artists to my friends' parents . . .

Then
I've got to explain myself
To Everybody

I do more translating
Than the Gawdamn U.N.

It was only with the advent of AIDS in the early 1980s that the new "co-sexualism" came into existence, uniting lesbians with expertise in activism and health care organizing and gay men in a medical crisis. The bonds became more firmly cemented as a new wave of homophobia revealed how deeply they were also connected in social and political crisis. Since then, what has come to be known as the new queer activism has proliferated, particularly among the generation now in its twenties and early thirties. At the same time, the production of new texts by academic insiders, the onset of more concentrated publishing of gay and lesbian work by academic presses, and a spate of new course offerings around the country explicitly geared toward issues of sexuality and identity mapped out the contemporary province of queer theory. So far, the 1990s have yielded queer series at several presses—Routledge, Columbia, and Duke have been front runners—with some of the other university and even commercial presses eagerly scrambling to catch up. The Center for Lesbian and Gay Studies—the first fully accredited research center of its kind—now exists at the City University of New York, the continuing ed-style Institute of Gay and Lesbian Education runs courses in Los Angeles, lesbian and gay caucuses sprout up at more conferences every year, more and more graduate students are writing dissertations in the field, and some anthologies for freshman writing courses are starting to include lesbian- and gay-themed selections (e.g., Colombo et al. 1989; McQuade and Atwan 1991).

With sexuality rather than gender as its distinguishing mark of allegiance, the new coalition has appropriated the old epithet of "queer" as a reclamation of power and a catchall term that purposely blurs the exact requirements for membership in the category. There is no consensus about whether homosexuality is a minority position—i.e., something that an estimated one out of ten people is—or a universal feature of life owned by many people in different forms. Bisexuality has been incorporated into the appellation "queer," and the precise credentials by which one is defined as queer have been admittedly impossible to adjudicate. Pertinently to this new lack of clarity, Diana Fuss (1991, 2) has recently written:

Interrogating the position of "outsiderness" is where much recent lesbian and gay theory begins, implicitly if not always directly raising the questions of the complicated processes by which sexual borders are constructed, sexual identities assigned, and sexual politics formulated. How do outsides and insides come about? What philosophical and critical operations or modes produce the specious distinction between a pure and natural heterosexual inside and an impure and unnatural homosexual outside? Where exactly, in this borderline economy, does the one identity leave off and the other begin?

Questions of classification and interpretive frameworks grow more complex when we look for evidence of lesbian and gay people and relationships cross-culturally. Anthropologist Saskia Wieringa (1989) has found "homosocial arrangements [that] are institutionalized in their respective societies and are surrounded by the accepted rituals of those cultures" among Native North Americans, in woman marriages and female "husbands" in Africa, and among Chinese silk workers in the last century (217). Yet she is quick to point out, drawing on the work of Ifi Amadiume on woman marriages in Nigeria, that "a female husband's social status and identity was not determined by her choice of a sexual partner . . . but by her wealth, her cleverness or trading skills, and the number of her wives or children" (223–24). The Native American *berdache* is one who adopts "the occupation, the behavior, the clothing and the marital status of members of the opposite sex"; yet as the choice of gender of a *berdache*'s marital partner is optional, and *berdaches* have made various gender choices without losing *berdache* status, it is clear that occupation and the adoption of particular gender-signifiers rather than choice of a sexual partner is the determining characteristic of the role (224–25). Native American writer Paula Gunn Allen (1990) has written of the Lakota word *koskalaka* to describe certain women—a word which she says "is translated as 'young man' or 'woman who doesn't want to marry,' in our terms, 'dyke.'"[3] She explains:

> These women are said to be the daughters (the followers/practitioners) of a Spirit/Divinity who links two women together making them one in Her power. . . . In a culture that values children and women because they bear them, two women who don't want to marry (a man) become united by the power of the Deity and their union is validated by the creation of a rope baby. That is, the rope baby signifies the potency of their union in terms that are comprehensible to their society, which therefore legitimizes it. (114–15)

Wieringa says that "a *berdache* [falls] into a *third* or *fourth* gender category, beside the more prevalent gender categories 'man' and 'woman'" (226). Both Wieringa and Allen caution, however, that the word *berdache* itself is French, an invention of ethnographers, and that as not only the anthropological gaze, but the practices and beliefs of Western intervention have imprinted themselves on native social systems, there are overwhelming difficulties in attempting to recover and perceive original native traditions. "Certainly," says Allen, "we are not in the position of our American Indian foresister who could find safety and security in her bond with another woman because it was perceived to be destined and nurtured by nonhuman entities, as were all Indian pursuits, and was therefore acceptable and respectable (albeit occasionally terrifying) to others in her tribe"(112).

Yet the very notion that the way a culture experiences a particular phenomenon can be interrupted or altered is itself an important reminder that these phenomena lack transcendent "truth," and are products of that culture's construction of reality. Such understanding can also help us to interrupt and alter beliefs within dominant Western culture that are stale or debilitating. For instance, countering entrenched convictions that certain gender or sexual attributes are simply "natural" properties (deviations from which are vilified as "unnatural"), theorist Judith Butler (1990, 1991) has described gender and sexuality as the products of strings of repeated psychic performances. The very possibility that the performance might at some point fail to repeat itself is evidence that lesbianism, for example, is not cosmically glued to the "self." These identities may *feel* like core essences inside of us, which we automatically project outward, she says, but they really work the other way around: gender, for instance, "*produces* on the skin, through the gesture, the move, the gait . . . the illusion of an inner depth" (1991, 28). In other words, gender is the *effect* of a socially learned performance—not the "inner reality" that prompts a performance. Butler believes that spectacles such as drag or lesbian butch behavior, despite old allegations that they are imitations of "real" sexual and gender selves, function as burlesques of compulsory heterosexual identities that are thus unmasked as "theatrically produced effects that posture as grounds, origins, the normative measure of the real" (1991, 21). Because they are performances that so deeply jolt social expectations, exposing heterosexuality as "an incessant and *panicked* imitation of its own naturalized idealization" that is "perpetually at risk" because it "'knows' its own possibility of becoming undone" (23), they have great subversive potential.

In an age when all identity categories have become suspect and their meanings interrogated, it is curiously more fitting than ironic that perhaps the biggest name in lesbian and gay studies is literary critic and theorist Eve Kosofsky Sedgwick, who is not a lesbian (yet who does claim a more complicated identification with the broader notion of "queerness"). In her landmark *Epistemology of the Closet* (1990), Sedgwick argues that the homo-hetero schism has been a major yet overlooked trope structuring knowledge in twentieth-century Western culture, influencing as much as gender, race, and class do the ways that people define and position themselves and create forms of social organization. She emphasizes that homophobia's role in regulating cultural representations and human behaviors is a fundamantal reference point not only for homosexual people, but equally for heterosexual ones, whose lives are schematized by a "homosexual panic" that induces them to configurate themselves in otherwise inexplicable ways.[4]

Sedgwick brings these premises to her queer readings of texts by James, Proust, Nietzche, Wilde, and Melville, examining the processes of knowing and of enforcing ignorance that both produce and are produced by homophobic culture. She emphasizes that there are no available means for comprehending what gay identity might mean outside of the proscriptions against it. She points out, for example, that despite increasing signs of "tolerance" or "acceptance" of gay people who are already perceived as having the misfortune to exist, the production of *more* gay people is not something the world is actively seeking: "Advice on how to make sure your kids turn out gay, not to mention your students, your parishioners, your therapy clients, or your military subordinates, is less ubiquitous than you might think" (42). Given these proscriptions, what we *can* do is explore what transactions such as coming out or being actively closeted mean when looked at as speech acts, contextualized by a host of social variables. Sedgwick, following Foucault, repeatedly returns to the ways that conditions usually understood as voids or absences—such as ignorance, closetedness—are in fact discursive presences anxiously structured by relations of power. Theorizing about the ways such conditions operate—are, in fact, regularly *performed* within the social repertory—is the essence of her project.

Unquestionably, lesbian and gay studies in the past decade has been deeply permeated by the experience of AIDS. Susan Sontag's *AIDS and Its Metaphors* (1989), Douglas Crimp's edited collection *AIDS: Cultural Analysis/Cultural Activism* (1989), Simon Watney's *Policing Desire: Pornography, AIDS, and the Media* (1989) and Cindy Patton's *Inventing AIDS* (1990) are all volumes that have been included in numerous course syllabi in the last several years and offer analyses of how AIDS has been not simply a medical, social, or political crisis, but on a larger scale the construct of culturally dominant systems of signification. All of these theorists use cultural criticism to investigate the specific ways that prejudice, ignorance, and moral irresponsibility have structured our society's response to AIDS; all also suggest that a shift in mass consciousness and a reconstitution of our forms of cultural representation are crucial to effectively fighting the disaster. In this sense, they force readers to probe and directly confront the matrices of AIDS much more actively than do more widely consumed depictions of the tragedy—such as, for example, the Names Project Quilt and the documentary film *Common Threads: Stories from the Quilt*—moving and important as those cultural artifacts certainly are. The Quilt, begun in San Francisco in the earlier years of AIDS, is "a national memorial" constructed by numerous individuals who have sewn panels honoring loved ones lost to AIDS. In the words of one of the project's early directors, the Quilt is meant to "creatively transform feelings of helplessness into hope" (The Names Project brochure). It has been used as a form of popular education and has traveled to numerous parts of the country, and is an important piece of social art operating within several traditions—including what might be described as the *Spoon River* tradition, in which the voices of the dead speak hauntingly out of the past, refusing to leave the sphere of human discourse; the *Leaves of Grass* tradition, which juxtaposes meanings of individual and collective identities; the American quilting tradition, in which pieces of fabric standing in otherwise accidental relationship to each other are recast, through the eye and hand of the quilter, into a constructed coherence; and the sentimental tradition, in which a metaphor is erected to elicit a response that a material tragedy of human bodies failed to provoke. The Quilt works on these and other levels to "haunt" or to "move" spectators; its tense is the past, its mode of operation affective. Similarly, the film *Common Threads* works primarily through its evocative portraits of individuals who have suffered the loss of someone close to them due to AIDS. Both Quilt and film are artifacts designed to garner empathy for people with AIDS so that the "general population" might be encouraged to stop blaming the victims and presumably unite in pushing the powers that be toward finding a cure.

Yet one pitfall of human empathy is that it is often evoked to provisionally *transcend* a prejudice or gulf of consciousness—leaving the prejudice or the gulf intact—rather than to deconstruct the processes whereby social dichotomies are created and the beliefs that desperately sustain such bifurcations. Throughout the thirteen-year history of AIDS, public representations of people with AIDS have rendered them as Other—in contrast to, as Larry Kramer made explicit in the set notes to his landmark AIDS play, *The Normal Heart* (1985), people with Legionnaires' disease or Tylenol poisoning, who were depicted as random, unfortunate subjects whose fate, but for a stroke of fortune, could have been yours or mine. Susan Sontag addresses this in *AIDS and Its Metaphors* when she describes the ways that political metaphors are used to talk about the body, so that we claim to be waging "wars" on diseases which are seen as "invading the society." The war metaphor

> implements the way particularly dreaded diseases are envisaged as an alien "other," as enemies are in modern war; and the move from the demonization of the illness to the attribution of fault to the patient is

an inevitable one, no matter if patients are thought of as victims. Victims suggest innocence. And innocence, by the inexorable logic that governs all relational terms, suggests guilt. (10–11)

Another highly influential metaphor that early on became attached to AIDS, says Sontag, is the plague metaphor, in which "mass incidences of illness are understood as inflicted, not just endured. Considering illness as a punishment is the oldest idea of what causes illness . . ." (45). A crucial component of the plague metaphor is that "the disease invariably comes from somewhere else . . . there is a link between imagining disease and imagining foreignness. It lies perhaps in the very concept of wrong, which is archaically identical with the non-us, the alien" (47–48). Thus the Eurocentric assumption about AIDS is that it started in Africa, a widespread African belief has been that HIV was a U. S.-engineered weapon of population control, many African Americans and others with memories of the infamous Tuskegee syphilis study are convinced that the CIA created and deployed the virus, and heterosexuals long conceived of AIDS as a homosexual disease (51–52). Events since the publication of Sontag's book have, unfortunately, not rendered her thesis obsolete; for instance, in 1993, Congress reaffirmed the ban on HIV-positive people entering the United States—even as most safer sex education projects within the country's borders continue to affirm abstinence as the best prevention.[5]

Watney, Patton, Crimp, and the contributors to Crimp's book have all produced texts offering critical perspectives on what AIDS signifies in the public imagination. Watney's thesis, for instance, leading and reflecting the philosophy of many AIDS activists involved with the arts, the media, and the academy, is that AIDS involves a "crisis of representation" and that it is this, at least as much as the infiltration of a virus into our social fluids, that has produced the contemporary phenomenon of AIDS. People with AIDS have been constructed as a new criminal class of the late twentieth century—as the language of the popular schism "innocent" and "guilty" victims clearly suggests. Viewed as criminal in their sexual practices, their drug addiction, their lack of containment within "safe" social structures, they have found that the consequences of their "crimes" have been enough to bolster a rigorous "morality" that has enjoyed a mandate to police most of society.[6] Yet Watney points out:

> Moral panics do not speak to a "silent majority" which is simply "out there," waiting to listen. Rather, they provide the raw materials, in the form of words and images, of those moral constituencies with which individual subjects are encouraged to identify their deepest interests and their very core of being. . . . The successful policing of

desire requires that we think of "the enemy" everywhere, and at all
times. (43)

The metaphors that have structured the public's (mis)understanding
of AIDS are, inevitably, the same ones that students bring into the
classroom and which undergird their attempts to speak and write about
AIDS. Particularly valuable for educators is Patton's chapter called
"Teaching about AIDS"—a pedagogy which she says involves "teaching
how to understand, how to *read* and *interpret* both the facts that bom-
bard us and the context of our own lives" (110). Yet complicating AIDS
instruction is the fact that students bring to the classroom expectations
already threatening to constrain what that pedagogy itself will mean
and should do, based on "a hidden ethical structure underlying infor-
mation-giving models of health education" in which the "general public" and "high risk groups" stand in distinctly opposite moral relationships to that information. Explains Patton, "Even though each group
receive[s] 'facts,' the 'public' is given information on the assumption
that they have a *right to know,* that is a right to 'protect' themselves,
while 'communities' are educated on the assumption that they have
an *obligation to know* and protect the 'public'" (103). In "AIDS 101,"
Peter Bowen attempts to help students recognize "their relation to
AIDS as both frighteningly real *and* discursively constructed" (1993,
141). Bowen describes frustration, rather than optimism, when he
hears the "media ventriloquism" students have clearly become adept
at performing—that is, the recapitulation of platitudes which tend to
certify their purveyors as "informed." These include items such as "If
you must engage in sex, use a condom" or "AIDS doesn't discriminate"
(154). Explains Bowen, "In reflecting—or better, refracting—the media's own doublespeak, students consistently constructed AIDS as a
controversial field of knowledge split between easily knowable facts
and incomprehensible practices" (144–45). Proudly demonstrating that
they knew better than to fear doorknobs, handshakes, or public toilets,
what Bowen's students missed in their enumeration of the things that
don't cause AIDS was that in mentally sanitizing their environment
they "imagine[d] a world made safe again for heterosexuality" and
invented a "negative utopia [which] eliminates those people for whom
AIDS remains an everyday crisis" (145). Bowen notes that items con-
spicuously absent from students' lists of how not to contract HIV are

> suggestions such as "you don't get HIV by jerking off your partner or
> by using a clean needle while injecting drugs." By worrying instead
> about such clearly innocuous and domestic acts like "washing clothes"
> or "combing hair," these disclaimers, even as they are proffered in a
> rhetorical gesture of confrontation, cautiously avoid any contact with,
> let alone mention of, precise descriptions of safer sex or clean needle

use. Instead of providing information about protection, such disclaimers offer students protection against AIDS information itself by emphatically resisting any identification with the practices that transmit HIV. (145–46)

Outside of the academy, the AIDS crisis has sparked the production of a new critical literacy in the gay community through the deployment of graphic images that publicly deconstruct mass social mythologies about sexuality, HIV, AIDS, and the benevolence and infallibility of governmental, media, medical, corporate, and religious institutions. Douglas Crimp and Adam Rolston's finely illustrated and explicated *AIDS Demo Graphics* (1990) is an excellent source for studying this surge of political/cultural production. Drawing heavily on metaphor, irony, puns, the lampooning of American iconography, selective highlighting of quotations and statistics, and bold direct statements, art collectives like the Silence=Death project and Gran Fury have used fusions of print and graphic art to challenge complacent notions of truth, objectivity, authority, and audience—much as we attempt to do in our own way, in our own classrooms, with our own methods. In contrast to the haunting quality of the Quilt, this art functions in a very immediate present tense. Working, in fact, in many ways at counterpoint to a Quilt sensibility, this art is confrontational and aimed directly at the policies, leaders, agencies, and institutions that have produced—and most importantly, continue to produce—AIDS as an epidemic. Crimp and Rolston contextualize the graphic images with descriptions of the demonstrations and direct actions conducted by ACT UP (AIDS Coalition to Unleash Power) for which they were created—actions whose effectiveness seemed paradoxical to many because they appeared designed to infuriate the public as much as to enlist its sympathy. ACT UP's actions irreverently targeted some of the most sacred institutions of our country—including the Catholic Church, the White House, Wall Street, the Board of Education, the Food and Drug Administration, specifically named pharmaceutical companies, the *New York Times,* and the philosophy of the Constitution itself.

One image in Crimp and Rolston's book which originally appeared in the New York City subway depicts the United States flag, except that substituting for the usual dense blocks of horizontal red stripes are lines of red letters which proclaim,"OUR GOVERNMENT CONTINUES TO IGNORE THE LIVES, DEATHS AND SUFFERING OF PEOPLE WITH HIV INFECTION BECAUSE THEY ARE GAY, BLACK, HISPANIC OR POOR. BY JULY 4, 1989 OVER 55 THOUSAND WILL BE DEAD. TAKE DIRECT ACTION NOW. FIGHT BACK. FIGHT AIDS" (108; see Appendix). The charge of genocide literally embedded in the familiar image of the flag disrupts and subverts the work the flag is dispatched to do, which is to metonymically invoke patriotic feeling and the concomitant belief that our government is altruistically and benevolently safeguarding the public good, providing "liberty and justice for all." Another poster, wheat-pasted around the city to advertise a protest at city hall, announces, "SINCE THE CITY CUT AIDS EDUCATION, MORE KIDS GET TO LEAVE SCHOOL EARLY" (92). The silhouette of a graveyard sprawls across the bottom of the page. Perhaps most confrontational of all is the poster depicting the head and upper torso of John Cardinal O'Connor beside a photograph of an unfurled condom scaled to the same size as the Cardinal, its pointed tip paralleling and absurdly resembling the Cardinal's high, pointed hat. Large block letters advise, "KNOW YOUR SCUMBAGS." Beneath the condom in small type is the caption, "This one prevents AIDS" (135; see Appendix).

As one returning student with a background in advertising suggested, unlike the Quilt, whose mood is one of sadness and solemnity, the mood of the ACT UP graphics is one of rage; and unlike the Quilt's encouragement of reconciliation and empathy, ACT UP's work shocks and offends viewers into factionalization and the taking of positions—breaking complacency by generating anger and discomfort that can't be easily forgotten. And while much of the emotional effect of the Quilt lies in the fact that it is handmade, a tangible artifact made by individuals working in community, ACT UP's work is reproducible, relying on the kind of anonymous technology that is usually devoted to colas and sneakers. The Quilt literally reveals its seams and the foibles of its makers, many of whom are novice sewers and designers, thus evoking the feeling of a very "human" enterprise; the ACT UP graphics, in the tradition of advertising, purvey the myth of a perfect world in which everything is under control—except that, unlike advertisements for consumer merchandise, they abrasively break the very myths they suggest by the intrusion of a tragic reality, which can produce in the spectator a desperate impulse to react. The students in my lesbian- and gay-themed classes expressed divergent opinions about the containment of these images in a book. One said she felt that the book domesticated the images by housing them within the safe structures of publishing—co-opting the raw power they wielded on the street. Another, though, felt that the book was like a documentary, capturing a particular period of time.

Lesbian and gay studies clearly has both a long history and a very short history. It has long existed as a diffuse relationship among readers and writers; events such as the opening of the first lesbian and gay bookstore, the Oscar Wilde Memorial Bookshop in Greenwich Village in 1967 (Duberman 1993, 163), were important in consolidating and mobilizing a critical, reflective, and politicized lesbian and gay literacy network. Courses with material about lesbians have existed in wo-men's studies programs since the 1970s, and scattered pioneering ef-forts to run courses about both lesbians and gay men (or only gay men) have been successfully launched from time to time. But now for the first time, lesbian and gay studies is poised at the threshold of institu-tional respectability, with the vital machinery—publishing venues in the traditional disciplines, its own conferences, journals, and imprints in mainstream presses, out faculty and students, a large number of courses being piloted on a number of campuses, even the first trickle of grant money—apparently firmly in place. What sort of field will this turn out to be? Whom will it serve? Who will fall inside, and who outside, its borders? (Will it *be* bordered, and where and how will those borders be erected?) The other interdisciplinary, identity-based "special studies" programs that have come before it—such as women's, African American, Latino, and labor studies—have contorted for more than two decades to locate themselves between the magnetic poles of com-munity and ivory tower, have debated the conflicting benefits of being *in* the multiple disciplines versus becoming their own entity *beyond and transcending* the individual disciplines, and have struggled to define their own constituencies, ideologies, epistemologies, and methodolo-gies. Now lesbian and gay studies has to invent itself—a reflexive, historically grounded process which should certainly yield considerable insight into the nature of constructing an identity.

Notes

1. Eve Kosofsky Sedgwick (1990, 43) has pointed out that in a technological era like ours, nature is often less intractable and more manipulable than culture, rendering claims to biological inevitability ironically ineffective.

2. D'Emilio (1983b, 108) cites a reference to the existence of classes in "ho-mophile studies" that *ONE* sponsored in the latter half of the 1950s.

3. "Dyke" is often used by lesbians in the same way that "queer" and "faggot" are used—as an appropriated term of resistance. Allen goes further by creating the distinction between the American Indian "dyke" who "bonds with women to further some Spirit and supernatural directive" and the "lesbian," a woman who is "emotionally and physically intimate with other women. (The two groups would not have been mutually exclusive.)" (114).

4. It should be noted that Sedgwick is writing about homosexual and hetero-sexual *men*. As with any form of male-focused analysis, lesbian experience shouldn't be assumed to generically tag along under the rubrics established, though in certain instances insights might be productively cross-referenced.

5. Ronald Reagan first instituted this ban by presidential executive order in 1987. Normally, the Public Health Service makes decisions about immigration

Chapter Four

Community Knowledge and Social Construction Theory in Composition

In *The Social Construction of Reality,* Berger and Luckmann (1967, 44) write, "The validity of my knowledge of everyday life is taken for granted by myself and by others until further notice, that is, until a problem arises that cannot be solved in terms of it. As long as my knowledge works satisfactorily, I am generally ready to suspend doubts about it." The interruption of uncontested knowledge has become the project of a substantial segment of composition theory. Those who bring a social constructionist—or, in James Berlin's (1988) related term, social-epistemic—perspective to composition research and pedagogy are concerned principally with how knowledge is produced and codified in social groupings through language. Although their goals range from the making of more sophisticated academics to the displacement of hegemonic political structures, they share a belief that writing instruction needs to remove itself from its conventional view of language as an ideologically neutral, individualistically navigated, transparent medium of thought and concern itself instead with the ways that communities bring knowledge into existence through fundamentally social discursive practices.

Dismantling the assumed global validity of heterosexual knowledge by exposing the machinery of its construction in thought, language, and textuality has been a major project of the lesbian and gay rights movement. A popular button often seen at queer marches and bookstores warns, "Don't presume I'm straight." The Gay and Lesbian Alliance Against Defamation (GLAAD) targets reference media as diverse as the *Reader's Guide to Periodical Literature,* the *Yellow Pages,* and *TV Guide* with letter-writing campaigns protesting the ubiquitously absent category, "Lesbian and Gay." Lesbian and gay activists denounce a Queens school board's refusal to let children know that a fictional character named Heather has two mommies. Queers add the kinship categories "life partner" and "lover" to the 1990 federal census when asked to list family members. "Nations are not communities and never have been," wrote historian Howard Zinn (1980, 9–10), rejecting Henry Kissinger's contention that states possess a unified consciousness and therefore a collective memory which is the substance of history. "The history of any country, presented as the history of a family, conceals fierce conflicts of interest (sometimes exploding, most often repressed) between conquerors and conquered, masters and slaves, capitalists and workers, dominators and dominated in race and sex." On many fronts, the lesbian and gay movement is concerned with disrupting the myth of collective heterosexual consciousness, and to a large extent it does so by creating metacommentary on mainstream culture's monopolistic methods of producing, obfuscating, and categorizing knowledge.

Sometimes, though, the very unilateral reality under attack is simply carved up into an almost equally unproblematized bilateral one. The presumable subtext of "Don't presume I'm straight" is "I'm gay"— but just what *that* means is in fact not at all clear, as has been demonstrated by the host of conflicting self-definitions recounted in the introduction to this book. (Neither is it usually considered that the caveat on the button might signify that I might be a bisexual transvestite or a man trapped in a woman's body.) In a sense, simply declaring oneself "lesbian" or "gay" is not necessarily to undercut the language, and hence the definitions, of dominant culture; often, in fact, it is to inadvertently reaffirm them by implicitly accepting the subaltern ontology conferred by conventional social partitioning. "We are just as married as any straight couple"; "We're Americans and we should have the right to serve our country just like anyone else"; "We are perfectly capable of raising kids and not influencing them to be gay." These sorts of statements, echoed across the liberal humanist sphere of gay equal rights organizing and the media that covers it, hardly begin to excise the familiar discursive formations of heterosexual ideology from the ostensibly "new" gay consciousness that seeks to break the former's hegemonic stranglehold on culture.

The ways one uses language to define and negotiate relationships—that is, to *have* relationships—with social practices and institutions has been richly addressed in more general terms in composition. In his influential article "Rhetoric and Ideology in the Writing Class," Berlin (1988) posited a tripartite taxonomy of rhetoric which included cognitive, expressionistic, and social-epistemic branches of contemporary rhetorical theory and practice. Cognitive rhetoric, for him, relies on scientific objectivism which "reflects the rationality of the world" because it sees "a beneficent correspondence between the structures of the mind, the structures of the world, the structures of the minds of the audience, and the structures of language" (483). The magic that enables this correspondence is the bracketing out of causal, predictive relationships among these entities. If, for example, General Westmoreland tells the American public that Asians don't value life as white Westerners do, and if schooling has inculcated in us the notion that the United States represents a moral, democratic world force, and if we bomb and kill the peoples of Southeast Asia and say that we are doing it for freedom, and if we interpret these actions as righteous, each of these events may be perceived to prove the logic of the others—though a different kind of scrutiny might interrogate the overarching discourses that serve to ratify each of them in the first place. In public discourse about homosexuality, cognitive rhetoric is often invoked to dismiss or affirm social entitlements for gays. For example, a currently popular movement to prove that homosexuality is an inherent biological condition is predicated on the idea that when gays are seen to have "no choice" about being gay because they are "born that way," they will be relieved of the social opprobrium which has underwritten disenfranchisement. Yet this reasoning, first of all, can only sustain itself by screening out vast social and historical evidence that discourses of prejudice specifically *aimed* at biological conditions—anatomical sex, skin color, nose shape, the ability to hear, see, or walk—have been foundational to exclusionary public policy since this country's inception. Even more basically, the argument fails to interrogate its own premises—that is, that human thought and behavior are reducible to biology, and that such a quest for biological causality is valid in the first place. As an op-ed piece in the *New York Times* (Hubbard 1993, A15) pointed out:

> [T]he use of the phrase "sexual orientation" to describe only a person's having sex with members of their own gender or the other sex obscures the fact that many of us have other strong and consistent sexual orientations—toward certain hair colors, body shapes, racial types. It would be as logical to look for genes associated with these orientations as for "homosexual genes."

Another example is the controversy over gays in the military, in which "studies" have shown that morale would be threatened by the inclusion of gay men.[1] The "scientific" incontrovertability accorded this sort of research and the "conclusions" that social scientists and military personnel believe they can safely draw from the "data" sidestep a basic fact: that these studies were premised on the idea that homophobic ideology is a legitimate factor in the shaping of social policy. The situation of gays in the military has often been compared to its antecedent, racial segregation in the military. Though of course racism still thrives, the main difference between any "study" about the effects of racial integration on troop morale now and several decades ago would certainly be that official discourses about racism as a valid determinant of public policy have changed. Thus that form of bigotry, however pervasive, can no longer *officially* be used as a referent or given credence in determining how governmental organizations will be regulated.

Expressionist rhetoric, according to Berlin, "has usually been closely allied with theories of psychology that argued for the inherent goodness of the individual, a goodness distorted by excessive contact with others in groups and institutions" (484). Yet precisely who or what any individual would be, removed from social contact, remains unknown and unknowable, since the human brain shows no promise of becoming impermeable to and independent of the forces of the social world. As Berlin describes it, expressionist rhetoric requires faith in a fundamental solipsism: "Discovering the true self in writing will simultaneously enable the individual to discover the truth of the situation which evoked the writing, a situation that, needless to say, must always be compatible with the development of the self. . . ." (485). In lesbian and gay coming-out narratives, for instance, there is often the declaration that one has now "discovered" or emerged into a special sort of "truth"—one forbidden by and sealed off from the social world—and that prior experience involved "living a lie." Underscoring this interpretation of personal development is the belief that social forces merely disinterestedly repress, and don't themselves comprehend and cultivate, gay feelings and experiences. In this construct, these feelings and experiences hatch independently and a priori from within *despite* the social world, and their expression itself is seen as an act of resistance to that world—not in any way as a product of it.

Social-epistemic rhetoric, the version Berlin values, is one in which "[i]deology is . . . foregrounded and problematized in a way that situates rhetoric within ideology, rather than ideology within rhetoric" (477). It is "an alternative that is self-consciously aware of its ideological stand, making the very question of ideology the center of classroom activities, and in so doing providing itself a defense against preemption and a strategy for self-criticism and self-correction" (478). Social-epistemic rhetoric views the writer as a social subject constructed by discourse and situated in discourse communities with and in which her knowledges are generated. Therefore, the writing class is a place that draws upon the writer's self-awareness of and interaction with myriad forces around her as she *constructs* meaning, and meaning is as provisional and reconstitutable as fluctuations of awareness and circumstances—as opposed to an expressionist class, in which it is believed that a core of "authentic" (and presumably eternal) meaning may be tapped and released in a one-way stream from the inside out. For this reason, Berlin feels that social-epistemic rhetoric has tremendous political importance, in that it "offers an explicit critique of economic, political, and social arrangements" (490). This was the rhetoric I attempted to foreground in the lesbian- and gay-themed writing courses I taught—one that would extrapolate from Foucault's analysis of the ways sexuality has been "put into discourse" by entrenched social institutions. (Expressionist impulses at times run so high in these sorts of classes, however, that whatever one's intentions, guiding rhetorics often get scrambled.)

In considering the impact social construction theory in composition might have on lesbian and gay writers, it is worth looking at some of the various other ways the theory has been invoked and deployed in the field. A key and oft-cited text in composition's discussion of social construction is Kenneth Bruffee's "Social Construction, Language, and the Authority of Knowledge: A Bibliographic Essay" (1986). In this essay, Bruffee's expressed intention is to import social construction theories from other fields into composition, since he feels that a number of different disciplines are doing exciting work but in fragmented, nonmutually illuminating ways. Here is Bruffee's definition of social construction:

> A social constructionist position in any discipline assumes that entities we normally call reality, knowledge, thought, facts, texts, selves, and so on are constructs generated by communities of like-minded peers. Social construction understands reality, knowledge, thought, facts, texts, selves, and so on as community-generated and community-maintained linguistic entities—or, more broadly speaking, symbolic entities—that define or "constitute" the communities that generate them, much as the language of the *United States Constitution,* the *Declaration of Independence,* and the "Gettysburg Address" in part constitutes the political, the legal, and to some extent the cultural community of Americans. (774)

Bruffee emphasizes that social constructionist ways of thinking and knowing are nonfoundational and anti-universalist, and thereby differ from both the Cartesian notion that some fundamental matrix of truth resides in the human mind and the cognitivist notion that it is located in the natural world. Social constructionist truth is, for Bruffee, "only an agreement, a consensus arrived at for the time being by communities of knowledgeable peers. Concepts, ideas, theories, the world, reality, and facts are all language constructs generated by knowledge communities and used by them to maintain community coherence" (777).

In contrast to Berlin, Bruffee is unconcerned with the political implications of social construction theory and vastly more concerned with the particular benefits it promises for composition professionals. For him, social construction has the potential to move us from the margin to the center of academic life, since it disengages language "skills" from their subservient position as "mere medium or conduit" (778) to knowledge and essentially merges language and knowledge—making reading and writing specialists indispensable. At one point, almost as an aside, he remarks, "[S]ome social constructionists go so far in their nonfoundationalism as to assume, along with the sociologist Erving Goffman for example, that even what we think of as the individual self is a construct largely community generated and community maintained" (777). Given that Bruffee is trying to connect the work that is being done in diverse disciplines, it seems strange that he would so easily brush off the notion of the constructed "self"—certainly one of the largest and most explosive features of social constructionist thought, one that *has* cut across disciplinary boundaries and has been of particular importance to those interdisciplinary studies involved with identity, such as women's studies and lesbian and gay studies. And given that so much of the work that is done in composition classes is involved, in some form, with the "self," why does Bruffee sidestep this issue? Compounding the mystery is the fact that the view of the self he describes seems to be supported by the theoretical principles he has laid out. Why does he use the pejorative phrase "go so far"—as if taking a construct to its logical end makes one an extremist? How far is one to go, and why is one to stop there?

Bruffee has, in fact, been criticized by John Schilb (1991) for "slight[ing] those who probe configurations of power based on gender, race, and class." Bruffee's essay, Schilb points out, "omits feminists (out of forty [bibliographic] entries, only three are by women), Marxists, African American theorists, Third World theorists, and other analysts of power like Michel Foucault and Pierre Bourdieu. . . . Bruffee's constant use of warm, positive words like *communities* and *conversation* also threatens to obscure processes of domination and struggle" (183–84). Needless to say, the debate over social construction that was at the center of theorizing lesbian and gay identities in the 1980s is also absent from Bruffee's discussion (and, in fact, from Schilb's enumeration of Bruffee's oversights—highlighting how far outside the sphere of academic discourse lesbian and gay issues have been even for progressive scholars). Sharon Crowley, in an essay included in and responding to the collection *Contending With Words: Composition and Rhetoric in a Postmodern Age* (1991, 195), similarly expresses skepticism about composition theory that "smacks of liberal social agendas" while ignoring work that has invigorated radical left perspectives in composition. Much of this work dismantles the notion that communities can actually be "like-minded" in the way that Bruffee's definition proposes and that "consensus" can ever be as uncomplicated as his filtered pool of sources would suggest. Crowley points out that the writing classroom "is populated by persons who may not be able to work in harmony, since they inevitably bring with them the patriarchal, racist, or classist discourses of the dominant culture—unless, of course, they identify primarily with one or another minority culture" (190). For Crowley, "harmony" is an obsolete pedagogical ideal, though she thinks that collectively reflecting upon the dystopic absence of harmony in a classroom might be extremely useful.

Looking at Bruffee through the lens of Schilb and Crowley, then, we find a very limited account of what social construction might mean in a writing class. If knowledge is produced by the consensus of "communities of knowledgeable peers," it would seem that Bruffee's knowledge is produced by the same old community that has historically held a monopoly on academic knowledge, and still tries to retain a controlling interest. Had Bruffee been more self-reflective about his own social location and its role in shaping his view of social construction, then this might be a different text, with a different sort of usefulness. Instead, the essay is an example of some specific ways that social construction theory is vulnerable to falling short of its own premises, leaving some of the same academic casualties who were veterans of earlier constructs and pedagogies on its newly formed margins.

Lester Faigley, in an article called "Judging Writing, Judging Selves" (1989), raises important questions about the construction of the "self" in student essays. Faigley's focus is primarily the perspectives of readers rather than writers, and the second half of his essay is concerned with teachers who commend their students for being "honest," "writ[ing] in a personal voice," or "possess[ing] integrity" in "personal experience" essays (404). Examining a collection of teachers' favorite essays in which personal experience essays clearly predominate, Faigley concludes that the writers succeed by inserting themselves into familiar discourses and constructing easily recognizable "selves," thereby making their experiences accessible to unknown readers. Faigley finds the very ease of these texts' reception troublesome, signaling something about their production—largely because the "natural and common-sense quality" of what the writers "expose" and "reveal" depends on the comfort and goodwill of the blandly imagined "general reader" of similar social identification (408–9). The impression of the teachers, then, that these student voices are simply "honest" expressions is questionable:

> [I]f one grants the possibility of an unconscious mind, then the question of insincerity becomes moot. How can one possibly express one's *full* self, including the unconscious part? And what if one is

sincerely expressing one's conscious self but unconsciously repressing something that remains unexpressed? Is the writer sincere or insincere? (409)

Faigley points out that "the self in student autobiographies, then, is not one that emerges like a butterfly from a chrysalis . . . but one that is discursively produced and discursively bounded" (411). Helping students to achieve critical awareness of the ways that definitions of the self emerge from discourse and of "how definitions of the self are involved in the configuration of relations to power" (411) is the closest we can come to "empowering" them; it is only when one is self-conscious about position and location in this way that one can act to *re*position and *re*locate oneself in the world.

To locate Faigley's point within the context of writing about lesbian and gay issues, consider the following student text excerpted in Ellen Louise Hart and Sarah-Hope Parmeter's essay, "'Writing in the Margins': A Lesbian- and Gay-Inclusive Course" (1992, 168). A man reflecting on how the course had changed his thinking begins:

> I have always equated homosexuality with only the sexual side of a relationship, and have never tried to see any other facet of a homosexual relationship. I was very uncomfortable with the thought of sex between homosexuals, and so I never looked beyond what I ridiculed, mostly due to what I didn't understand.

He goes on to explain that by reading an AIDS memoir and, consequently, analyzing through new eyes a relationship between two gay men he has known for a long time, he has come to realize that there is much more to the men's relationship than sex. His frank reflections on his prior homophobic misconceptions and his arrival at a place of greater enlightenment are the essential material of his story. This is certainly "honest" writing by many people's standards. Yet the piece may look different when cast within the terms of Faigley's critique. What, for instance, are we to make of his passing remark that he had *never tried* to see gay relationships differently? Is there perhaps a level at which his admissions of discomfort, shortsightedness, a propensity to ridicule gays, and lack of understanding are being offered not *only* as regrettable vestiges of his ignorant past, but also as criteria for his recertification as insider in the heterosexual discourse community—even *with* or *despite* his newfound sensitivity? In other words, alternatively to reading discourses of "openness" and "sensitivity" as empathetic steps *toward* the Other, how might we read them as signposts safely demarcating the space that exists *between* a speaking subject and the Other? Beyond being the *narrative* of a *nice* guy, to what extent is this essay also the *performance* of a *straight* guy?

Marian Yee's essay "Are You the Teacher?" (1991) also deals with issues of representation in autobiography, but this time the autobiographical experience is her own in the classroom. This piece is a rather extraordinary manifestation of Faigley's wish for the "personal experience" essay that reflects upon the discourses that are inscribed upon the "personal experience" and that brought it into existence. Yee writes of her students' confusion each term as they encounter what seems to them like an oxymoron: a Chinese English teacher. When they ask her, "Are you the teacher?" she knows what they mean, because her images of English teachers have been shaped by some of the same forces as theirs. She thinks of the movies that created her own visual images of teachers—*The Paper Chase, Dead Poets Society, Stand and Deliver*—as well as the "steamy dragon-ladies from kung-fu movies" and the "small, dark-haired women like my mother and her friends, who work as seamstresses in sweatshops" who formed her visual associations with the category "Chinese women" (25). It is difficult even for her to imagine conflating the categories "English teacher" and "Chinese woman." With this cultural knowledge, she is able to regard the students who have asked the question and wonder: "Who is this 'you' that they are looking at? Who is the 'teacher'? What images, associations, separate the two? Do Chinese women inhabit a different sphere than English teachers? What are those spheres like? How do we know about them? From whose point of view do we see them?" (24–25) Rather than simply answering the students and effacing the deep importance of their question, Yee permits the complications of her own identity as it is constructed in various public spheres, including the classroom, to play a heuristic role in the class. She writes:

> I am a "text" in the sense that I represent a particular group that is publicly inscribed within powerful cultural narratives. The point, however, is not to correct these narratives. The process of rejecting one narrative and replacing it with another will not give me or my students a truer or more complete account of who I am or of who they are. It is necessary for me to hold many narratives within me at once, for I am composed of many parts. Each student is, himself or herself, composed of multiple narratives that compete with each other to tell the main story. . . . Teaching students how to recognize and read the dominant cultural narratives that construct their identities and their views of the world is a way to help them rethink writing, not as an act of recording those narratives but as acts of resisting and reevaluating those narratives, and of recovering other narratives that have been suppressed or ignored. . . .(29)

The sensation that "I am a 'text'" hovers around lesbian and gay people all the time, monitoring their acts of coming out and structuring coming-out speech acts in a variety of contexts. As Simon Watney (1991) has pointed out, school is a context in which the discourse of "promotion" has historically stifled potential acts of self-identification by gay adults, and has contingently "denied [young people] . . . an identity in relation to their sexuality" (397). In the absence of any speaking homosexual subjects, gays and lesbians have easily been "depicted as a uniform type, an abstract, generalized, and thus dehumanized menace" (394). Once members of any group are dehumanized, the next steps to marginalization and persecution are easy to make. The contemporary lesbian and gay rights movement has managed to subvert the anonymity of closetedness and replace its abstractions with actual names and faces (at least on TV and in the morning paper, if not in your neighborhood). Still, many people fear coming out in school (and elsewhere) because they don't want to watch themselves being reread within that cultural fiction of demonization; it can be overwhelming to contemplate the gulf between what one may signify to others and how one experiences oneself.

As increasing numbers of teachers and students do choose to come out in school, though, the nature of their "textuality" will inevitably change. Up until now, the rare visible lesbian or gay person in school—whether the guest lecturer or the freshman writer—has often played the objectified role of the "teaching aid," cheerfully supplanting "myths" with "facts" and, supposedly by his or her sheer presence, "bursting stereotypes." But as a proliferation of identifiably queer bodies begins to inhabit everyday space, the "gay person as text" may finally be in a position, as Yee found herself, to move beyond simplistically refuting the powerful narratives which have been written about her and instead to "hold many narratives within [herself] at once." For the lesbian or gay student, this may mean finally having the luxury to examine the multiple discourses that have shaped "personal experience," rather than perceiving the necessity to always react to pervasively negative discourses with overdetermined "corrective" counterdiscourses—proclaiming, as one T-shirt says, "I am out, therefore I am."

In the hit musical *La Cage Aux Folles,* gay men in drag sing the lyrics:

> *I am what I am*
> *I am my own special creation.*

Social construction theories in composition have important uses for lesbian and gay student writers because they take them beyond the tautological first line of the song and locate them more productively in the second. They presume that what gay people are needs some explaining—not within the stale conventions of etiology ("What makes people gay?") but in ways that account for how concepts such as "gay" and "straight" and the values that encompass them have been constituted in human discourse. It is empowering to conceive of oppressive forces as constructed and of homosexuality as a contested identity; thinking, let alone acting, can be a stultifying project if one is convinced that social laws and opinions are calcified and one's identity simply "is." Expressionist approaches to composition might under ideal circumstances provide a forum in which students could feel free to vent their anger and sorrow about homophobia, generate narratives about their relationships, or perhaps write informative advocacy pieces about gay political issues. What such a class is less likely to provide is the opportunity to excavate the meanings that underwrite these positions, the beliefs that yield these beliefs. Homophobia is bad; we want it to go away. But what exactly *is* that thing—or those disparate things— that we call "homophobia"? In what forms does it exist? How have we come to know it? What has defined our relationship to it? What gives it such power in so many spheres of human activity? What new meanings might replace it if it went away? How did human sexuality get bifurcated in this way—gay and straight—when, as Eve Sedgwick has pointed out, so many other categorical cleavages are possible—people who like to do it with people versus people who like to do it with animals or with objects; people who do it for money versus people who do it for free; people who are into bondage versus people who are into feet? What do people get out of homophobia in our society? How does queerness locate someone as a reader and a writer in a homophobic culture? If many of the truths promulgated by our culture don't apply to lesbians and gays—such as, for example, "Your family will always be there for you, no matter what"—in what ways does the "exception" of lesbian and gay experience cast new light on those truths for all people?[2] What does it mean to "come out"? (Out of what? Into what?) How have discourses of AIDS affected, and been affected by, discourses of homophobia?

What conditions must be present in order for a lesbian or gay student to consider these questions, to speculate about them in ways that will inform her or his narratives, arguments, and analyses?

Foremost, something in the composing context must position the writer beyond the most basic moment of "coming out" to teacher and peers in a writing class. Coming out in such situations usually entails some combination of announcement and persuasion—"I am" and "This means"—the point being, of course, to convince an audience to relinquish old images and meanings of queerness and replace them with affirmative new ones. Coming out in a mainstream class requires courage and stamina, and usually too the deployment of available meanings from the gay community arsenal. The occasion hardly affords the luxury of interrogating those meanings or inventing new ones; "gay is good" is too precious a concept to sacrifice to the ostensibly greater good of deconstruction at such a moment. If straight people in

shared basis for the production of linguistic artifacts, there are shared ways of construing them. At the same time, Bizzell isn't altogether sure about exactly what sort of "language-using practices" discourse communities share. She's not referring to patterns of utterance or pronunciation, such as those used by communities grouped in a particular region. But do they have in common a corps of lexical terms, as do doctors or computer programmers? And if "canonical language regulates the world views of group members," can this "canonical language" be defined at the level of rhetoric, rather than just syntax or semantics? Presumably it can, since Bizzell draws on Bruce Herzberg's (1986) observation that a discourse community is the "center of a set of ideas" and that "discourse is epistemic or constitutive of the group's knowledge" (223), and she contends that conflict is an inevitable component of interactions among discourse communities because of the "value contradictions that arise when discourse communities overlap" (224, 232).

Bizzell considers, too, six criteria that the applied linguist John Swales developed to determine whether a group in fact constitutes a discourse community. Bizzell understands Swales's discourse communities to be constellations formed to enact some project—she calls it work—that members could not accomplish alone. If one interprets "work" broadly (in the sense that undergoing psychotherapy or maintaining a relationship entails "work"), then lesbian and gay communities are joined together in "work"—the work of personal and social transformation. Consider how the lesbian and gay community might qualify according to Swales's criteria (as related by Bizzell, 225–26) as a discourse community:

> 1. There must be some common, public "goal" the group seeks to accomplish, some work the participants are trying to perform together.

The lesbian and gay community, as I have indicated in my introductory chapter, is quite divided on many levels about the precise nature of its goal. The majority want, at the least, equal rights with heterosexuals in terms of such things as legal marriage, health benefits, child custody, and legal protection from housing and job discrimination—though many others would prefer to see the institution of marriage as we know it dissolve altogether, some would like to see society rearrange itself into communal or nonmonogamous domestic arrangements, and some feel that sexual liberation for all rather than redistributed social benefits is the key issue. However, there is probably a consensus that a common goal is the eradication of homophobia. Under that rubric, we may not all understand each other, but for the most part we hear each other.

> 2. There must be some discursive "forum" accessible to all participants; oral, visual, and or/print media may be involved.

The lesbian and gay community has developed an extensive network of media—books, newspapers, magazines, academic journals, films, artwork, music, television shows, and computer networks—as well as vehicles for their dissemination, such as bookstores, record companies, theatres, production companies, music festivals, professional associations, social and political organizations, community centers, college courses, comedy clubs, annual Gay Pride celebrations, and the like.

> 3. The group must use its forum to work toward its goal by "providing information and feedback."

Using the above-mentioned media and distribution networks, as well as individual newsletters, national organizations such as the Human Rights Campaign Fund, the National Gay and Lesbian Task Force Policy Institute, the Gay and Lesbian Alliance Against Defamation, and the Lambda Legal Defense and Education Fund report to the community on their work in lobbying, grass-roots organizing, challenging homophobic images (and homosexual absences) in the media, and fighting homophobic injustice through the courts.

> 4. The group develops expectations for how productive exchanges of information should proceed, which is to say that the group shares discourse conventions or "genres."

As conveyed in Item 1, a national "community" based on a single characteristic of shared identity and having much else *not* in common has, of course, a variety of ways of communicating. However, it is probably safe to say that there are shared understandings of at least two discourse conventions: the speech acts of being closeted and of coming out. Eve Sedgwick has argued that the former constitutes a speech act in the sense that it is a particularly structured form of silence, which is itself a discourse. As for the latter, the lesbian and gay community ritually utilizes specific speech genres, such as narratives built around the questions "Are you out to your family?" and "Are you out at work?" as well as coming-out stories of a more general nature. The color lavender, the pink triangle, pinky rings, the rainbow flag, the Silence=Death logo since AIDS, and other iconography have been used to communicate group membership. "Lover" and "partner" are the words usually used in reference to a mate, whether in a relationship of long or short duration. ("Companion" and "friend," on the other hand, are strictly words of the closet or of outsiders.) Many gay men have long used terms such as "girlfriend" and "Mary" to refer to one another. Lesbians have used the terms "butch" and "femme" since the 1950s; lesbian psychotherapist Joann Loulan maintains that all lesbians, even those who eschew roles, know very well to whom they apply. A new lesbian and gay television variety show is called "In the Life," after the traditional expression denoting membership in the pre-Stonewall subculture. Nonverbal signs such as handkerchiefs (rear pocket means gay; specific colors and sides advertise specific sexual behaviors or roles, such as active or passive) and keys hanging from a belt loop have been staples of (primarily male) gay communication since the early 1970s. As Hal Fischer has observed in *Gay Semiotics* ([1977] 1991, 44):

> Traditionally, western societies have utilized signifiers for non-accessibility. The wedding ring, engagement ring, lavaliere or pin are signifiers for nonavailability which are always attached to women. Signs for availability simply do not exist. . . . In gay culture, the reverse is true. Signifiers exist for accessibility. Obviously, one reason behind this is that gays are less constrained by a type of code which defines people as property of others or feels the need to promote monogamy. . . . Gays have many more sexual possibilities than straight people and therefore need a more intricate communication system.

5. The group's discourse not only is thus specialized, but exhibits a tendency to become increasingly specialized; there is "an inbuilt dynamic toward an increasingly shared and specialized terminology."

Beyond some of the above examples, new words have come into the community's vocabulary concomitantly with increasing politicization: "dyke" and "faggot" were "appropriated" pejoratives of the 1970s; "queer" functions in the same way in the 1990s. "Michigan" is used in certain circles of lesbians to denote the huge annual Michigan Womyn's Music Festival, not only as event, but as definitive cultural experience (in the same way that "Cannes" is used in the film world). The word "out" has been used in numerous titles of publications—*OutLook, Outweek, Out, Out & About*—and sends a clear signal about the magazine's contents. "Gaydar" refers to a gay person's ability to intuit the presence of other gays. A teenage lesbian is a "baby dyke." A post-1970s lesbian who wears makeup, heels, and other traditional feminine accoutrements is a "lipstick lesbian." A working class, nonpoliticized lesbian is a "bar dyke." A particular form of lesbian and gay studies is "queer theory."

6. There must be a "critical mass" of experts in the group at any given time: people who are intimately familiar with the specialized genres with which the group seeks to accomplish its goals and who thus can

initiate novices. The "survival of the community depends on a reasonable ratio between experts and novices."

Chief induction centers are bars, social and political organizations,
community centers, and campus organizations and courses. These are
places where newcomers—often people who "want to come out"—
come to join and learn the customs of "the community." Lesbian and
gay community centers schedule "orientations" for new folks in town
as well as for the newly out. There are now many lesbian and gay
psychotherapists and counselors who advertise themselves as such;
they, as well as support groups and other services of community centers, help new initiates become acculturated to the community and
navigate the sometimes difficult transition into identification with it.
Often such a sense of identification is indicated by wearing one's first
gay button, T-shirt, or pinky ring—nonverbal signals of membership.
Increasing identification with the community can be indicated with
shorthand references to such things as "The March" (on Washington
in April, 1993); "Pride" (the annual parade and/or festival); "the ban"
(against gays in the military); "Colorado" (Amendment 2); or, for the
sophisticated, "Bowers" (the 1986 *Bowers v. Hardwick* Supreme Court
sodomy ruling; referred to as feminists do to "Roe"). "Before Stonewall" and "since Stonewall" both invoke the Great Divide of queer
existence and signal, respectively, the great dismal past and the vast
open road of gay liberation along which anything is possible.

The lesbian and gay community would seem, then, at least in
Swales's scheme, to constitute a discourse community. Yet, like virtually any large community, this one is far from homogeneous, and many
of its members feel allegiance to other identity-based communities,
too—groups based on such things as gender, race or ethnicity, physical
ability. So what do these criteria actually add up to when we think
about lesbian and gay students in writing classes? What do they suggest
about the ways that these students might draw upon their group
membership in their literacy acts?

Joseph Harris, in his essay "The Idea of Community in the Study
of Writing" (1989), agrees that the uses of the concept "discourse
community" as it appears in scholarship on writing are contradictory
and confusing,

> drawing on one hand from the literary-philosophical idea of "inter-
> pretive community," and on the other from the sociolinguistic concept
> of "speech community," but without fully taking into account the
> differences between the two. "Interpretive community," as used by
> Stanley Fish and others, is a term in a theoretical debate; it refers not
> so much to specific physical groupings of people as to a kind of loose
> dispersed network of individuals who share certain habits of mind.

> "Speech community," however, is usually meant to describe an actual group of speakers living in a particular place and time. Thus while "interpretive community" can usually be taken to describe something like a world-view, discipline, or profession, "speech community" is generally used to refer more specifically to groupings like neighborhoods, settlements, or classrooms. (14)

Despite the multiple categories available to describe collectives of language users, Harris still finds some common threads running through descriptions of "discourse communities" that indicate a sense of common enterprise, or purposeful social bonding:

> A . . . stress on a shared or collaborative project runs through most . . . attempts to define "discourse community." Thus while *community* loses its rooting in a particular place, it gains a new sense of direction and movement. Abstracted as they are from almost all other kinds of social and material relations, only an affinity of beliefs and purposes, consensus, is left to hold such communities together. The sort of group invoked is a free and voluntary gathering of individuals with shared goals and interests—of persons who have not so much been forced together as have chosen to associate with one another. . . . (15)

Harris concludes, though, that "consensus" rather misstates the fundamental conditions required for community, since "matters of accident, necessity, and convenience hold groups together as well" (20), internal dissonance is endemic to community, and the identifications that forge community are multiple and overlapping, thereby rendering its functional cohesion always tenuous. In other words, the "organic unity" of a community is a myth, and consensus without conflict a utopian ideal. However, the fact that communities form in response to sociopolitical conditions and can re-form as these conditions shift makes their discursive and interpretive functions no less powerful. The problem, as Harris sets it out, comes when teachers regard discourse communities—the communities from which our students come and the academic community—as fixed rather than dynamic. Such a view of communities reifies divisions between insiders and outsiders and erases the possibility of discursive cross-fertilizations that yield new knowledge.

Harris's essay is partly a response to David Bartholomae's well-known and controversial essay "Inventing the University" (1985), which according to some readings (mine included) fashions the university as an induction center in which the civilian languages of the students' home communities are shed and the uniform of academic language is donned. Harris highlights the language of Bartholomae's opening paragraph to illustrate the schism of "us" and "them," of missionaries and natives, immediately invoked:

> Every time a student sits down to write for us, he has to invent the university for the occasion—invent the university, that is, or a branch of it, like history or anthropology or economics or English. The student has to learn *to speak our language, to speak as we do,* to try on the peculiar ways of knowing, selecting, evaluating, reporting, concluding, and arguing that define *the discourse of our community.* (Bartholomae quoted in Harris 1989, 134, Harris's emphases)

Though Bartholomae does, in his next sentence, amend "the discourse" to "the *various* discourses of our community" (134–35), the scope of these various discourses includes only the academic disciplines of the liberal arts. His examples are further restricted to the traditionally bounded academic departments whose discourses are rooted in specialization—history, anthropology, economics, English—while the newer interdisciplinary fields that have both inherently and self-consciously problematized the notion of discrete discourses, such as women's or ethnic studies, go unnoticed. In addition, Bartholomae's language at times suggests a militaristic imperative regarding students' surrendering of old discursive paradigms and appropriation of new ones—the student *has to* invent, *has to* learn (emphases mine)—creating a sense of tremendous authority on the part of the institution, and a corresponding relinquishing of authority on the part of the recruits who enter.

In later portions of the essay, Bartholomae explains his criteria for evaluating student writing:

> In general, as I reviewed the essays for this study, I found that the more successful writers set themselves in their essays against what they defined as some more naïve way of talking about their subject—against "those who think that . . ."—or against earlier, more naïve versions of themselves—"once I thought that . . ." By trading in one set of commonplaces at the expense of another, they could win themselves status as members of what is taken to be some more privileged group. The ability to imagine privilege enabled writing. (153)

> The more advanced essays for me, then, are those that are set against the "naïve" codes of "everyday" life. (I put the terms "naïve" and "everyday" in quotation marks because they are, of course, arbitrary terms.) In the advanced essays one can see a writer claiming an "inside" position of privilege by rejecting the language and commonplaces of a "naïve" discourse, the language of "outsiders." The "I" of those essays locates itself against one discourse (what it claims to be a naïve discourse) and approximates the specialized language of what is presumed to be a more powerful and more privileged community. There are two gestures present, then—one imitative and one critical.

> The writer continually audits and pushes against a language that would render him "like everyone else" and mimics the language and interpretive systems of the privileged community. (157)

For me, there is an odd element of religious mysticism in Bartholomae's portrayal of academic discourse—perhaps because his account of the discursive acts that most impress him strangely evokes the lines, "I once was lost but now I'm found, I was blind but now I see." Though he does make the token parenthetical gesture of acknowledging that "naïve" and "everyday" are "of course" arbitrary terms, he does not exploit or indeed ever again refer to the existence or uses of their indeterminacy. Neither does he interrogate the socially charged terms "status" or "privilege"—nor his assumption that they always represent the goals of student writers. Is there anything, to him, "naïve" about accepting the need to mimic a privileged system? About desiring to enter it? Bartholomae's "successful" writers' strategies resemble those of successful players in corporate capitalism—an analogy that borrows from Berlin's (1988) description of the veiled operations and agendas of cognitive rhetoric. For Berlin, corporate workers' "work life is designed to turn goal-seeking and problem-solving behavior into profits . . .," while

> the rationalization of the writing process is specifically designated an extension of the rationalization of economic activity. The pursuit of self-evident and unquestioned goals in the composing process parallels the pursuit of self-evident and unquestioned profit-making goals in the corporate marketplace. . . . The purpose of writing is to create a commodified text . . . that belongs to the individual and has exchange value . . . just as the end of corporate activity is to create a privately owned profit. (483)

The discursive positioning that Bartholomae favors seems to be precisely the contrary of that encouraged by liberatory pedagogy, whose aim is to help students *transcend* the naïve belief that they can—or should—magically enter mainstream culture by "mimicking" its mass discourses and behaviors, as mass media, schooling, advertising, and other institutions encourage them to do. What are our students learning when they learn to mimic a discourse, a posture, a stance? What aren't they learning? Might they learn something very different if they were to examine the ways in which the privileged discourse of the university represents particular agendas, perspectives, and principles, and contrasted these with the ways other discourses—in which they play a part—represent particular agendas, perspectives, and principles? Might they learn something about the etiology of these discourses, discover that they are in fact malleable and fluid, that no one discourse need pose as "the" authentic one that must be imitated or eternally constituted as the sole arena of power and agency? Bartholomae continues:

> It may very well be that some students will need to learn to crudely mimic the "distinctive register" of academic discourse before they are prepared to actually and legitimately do the work of the discourse, and before they are sophisticated enough with the refinements of tone and gesture to do it with grace or elegance. (162)

If they "will need to learn to crudely mimic" before they are proficient in the discourse, isn't Bartholomae really suggesting that we teach them to perform surface functions that are essentially rote, conformist, and compliant? Though the "surface" features of writing have long been viewed by compositionists at counterpoint to "deeper"-level operations such as "critical thinking," Bartholomae threatens to merge the two. I can't help but think that all of this seems to have something to do with the preservation of his own institutional authority. There simply doesn't seem to be room in this scheme for students—or faculty—to question it. Is there any realm in which Bartholomae lacks authority? What might he learn from examining what happens to him there? Does he necessarily mimic the behavior or discourse of insiders in every community he enters? Might he value his own discourse so much that he might choose in those situations to remain on the margin, finding it a more rewarding or even powerful place? Might he undergo a kind of mental split, faking the alien discourse for the moment but remaining conscious that he is performing only to achieve particular ends? How does he decide what those ends are, whether they are worth it, how far he will go with the project, what alternative strategies exist? What might he lose in such a situation? How would he feel? What would he learn from reflecting upon all of these choices, from self-consciously manipulating all these variables? Perhaps most important—and most absent from Bartholomae's discussion—what larger social and political structures might he discover serve to bolster the privilege and authority of his own academic discourse community, and in what ways has he come to rely on that support in his daily discoursing?

Bartholomae's scheme also forecloses on the possibility that alternative discourse communities might breed alternative sorts of privileges—and that those benefits might be seductive enough to deter students from trading them in for the "insider'" benefits of the academy. I am thinking particularly of M. A. K. Halliday's (1978) description of *antilanguages,* which he says are generated by *antisocieties.* He defines an antisociety as "a society that is set up within another society as a conscious alternative to it. It is a mode of resistance. . . ." (164). He cites as examples of antisocieties groups of vagabonds, prisoners, and reform school students—all of which carry negative social values—yet some of the social configurations based on identity politics since the 1970s would also seem to fit his description. Halliday isn't describing groups of people who are merely outsiders; he is describing people who have chosen to invert discourses about their outsider status in relation to the dominant society so that, as Diana Fuss says, "to be out is to be in." According to Halliday, "the simplest form taken by anti-languages is that of new words for old; it is a language relexicalized" (165). In certain sectors of the lesbian and gay activist movement, for example, words such as "queer," "fag," and "dyke" have been "reclaimed" for their "in-your-face" power, or as terms signifying camaraderie among members (in somewhat the same way that "nigger" can function positively in certain situations for African Americans). Halliday stresses that antilanguages are not only for the down-and-out or even for those engaged in social protest; mysticism and literature, for example, can be conceived of as antilanguages within rationalist Western culture. What is significant about an antilanguage is that it is a necessary "vehicle of . . . resocialization" for members of a community, and that it is "a *counter*-reality, set up *in opposition to* some established norm." Thus "[i]t is not the *distance* between the two realities but the *tension* between them that is significant" (171; emphasis Halliday's).

Halliday's account of antilanguages suggests that to enter the academic discourse community and, in Bartholomae's words, "trad[e] in one set of commonplaces at the expense of another" might be a transaction that one makes at tremendous personal cost—and one that, furthermore, some may be staunchly unwilling to enact. Yet one of the ways that hegemonic discourses defuse resistance is by failing to participate in discourses *about* tensions between discourses (and thus between communities). Linda Brodkey (1989), for instance, suggests:

> Those who occupy the best subject positions a discourse has to offer would have a vested interest in maintaining the illusion of speaking rather than being spoken by a discourse. . . . Hence, it is at least plausible to expect most, though not all, of those individuals whose subjectivity is the most positively produced by a discourse to defend its discursive practices against change. And it is equally plausible to expect some, though again not all, of those individuals whose subjectivity is the most negatively produced to resist its discursive practices. (126–27)

Resistance, then, comes from two sides—outsiders may form antisocieties whose discursive practices disrupt that which seems inevitable, impermeable, and even beneficent about regimes of dominant subjectivity; and insiders, if no longer able in a postmodern world to hitch the yoke of universality one notch more tightly around everyone, may still stake out fiefdoms of hegemonic subjectivity in particular socially desirable and guarded domains such as the academy. The real battle becomes not so much one over turf and inclusivity—in the age of multiculturalism, all are welcome, even if only in the blandest sense— but one over the naming or erasure of tensions.

Interpretive Communities: Is There a Queer in This Class?

The very notion of "interpretive communities" has come to be inextricably linked to Stanley Fish. Yet despite the fact that the term has come to take on a specialized meaning based on its association with Fish, particularly within the context of literary criticism, I am going to appropriate it here to discuss more broadly, and from several angles, social or community issues involved in the interpretation of texts, utterances, or discourses.

To begin, though, with Fish—"Is There a Text in This Class?" (1980) is a text written on the defensive, being Fish's attempt to absolve himself of charges of solipsism and relativism leveled at him because of his—and deconstructionists'—claim that language is indeterminate and interpretation situational. Fish seems primarily to be saying one thing, though he ends up suggesting quite another thing—the latter being that "an individual's assumptions and opinions are not 'his own'" in the sense that "*he* is not their origin (in fact it might be more accurate to say that they are his); rather it is their prior availability which delimits in advance the paths that his consciousness can possibly take" (320). In this late instance, Fish seems to be making the Foucauldian observation that individual consciousness is "written" by the various discourses it has occupied—or that have occupied it. Such a view would suggest that interpretation is a highly individualized, though deeply social, activity—individualized in the sense that we each have our own particular set of accrued discursive experiences, garnered from the communities we have entered, and social in the sense that comprehension would be impossible if not for our excursions in the world. In this view it would seem that interpretation depends not so much on where you *are* as on where you *have been*.

Throughout most of his essay, though, Fish seems to be arguing for a view of interpretation that is situational in a very present tense. Eternal, normative meanings of utterances are impossible, he says, because

> sentences emerge only in situations, and within those situations, the normative meaning of an utterance will always be obvious or at least

accessible, although within another situation that same utterance, no longer the same, will have another normative meaning that will be no less obvious and accessible. . . . This does not mean that there is no way to discriminate between the meanings an utterance will have in different situations, but that the discrimination will already have been made by virtue of our being in a situation (we are never not in one) and that in another situation the discrimination will also have already been made, but differently. (307–8)

Fish clearly sees the situation, and not the individual receiver of the utterance, as the crucial factor determining meaning. Yet it seems to me that several receivers of an utterance, positioned within the same immediate situation but also within diverse wider social contexts, will construe the same utterance differently—and may *never* discover a common denominator that might yield even provisional consensus. The meaning of the eponymous question, "Is there a text in this class?"—by which the student asking the question meant "Is this a class which assumes the instability of texts?" and to which Fish's colleague confidently responded, "Yes; it's the *Norton Anthology of Literature"*— would hardly be settled so easily if the colleague were a complete stranger to postmodern literary theory, or illiterate.

Or take an incident that occurred more than ten years ago, when a coworker in an office in which I was temping complained to me all morning about the dearth of straight men in New York. Near lunchtime, she asked me if I was in a relationship, and I said I was. "You mean, you actually found someone straight?" she said. I said no, I hadn't. She gasped in surprise. "You mean, he's gay?" I said, "No, *she* is." Because she was conversant with the diverse sexual/affectional cultures of New York City, there was only a short time delay—much as there probably was for Fish's colleague—before this information sank in and she began to laugh, recognizing that she had circumnavigated the sphere of possibilities rather than land directly on the one that should have been obvious. Yet clearly, the different spheres we inhabited and our daily experiences and expectations in the world transcended in interpretive importance the fact that we were both situated in a New York office discussing relationships and homosexuals. At the same time, she *was* able to quickly realize that the joke was on her; her confusion was followed by an "Of course!" and though the cohesion of the premises underscoring her automatic identification with me was dismantled in one way, she used her claim to sophisticated knowledge and experience to reconstitute it in another. Often, with people who lack such knowledge and experience, relaying this kind of information simply results in an immediate gulf, a blank look that seems to say, "That's not possible" or "You are immoral" or "You don't exist for me as you did a minute ago."

Another idea of what might constitute an interpretive community comes from schema theory. Described by Mary Crawford and Roger Chaffin (1986) as a cognitivist approach to reading, schema theory nevertheless seems philosophically related to (though methodologically different from) social constructionist views of the relationship of discourse to comprehension. Crawford and Chaffin explain that "comprehension is an active process of matching information in a text or utterance with the knowledge structures, or schemata, that the understander brings to the task" (3–4), and that because people are the products of different experiences which have formed diverse schemata prior to any one task of reading, understanding is necessarily variable. Schema frame the interpretive experience:

> A schema is activated when part of the incoming information matches part of the schema in memory. . . . If particular slots are not filled by information from the text, the schema will provide the necessary information. . . . In a similar way the schema fills in gaps in the narrative. Any events not explicitly mentioned are assumed to have occurred in the normal way. . . . The schema fills in missing information, and later the memory trace may not distinguish between the information provided by the sentence and information "read into" it. (4–5)

In a certain sense, Crawford and Chaffin are presenting in cognitivist language something also expressed, though in different terms, in postmodern discourse theory: that understanding never exists in a pristine state unmarked by prior or concurrent contextualizing experiences, and that construing is in fact an act of constructing. The main difference is that Crawford and Chaffin's focus is on discrete, finite, individual and measurable sources of knowledge, while the focus of much postmodern discourse theory is the ways that knowledge is inscribed through language in larger and virtually inescapable societal structures. Consider, for example, this story:

> [A researcher] showed people a film of a collision between two cars and then questioned them about what they had seen. Memory of the accident was found to have been affected by the question that had been asked immediately after the film. People who had been asked, "About how fast were the cars going when they smashed into each other?" were more likely, one week later, to answer "Yes" to the question "Did you see any broken glass?" than were people who were asked, "About how fast were the cars going when they hit each other?" The people who were asked the "smashed into" question also gave higher estimates of the speed of the car. Information presupposed by the question was incorporated into the memory of the accident. The memory was thus seen to be a dynamic structure subject to change. (6–7).

Crawford and Chaffin's accounts, such as this one, of how experience structures perception provide useful frameworks for considering the roles particular communities might play in interpretively situating their members. My office coworker's assumption that the gay person I was involved with was a man, unlikely as that must have been even to her, could be understood to stem from the heterosexual "schema" she brought to the conversation. This schema could also account for her difficulty in recognizing me as someone from outside her interpretive community; nothing in our immediate situation had clued her in. In a certain sense, it was not that different than the response of many people to the riddle about the father and son who are in an automobile accident together. The father is killed, and the son, seriously injured, is taken to a hospital. In the operating room, the surgeon looks down at the patient and says, "I can't operate on him. He's my son." How is this possible? The answer, of course, is that the surgeon is the patient's mother, and the point is that anyone who has only had experiences with and been exposed to representations of surgeons who are male is likely, like my coworker, to miss the obvious.

Crawford and Chaffin do, in fact, use schema theory to look at the relationship between gender and comprehension. They refer to gender as "a high-level schema" (25), and point out that within the women's movement, "[t]he experience of having one's consciousness raised is explained very well as the acquisition of a new schema that fits the experience" (25). Although I would question whether it in fact "fits" the experience or rather "reconstitutes" the experience, the idea that the experiences which yield a social identity serve as schema for comprehension seems like a highly useful one for understanding what happens for lesbian and gay students engaged in academic acts of interpretation.

Patrocinio Schweickart's (1986) reader-response account of reading as a woman makes it possible to consider from another angle what an interpretive community might be. She writes from a perspective that Jonathan Culler (1982) has characterized as belonging to "the second moment" of feminist criticism, in which the critical task is to confront the problem of "how to make it possible to read as a woman" and in which "the possibility of this fundamental experience induces an attempt to produce it" (63).[3] For Schweickart, many male texts require of women a "bifurcated" reading, or "a dual hermeneutic: a negative hermeneutic that discloses their complicity with patriarchal ideology, and a positive hermeneutic that recuperates the utopian moment—the authentic kernel—from which they draw a significant portion of their emotional power" (41–42). Schweickart doesn't question or define the categories "female" and "male" (though it is clear that "male" texts manifest varying degrees of sexism), but accepts each as an already-produced given. In her account, genders seem to be composed of natural confluences between biological sexual characteristics and epistemological location, and there are no markings of difference within the categories. Thus, within this scheme it *is* possible to find "an authentic kernel" reflecting the truth of one's experience.

As Culler has pointed out, "Even the most sophisticated theorists make this appeal—to a condition or experience deemed more basic than the theoretical position it is used to justify" (49). While postmodern feminist theory since Culler has grappled extensively with this problem, the extensive body of theoretical and critical work that came out of this "second moment" together with the wide audience that received it provide evidence of a community trying to define a collective interpretive framework based on the idea of shared gender. If I can, for the moment, set aside the obvious problems that Schweickart's text poses for me as a postmodern reader, and concentrate on reading it simply as the story of her own subjective experience reading as an Other negotiating with objectifying textual representations of herself, I discover some interesting things about her interpretive process as she casts it within the interests of a gendered community. Most notably, she sees interpretive acts not only deriving their existence from gender-community identification, but also generating it: "Feminist reading and writing alike are grounded in the interest of producing a community of feminist readers and writers, and in the hope that ultimately this community will expand to include everyone" (56). For Schweickart, then, the interpretive community is an at least hypothetically homogeneous grouping of women whose collective experience as women in sexist society leaves them with a sort of shared schizophrenia as readers; but at the same time, they have the ability to alter their affective textual experience by collectively producing a new kind of community literacy.

In a way, Schweickart poses a huge problem for me as I consider the forms and meanings an interpretive community might take, because even as I reject her premises and consequently have trouble with her conclusions, another part of me can't help feeling that *I know exactly what she means.* I, too, have felt like a schizophrenic reader—as a woman, as a lesbian, as a Jew, and at times in other ways. I recognize instantly what Schweickart means when she describes her "bifurcated" readings, and I have also heard my lesbian and gay students describe similar experiences as readers of heterosexual texts. I have additionally observed them responding to a syllabus full of lesbian and gay texts, heard them talk about what it meant to them as readers and writers to encounter such texts, seen the texts they produced in response, and—just as Schweickart said—watched new formulations of identity and community ensue. Was this an interpretive community? Did it really have to do with our being lesbian and gay? How about the fact that straight people were there, too?

What about textual experience made community happen? What about community experience made textuality happen?

A difficulty that comes up when trying to account for the nature and mechanisms of interpretive communities, then, is one of being caught between two forces. On the one hand, there is the drive to move beyond reliance on received categories of identity in formulating the structures that make us understand one another—the postmodern gesture of decentering the subject. Yet as feminist Susan Bordo (1992) has pointed out, this "decentering" is often painful when moved off the theoretical page and experienced as "part of the lived experience of acting, thinking, writing in fragmenting times," for "in human communities it has often meant homelessness, dislocation from history, a sense of political and intellectual vertigo and paralysis, and the replacement of lost human bonds by the individual search for stimulation and material gratification" (163–64). Therefore we encounter, in the words that Adrienne Rich used in a much earlier feminist "moment," the ineluctable "drive/ to connect. The dream of a common language" (1978, 7). It is possible, in fact, and worth exploring the idea that truly dynamic interpretive communities get formed at the point where massive weather fronts of theory and the complications of human need collide.

Notes

1. Lesbians rarely enter the discussion and are widely considered not to be the real point of contention. As Alisa Solomon has pointed out in her article "An Army of Others: Why the Gay Ban Makes the Man," "They'll ogle us, put naked pinups around the barracks, sexually harass us, maybe even rape us: so say military men at bases around the country who are terrified that the ban against homosexuals will be lifted. They're afraid, in other words, of being treated like women. . . . What's so striking about these fantasies . . . is how these straight men are projecting the culture of military macho onto gays. It's an extraordinary reversal. [They] are imagining gays as the most manly of men—and themselves as prey. *This* is the threat to morale" (1993, 25).

2. For an excellent discussion of this issue, see Kath Weston's *Families We Choose: Lesbians, Gays, Kinship:* Chapter 3, "Coming Out to 'Blood' Relatives" and Chapter 4, "Kinship and Coherence: Ten Stories."

3. For Culler, the "first moment" of feminist criticism is that which is involved with "investigating attitudes to women or the 'images of women' in the works of an author, a genre, or a period" (46).

Chapter Five

The Politics of Outsiderhood Go to School
Liberatory Pedagogy

As James Berlin (1988) has defined it, social-epistemic rhetoric posits knowledge as a product of a dialectic between a subject, the discourse community in which the subject is located, and the material world. This dialectic, grounded in language, socially constructs the subject as well as all that is thinkable by that subject. A pedagogy predicated on such a view therefore moves students toward a perception of themselves and their beliefs as discursively produced rather than naturally or even culturally determined.

Liberatory pedagogy at its best operates on somewhat similar principles, but its goals are often more pragmatically geared toward the alteration of material conditions. Whereas social-epistemic rhetoricians are largely concerned that students *understand how* social knowledge gets produced (and presume that with this understanding students will choose to position themselves in the world differently than they would have without it), liberatory pedagogues are specifically interested in the application of this knowledge beyond the academy in the form of social transformation. Put more simply (and perhaps at the risk of oversimplifying), social-epistemic rhetoricians want to fashion their students as critical intellectuals; liberatory teachers want to bring their students to self-realization as actors in history and "empower" them (key word!) to change the conditions of their lives.

These categories are really not mutually exclusive, and the schismatic definitions I've just set out contain more than a grain of falsehood; indeed, increasingly in the last few years the two categories have almost conflated within composition. What may be more important at this point is the fact that they have somewhat different histories, giving them somewhat different flavors even at their point of convergence. Social-epistemic rhetoric has a good many of its roots in European and North American poststructuralist theory, while most people trace liberatory pedagogy back to the 1960s work of Brazilian educator Paulo Freire (though, as I shall illustrate, forms of it made appearances here in earlier parts of this century). Right now, in composition at least, they might be formulated together as a continuum, with the liberatory dimension aimed at breaking through the academy's walls and bringing theory into the realm of social action.

The primary work that has been done in these two areas has focused on class and economic issues; secondary focuses have been issues of gender and race. Virtually no attention in the main current of liberatory education has been directed to issues and politics of sexual identity. Adding sexual identity to the list of concerns of social construction and liberatory pedagogy is not just a matter of squeezing another item onto a menu, but of recognizing the ways that sexual identity intersects with every other aspect of identity and social organization, and thus is a prime source of the very arrangements that are at the heart of social-epistemic and liberatory pedagogical inquiry. Within the emerging field of lesbian and gay studies, issues of family, identity, community, history, sexuality, psychology, and education are being alternatively constructed and interpreted from lesbian and gay subject positions; yet this new work has yet to be connected to composition. In this chapter I will describe some basic strands of thought and counterthought that have been influential in liberatory pedagogy, working on the premise that a knowledge of the history and philosophy of liberatory learning is indispensable to conceiving viably antihomophobic classrooms.

Two early incarnations of liberatory pedagogy in the United States that preceded the Freirian projects which have dotted the educational landscape since the sixties were the Modern School movement from 1910 to 1960 and the Highlander Folk School, which began in the early 1930s in Tennessee and still continues. The Modern School movement was an educational experiment inspired by the work of Francisco Ferrer, a Spanish anarchist and educator (Avrich 1980). Ferrer was executed by the repressive Spanish regime in 1909 on trumped-up charges after years of political activity which had gained him notoriety with the church and the reactionary government. He openly opposed both these forces and worked to free schooling from their influence. Ferrer's goal was to bring literacy and Enlightenment rationalism to adults and children of the working class, and he saw his project "not only as an educational institution but as a center of propaganda and agitation, a training ground for revolutionary activity. . . . [He] was applying the principles of syndicalism to educational practice, with the school, the counterpart of the union, acting as a vehicle for social transformation" (23–24). In the wake of international protests that followed his execution, anarchists and other civil libertarians in the United States—Emma Goldman and Alexander Berkman principals among them—founded the Ferrer Association to honor his ideals and a network of schools to implement them. At the Ferrer School in New York, according to Avrich, "Anarchism, socialism, syndicalism, revolution, birth control, free love, Cubism, Futurism, Freudianism, feminism, the New Woman, the New Theatre, direct action, the general strike . . . were [all] intensely discussed. . . ." (111).

The Highlander Folk School was founded and led for decades by Myles Horton, who originally wanted to create a school for Appalachian mountain people in a time and place where most of the local population was on relief. Modeling his program on the folk school tradition which had begun in nineteenth-century Denmark, Horton promoted the idea of adult education as worker education, and tapped an incipient revolutionary consciousness by using the conditions of students' lives as the source material of literacy and learning. Highlander worked with unions and farmers' organizations, often educating on the picket line. The school openly violated Tennessee's Jim Crow laws and worked to open the labor movement to all working people. Among the creative fruits of the Highlander community was an early incarnation of the song "We Shall Overcome." In the 1950s and 1960s the school's focus shifted to the civil rights movement—Rosa Parks and Septima Clark were among the leaders who emerged—and in the 1970s to community organizing around regional issues. Since then, Highlander has continued to host community activists from a variety of geographic regions in workshops and courses centering on critical problems and conflict situations in students' lives. Recently the school has added lesbian and gay issues to its roster of programs (Adams 1972; Graves 1979; Brown 1990; Highlander Reports Fall 1992).

An offshoot of Highlander back in 1954 was the Citizenship Schools, started in the racially segregated Sea Islands of South Carolina to teach literacy skills when they were still required for voter registration as a way of obstructing African Americans from voting. The Citizenship Schools later ended up under the auspices of the Southern Christian Leadership Conference, and by 1963 SCLC reported more than 400 schools across the South, with an estimated 100,000 who had learned to read and write through the program (Graves; Adams; Brown). Asked to explain the success of this program where other literacy projects had failed, Horton said:

It isn't a kind of mass education gimmick that you can plunk down anywhere and it works. That's why they couldn't get people to come to those state-financed literacy programs. It wasn't that people wanted to read and write because it was a good thing. They wanted to read for a purpose. That's why so many programs don't work; they are based on the thought that everybody if given a chance would learn to read and write. It's obviously not true . . . you must start where people are. That means their perception of where they are, not yours. . . . In the case of the Citizenship School, the basis was their everyday experiences and their ambition, their goal, which was voter registration. The content comes from what the people want to learn. (Quoted in Graves, 4)

The inspiration for most current efforts in liberatory education is Paulo Freire, whose 1968 *Pedagogy of the Oppressed* and subsequent writing (Freire and Macedo 1987; Freire and Shor 1987) offered a radical analysis of the politics and hidden agendas of conventional modes of instruction. Drawing on his work with illiterate peasants in Recife, Brazil, Freire articulated with greater theoretical complexity some of the same principles Horton used to explain the success of the Citizenship Schools. Like Horton, Freire feels that literacy as the mastery of "basic" discrete skills constitutes an arcane and alienating educational objective, one which is hardly likely to motivate adults to learn and in which the role of the student can only be to remain passive, receptive, and uncritical. He invokes in contrast the notion of critical literacy, which becomes manifest through what he calls "problem-posing education" grounded in the issues, concerns, conflicts, and questions with which students are personally moved to enter into active relationship. This sort of literacy has no moment of closure, no point at which "achievement" is signalled; it is a process of becoming, of ongoing inquiry and engagement with the world—of actively "reading" the world as well as the word, in Freire's famous phrase.

For Freire, education can either be an instrument of *subjection* or a catalyst for the development of conscious *subjects* who dialogically and transformatively interact with their world. Freire calls the process of critical reflection and the knowledge that one has agency in the world which results from liberatory education *conscientizaçao,* and the achievement of this agency *humanization.* Dehumanizing education relies on the "banking concept" of education, in which teachers make deposits of knowledge in students' heads "as if [reality] were motionless, static, compartmentalized, and predictable" (1970, 57), in the process turning students "into 'containers,' into 'receptacles' to be 'filled' by the teacher" (58). The harder students strive to "succeed" at this kind of education, the more effectively they are distracted from the possibility of intervening in the making and remaking of reality. This serves the needs of the oppressive class, in that it retains its control over descriptions of reality and the hegemonic social structures that are legitimated and locked in place by those descriptions. As Freire puts it, "Banking education (for obvious reasons) attempts, by mythicizing reality, to conceal certain facts which explain the way men exist in the world; problem-posing education sets itself the task of demythologizing. Banking education resists dialogue; problem-posing education regards dialogue as indispensable to the act of cognition which unveils reality" (71).

Ira Shor has been one of the foremost importers and transposers of Freire's work in the United States. In *Critical Teaching and Everyday Life* (1980) he explores what liberatory education could mean for working class students in public higher education in this country. His account of these students' experience of "banking" education is one in which even liberal studies have been "vocationalized" (30), and in which alienating work, patriarchal family structures, and the pervasive forces of mass culture and ideology have performed many of the "deposits" that clog students' thought processes. As a result, students retreat from critical scrutiny of the circumstances of their lives, taking recourse in ascribing poverty, war, and murder to "human nature," monetary gain to "luck," and survival to "common sense." Says Shor, "The flight from understanding cause and effect is a defense against confronting the social process which has infantilized and disempowered you, thus avoiding the facts of weakness out of which strength can grow" (61–63). Shor's liberatory writing class attempts to meet false consciousness head-on by having students "extraordinarily re-experienc[e] the ordinary"—i.e., critically interrogate some of the blindingly familiar, seemingly benign, but subtly problematic artifacts in their lives, such as nonnutritious, overpriced hamburgers from the school cafeteria and rigid, uncomfortable student chairs. By questioning the logic whereby these artifacts are deemed adequate by college authorities and alternatives are made to seem unavailable, students move beyond reifying these conditions ("That's just the way it is") to mentally and tangibly involving themselves in the processes of production of their own environment. Through this involvement, Shor contends, they don't simply solve problems; they come to see that reality *can* change when it is intervened with, and that through induced passivity they have been made unwitting coconspirators in their own victimization.

In his introduction to *Freire for the Classroom* (1987), an anthology of essays on liberatory teaching, Shor proposes that teachers join students in creating a Freirian pedagogy that is "participatory, critical, values-oriented, multicultural, student-centered, experiential, research-minded, and interdisciplinary" (22). Shor's "desocializing model for teacher education" is one in which teachers ground themselves in modes of dialogical inquiry, in ethnography and cross-cultural communication, in an understanding of inequities in society, in the history of egalitarian movements that have been socially transforming and in models of community change. Contributors to the volume demonstrate their application of Freirian pedagogy in such diverse areas as math, ESL, women's studies, and high school reading classes. Kyle Fiore and Nan Elsasser (1987, 87–103) describe a course they taught at a community college in the Bahamas, in which they used Freire's idea of a generative theme close to the students' concerns as the focal point of instruction. In this case, the all-women's class chose the theme of "marriage." Through the process of examining in depth the subtopics *housework, divorce, sexuality,* and *domestic violence* and concluding the term with a collective letter addressed to Bahamian men that ran in both Nassau daily papers under the headline "Bahamian Women Deserve a Change," the women became able to reflect upon, articulate, and issue a public protest about oppressive features of their lives.

While Shor and his contributors describe the practice of activist pedagogies in which students are guided toward modes of re-envisioning conditions of their lives, Henry Giroux presents, I believe, a more complex reading of the social forces that coalesce in school and manifest ideology through education. In *Theory and Resistance in Education* (1983), he attempts to relate "the deep grammar of the existing social order" to the surface structures and practices of alienating schooling, and identifies schools as "cultural and political sites" that "represent arenas of contestation and struggle among differentially empowered cultural and economic groups" (3). Giroux also observes that much radical pedagogical theory has been "much too cognitive in its orientation" and has focused overwhelmingly on class oppression, eliding the equally pervasive presence of racial and gender discrimination [add: homophobia] (39, 59). He writes of "those students who experience daily the pain of humiliation and powerlessness because their own lived experiences and sedimented histories are at odds with the dominant school culture," and says that radical teachers, rather than either reproducing the conditions of enforced powerlessness or trying to simply redress them, will recognize that "[t]he contradictory nature of school life provides a site for teachers to explore how the knowledge and meanings of subordinate groups are experienced and interpreted both within and outside of discourse"(68). Knowledge is politicized for Giroux not merely through recognition that schools attempt to reproduce the conditions of capital and hence the labor force that will support the perpetuation of systems of domination (222–23), but also through the development of "a theory of domination that incorporates needs and wants" of diverse groups, that "points to the importance of the sensual and imaginative as central dimensions of the schooling experience," and that touches "those pockets of desires and needs that harbor a longing for a new society and new forms of social relations" (39, 35). Thus, says Giroux, a legitimate pedagogy of resistance is one in which

> students come to grips with what a given society has made of them, how it has incorporated them ideologically and materially into its rules and logic, and what it is that they need to affirm and reject in their own histories in order to begin the process of struggling for the conditions that will give them opportunities to lead a self-managed existence. (38)

Giroux's account, in my view, is a step closer toward relevance for lesbian and gay students than Shor's or even Freire's models (though he, like Shor, is deeply influenced by Freire) because it transcends their schismatic, adversarial schema of oppressors and oppressed as two fairly well-delineated, respectively unified groups whose interests are clearly at odds with one another. It isn't easy to translate the "oppressor/oppressed" binary into a form helpful to understanding the homo-hetero opposition, since the classification of anyone in this scheme is always questionable due to the ill-defined contours of the categories.

But I find other problems with Shor. Particularly as he constructs it, what liberatory pedagogy "liberates" is the consciousness of the oppressed from a false identification with the oppressors, which has kept the oppressed ensnared in a perpetual hegemonic trap. The liberated teacher is, to borrow Freire's terminology, the "humanized" agent who is cognizant of the forces and contradictions that sustain a repressive social order and is in a position to guide students through the necessary processes leading to similar awareness. Yet it is hard for me to accept that Shor's students are quite as dehumanized as he thinks they are—or that he himself is so fully *conscientização* as to know the particular arenas in which his students require conscientization. His dichotomy of critical consciousness as an objective ideal on the one hand and students' "pre-scientific," reified constructions of reality on the other erases the sorts of knowledge students bring to the classroom from their own communities and from their daily experiences of marginalization. In other words, he seems to be working according to a deficit model for worker-students, rather than with the belief that they already *do* apprehend certain contradictions in their lives that are fertile source-material for critical academic analysis. Thus, although it is ostensibly part of Shor's project to help students critique distorted cultural representations of themselves and others, he seems at the same time to appropriate the "oppressor's" privilege of devaluing and delegitimizing their interpretations of their own lives, based on the world view from his own privileged subject position. Furthermore, though he does describe some class work based on the sexism inherent in marriage, he overwhelmingly privileges the economic realm as the site of critical renegotiation. Significantly, too, heterosexism is absent from Shor's critique of marriage. He opens his description of that course unit confidently, stating, "Marriage is an obvious subject around which to design problematic study in virtually any academic discipline. It is such a familiar part of everyday life. . . . Students come to class with a multitude of opinions and expectations concerning marriage. They bring to this problem-theme a special form of false consciousness: their conditioned sexist behavior" (218). Shor's own conditioning has obviously played a role in course design and, consequently, in the role that a lesbian or gay student in the class can play in this group exercise of critical inquiry, due to Shor's rather annihilating failure to imagine the presence of such a student. He defines all the women in the class by their relationship to marriage—present or future—yet doesn't consider how such limited framings of the group might be connected to his regret that "there is virtually no mature thought on the problem" in the class (220). In fact, there is nothing in his book that suggests ways of tapping the kind of heightened awareness that lesbian and gay students bring from their daily experience of violating social expectations and of finding themselves either absent or demonized in cultural myths and narratives—those about marriage, dating, and the nuclear family foremost among them.

Shor also points, Orwell-like, to "the electronic mass media" as an agent of "the mass denial of reason" and as part of the "complex machinery [that] effect[s] thought-control" (49), and laments the fragmentation in students' lives wrought by fast food, advertising, and TV—as if to suggest that postmodernization is the diabolical weapon of the oppressor and a pre-electronic, pre-industrial Eden-state the telos of humanization. However, others have suggested contrasting interpretations of the politics of empowerment in contemporary culture, such as postmodern feminist Donna Haraway in "A Manifesto for Cyborgs" (1990):

> Communications technologies and biotechnologies are the crucial tools recrafting our bodies. These tools embody and enforce new social relations for women worldwide. Technologies and scientific discourses can be partially understood as formalizations, that is, as frozen moments, of the fluid social interactions constituting them, but they should also be viewed as instruments for enforcing meanings. The boundary is permeable between tool and myth, instrument and concept, historical systems of social relations and historical anatomies of possible bodies, including objects of knowledge. Indeed, myth and tool mutually constitute each other. . . . The machine is not an it to

be animated, worshiped, and dominated. This machine is us, our processes, an aspect of our embodiment. We can be responsible for machines; they do not dominate or threaten us. We are responsible for boundaries; we are they. (205–6, 222)

Haraway believes that the "cyborg"—which she describes as "a cybernetic organism, a hybrid of machine and organism, a creature of social reality as well as a creature of fiction . . . that changes what counts as women's experience in the late twentieth century" (191)—represents new ways of making social meanings, and that this has significance for writing:

Cyborg writing is about the power to survive not on the basis of original innocence, but on the basis of seizing the tools to mark the world that marked them as other. . . . The tools are often stories, retold stories, versions that reverse and displace the hierarchical dualisms of naturalized identities. In retelling origin stories, cyborg authors subvert the central myths of origin of Western culture. . . . Feminist cyborg stories have the task of recoding communication and intelligence to subvert command and control. . . . Cyborg imagery can suggest a way out of the maze of dualisms in which we have explained our bodies and our tools to ourselves. This is a dream not of a common language, but of a powerful infidel heteroglossia. (217, 223)

Shor's dialectical relationship with "things," then, seems circumscribed by a particular set of intentions—i.e., to move students toward recognition of the ways that their interests have been harnessed and co-opted by the interests of corporate greed—while the multiplicity of other meanings attached to "things" and even to living in a post-industrial, high-tech, goods-rich, fast-paced society remain unexplored. For women, the fast-food hamburger floats in history not only as a signifier of deteriorating health and environmental conditions but *also* as a marker of women's liberation from the time-consuming responsibilities of food production. And while some may rue the fact that the formerly warm, community-centered nature of leisure activity has been displaced by alienating, atomizing technological apparatus such as modems and VCRs, for lesbians and gays already alienated in small-town culture around the country, technology can mean the chance to communicate with one another via computer networks and to encounter forms of queer cinematic representation other than the *Basic Instinct* variety that monopolizes the mall. Giroux's injunction to develop "a theory of domination that incorporates needs and wants" seems to offer greater possibilities for looking at cultural facts and artifacts as multiply signifying entities that intersect with students' multiple identities in complex ways and thus command a variety of (sometimes contradictory) values and interpretations. Such a pedagogy would seem to offer more students the chance to "come to grips with what a given society has made of them" than a largely class-based, tech-wary liberatory pedagogy like Shor's.

More recently, Giroux has written that the university is "a place that produces a particular selection and ordering of narratives and subjectivities. It is a place that is deeply political and unarguably normative" (1992, 120). Of course, even in liberatory classrooms, lesbian or gay subjectivity is often still the one that dare not speak its name. But Giroux's attention to that process of selection and ordering, along with his recognition that there are *many* possible narratives and subjectivities and thus what we need is "a public philosophy that legitimates a politics and pedagogy of difference" (133) makes his liberatory pedagogy more suitable for the 1990s than Freire's or Shor's. (In all fairness, the text of Giroux's I am drawing on in this paragraph was *written* in the 1990s.) Giroux envisions a pedagogy that acknowledges the rich traditions of alternative "cultures," one in which

> there is a questioning of the omissions and tensions that exist between the master narratives and hegemonic discourses that make up the official curricula of the university, department, or program and the self-representations of subordinate groups as they might appear in "forgotten" histories, texts, memories, experiences, and community narratives. A pedagogy of difference not only seeks to understand how difference is constructed in the intersection of the official canon of the school and the various voices of students from subordinate groups, but also draws upon student experience as both a narrative for agency and a referent for critique. . . . Such a pedagogy contributes to making possible a variety of human capacities which expand the range of social identities that students may become. It points to the importance of understanding in both pedagogical and political terms how subjectivities are produced within those social forms in which people move but of which they are often only partially conscious. (136–38)

Lesbian and gay studies has certainly been consumed with, more than anything else, the ways that subjectivities are produced, and Giroux's increasingly postmodern liberatory pedagogy probably comes closest of the ones I have mentioned to describing what I hoped would be the liberatory dimension of the lesbian and gay writing classes I taught. Lesbians and gay men are used to functioning as negative metaphors and as a result brought to the class a wry consciousness of the semiosis of everyday life. Many of them were also connected to informal educational networks such as the prolific gay press and a network of social and political organizations that kept them informed about legal, media, and AIDS-related issues. What I believe was "liberatory" about our class was that their intuitive understanding and the understanding that came from community identification and affiliation could be put through the sieve of critical analysis, that critical analysis could find expression in social action (including both events pertaining primarily to their own personal social existence and organized, mass mobilizations), and their experience of social action or interaction could be brought back into the class and subjected to further critical analysis, informing their approach to future action. In short, it was a class that I hoped would help people create a viable place for themselves in the world, partly by helping them find ways of rethinking themselves through language and, consequently, by using new language to find ways of reconstituting the world.

Liberatory Principles in Women's Studies

I have given examples of a few salient exponents of liberatory pedagogy, and before I go on I want to account for why I am leaving out of this discussion the entire enormous discipline of women's studies, which was founded on liberatory principles—even, in part, Freirian ones. Much of women's studies in fact overlaps with lesbian and gay studies; the question of gender permeates both disciplines, and lesbians especially often keep one foot in each classroom. The reason I am choosing not to discuss women's studies here has everything to do with both its sheer enormity and at the same time its correspondence to areas I have discussed. For many years what was called "feminist pedagogy" by academics in women's studies was not extremely different from the pedagogies of Freirians or even compositionists. Notions of process-oriented, student-centered, nonhierarchical and nonauthoritarian classrooms which were sites of critical thinking and collaborative learning were characteristic, to varying degrees, of all of those arenas, except that often in women's studies these were values and practices talked about specifically in relation to gender. Feminists, Freirians, and compositionists also shared a self-consciousness about the relationship of theory to practice, both inside and outside the classroom. For Freirians and feminists, the "outside" practice had to do with involvement in movements for social change (for feminists, in fact, it had to do with the quality of their involvement with virtually everything!); for compositionists, writing was also, though usually in a far less radical way, linked to issues of good citizenship and social responsibility. What has distinguished feminists from Freirians and compositionists is a belief in personal self-scrutiny as a matter of political and pedagogical significance. It has been common for feminists who are involved with antiracism work, for example, to engage in consciousness-raising sessions in which their own relationship to racism can be examined, and for them to confront the racism or internalized racism that is still, however uncomfortably, present inside them. This confrontation is not seen as an impediment to performing antiracist work, but rather as an enabler of it. That is, it is considered important to examine the way contradictions are lodged in, and actively dealt with inside, oneself, and this process itself becomes a model for social change.

In women's studies the relationship between method and content has often been foregrounded and has led to the creation of frequent metanarratives about process even in undergraduate courses. Collections such as Charlotte Bunch's and Sandra Pollack's *Learning Our Way: Essays in Feminist Education* (1983), Gloria Bowles's and Renate Duelli Klein's *Theories of Women's Studies* (1983), and Margo Culley's and Catherine Portuges's *Gendered Subjects: The Dynamics of Feminist Teaching* (1985) are a few textual manifestations of the ongoing conversations that have often involved faculty, administrative staff, and students at all levels about what kind of pedagogical practice would best represent the integrity of women's studies. Many of these discussions have been gender-specific—what kind of practice befits a *women's* classroom, learning about *women's* lives? Although in recent times some women's studies courses have been formulated in line with what would once have been called "male" poststructuralist theory (and many would still call it that) and some modes of instruction have reformed within the context of a new philosophical era and a new generation of students, there is still in most cases the galvanizing question of "How will this help women to live better?" In fact, I believe that most of these classes are informed in some manner by questions that Adrienne Rich posed in her commencement address at Smith College in 1979. Said Rich (1986) at that time:

> Suppose we were to ask ourselves simply: What does a woman need to know to become a self-conscious, self-defining human being? Doesn't she need a knowledge of her own history, of her much-politicized female body, of the creative genius of women of the past—the skills and crafts and techniques and visions possessed by women in other times and cultures, and how they have been rendered anonymous, censored, interrupted, devalued? . . . [D]oesn't she need an analysis of her condition, a knowledge of the women thinkers of the past who have reflected on it, a knowledge, too, of women's worldwide individual rebellions and organized movements against economic and social injustice, and how these have been fragmented and silenced? . . . Without such education, women have lived and continue to live in ignorance of our collective context, vulnerable to the projections of men's fantasies about us as they appear in art, in literature, in the sciences, in the media, in the so-called humanistic studies. I suggest that not anatomy, but enforced ignorance, has been a crucial key to our powerlessness.

Problems with Liberatory Pedagogy

Rich's questions are important and can be translated, I believe, to serve as models for any liberatory intellectual project. They are important largely in their specificity, and for the fact that they are asked not by someone designing a curriculum for a body of unknown and undefined strangers, but by one longing to know for herself. Lack of specificity has been a hallmark of the main current of (white, male) liberatory pedagogical theory. I once heard Joseph Harris exclaim about Henry Giroux at a conference, "All those books and never a single classroom experience!" It isn't surprising that liberatory theory doesn't invoke mental images of lesbians, gays, or anyone else; the abstractions are not populated by real people. The result is not only that it's hard, as a reader, to grasp just what it all might mean when played out with live human beings; it's also that in such ungrounded theory many parts of human beings easily remain unimagined, their transformative power untapped, and the reader/teacher as would-be liberator trying to implement the ideas ends up, unexpectedly, "banking" whatever form of liberation *he* thinks is appropriate in students' heads.

Elizabeth Ellsworth, in an essay called "Why Doesn't This Feel Empowering? Working Through the Repressive Myths of Critical Pedagogy" (1989), levels precisely this charge. Reviewing the literature on critical pedagogy, she finds that theorists of critical pedagogy "consistently strip discussions of classroom practices of historical context and political position," and use words such as "critical," "empowerment," "student voice," and "dialogue" in ways that actually camouflage and defuse real political positions such as antiracism, antihomophobia, antineoconservativism, etc. (300). As a result, she feels that "the critical education 'movement' has failed to develop a clear articulation of the need for its existence, its goals, priorities, risks, or potentials," and leaves one wondering, "Empowerment for what?" in the absence of a challenge to "any identifiable social or political position, institution, or group" (301, 307).

Ellsworth finds critical pedagogy's excessive rationalism paternalistic and its claims to teacher-student egalitarianism shallow, given that students are only seen as "empowered" "when the teacher 'helps' [them] to express their subjugated knowledges" (308–9). Beyond that, it lacks a recognition that consciousness of anything is always partial, as well as the fact that the part of our identity that is "oppressed" by a particular situation is just a *part* of who we "are," and other parts may be standing by, unaddressed and unaccounted for. The goal of eliciting "student voice"—generally discussed as an expression of unified subjectivity—is a naïve one because "[i]t is impossible to speak from all voices at once, or from any one, without the traces of the others being present and interruptive" (312). Because liberatory pedagogy tends to lump not only whole consciousnesses, but whole classes of students, into falsely unified masses, it "fails to confront dynamics of subordination present among classroom participants and within classroom participants in the form of multiple and contradictory subject positions" (315).

Besides that, Ellsworth feels that critical educators ignore their own often threatening role as observers of students' processes, assuming that students who don't evince particular signs of awareness are simply unaware, rather than simply feeling vulnerable about the risk of revealing too much of their Otherness in situations that seem to replicate the usual social dangers of, for example, sexism, racism, and homophobia. Partly for this last reason, Ellsworth finds the critical pedagogue's lack of specific self-portraiture particularly troublesome.

> When education researchers writing about critical pedagogy fail to examine the implications of the gendered, raced, and classed teacher and student for the theory of critical pedagogy, they reproduce, by default, the category of generic "critical teacher"—a specific form of the generic human that underlies classical liberal thought. Like the generic human, the generic critical teacher is not, of course, generic at all. Rather, the term defines a discursive category predicated on the current mythical norm, namely: young, White, Christian, middle-class, heterosexual, able-bodied, thin, rational man. (310)

The generic teacher invents generic students notable for their lack of consciousness. Yet Ellsworth found in her experience teaching a course called "Media and Anti-Racist Pedagogies," as I found in my lesbian- and gay-themed writing courses, that many students entered the class "with oppositional voices already formulated within various antiracism and other movements. These movements had not necessarily relied on intellectuals/teachers to interpret their goals and programs to themselves or to others" (311).

Another useful critique of liberatory pedagogy is the more recent "Considerations of American Freiristas" by Victor Villanueva, Jr. (1991). Villanueva argues that "history and culture alone do not make for a political sensibility," and that "such a view is reductive of the complex combinations of cultures and histories in American minorities. . . ." (249). He, like Ellsworth, highlights the fact that human subjects are split, and contends that even the most enlightened among us harbor some secret acceptance of traditions and national-cultural norms. He is skeptical that any freshman composition class will accept the counterhegemonic positions encouraged by Freirians, and illustrates this view by a description of a "Freirian" teaching experience in a Writing Project class that he observed over the course of a term which did not produce the utopian results that it was intended to. The students were low-income adolescents and young adults, almost all Black, and, according to Villanueva, the class was "Freirian" principally because Floyd, the teacher, described it that way. Yet he says of Floyd:

> His method was explicitly propaganda. He said so. Floyd would impart what he knew. . . . [T]here was no dialectic in this class. The hegemonic and counterhegemonic were not allowed evaluation. (256)

In Floyd's class, students resisted the master liberatory narratives of alienation and collectivity, writing contentedly of their attractions to mainstream culture and their desires to enter it and eschewing the call to revolution in favor of the usual route of individual access through hard work. Villanueva perceives that students failed to identify with the persona of "alienated man" in mainstream society because "[o]ppressor and oppressed have histories, cultures, ideologies, traditions in common. This is the tug inherent in hegemony" (256), and they were unpersuaded that collective action held out much hope of advancement because their observations of successful minority figures—movie stars, athletes, politicians—indicated that "individuals have gone farther than the race" (257).

Villanueva ultimately developed a course in which, rather than taking a firm counterhegemonic stance, he promoted a dialectical relationship between tradition—which has deep affective and historical importance for students—and changing worldviews. By writing about the tensions between tradition and change, students developed their own critical positions vis-à-vis traditions as their own antagonisms became revealed through writing—a distinctly different enterprise than being politely but firmly escorted toward a new worldview.

Villanueva's portrait of the dogmatic Freirian teacher and Ellsworth's depiction of liberatory pedagogy's failings both, in some sense, caricature the pedagogy by portraying it at its most sententious and fatuous level; both, at the same time, ring true for me because they pull back the curtain on the uneasy allegiances all of us have, as multidimensional beings, to the very forces that "oppress" us. It is difficult to live in a country that advertises its consumer products as seductively as ours does and not be seduced; it is also difficult to have been raised in a family, community, and society and altogether resist identification with them, even if the very modus operandi by which each shores up its identity is the repudiation of queerness. Liberatory pedagogy has not, it is true, adequately dealt with these contradictions inside us. Nevertheless, I believe that Villanueva's, Ellsworth's, and my own pedagogies are all in significant ways derivative of liberatory principles and ideology. Like Freudian psychoanalysis, Marxism, pizza, and mah jong, most imports are enthusiastically received and then just as enthusiastically altered when they cross borders and must adapt to serve the needs of a new clientele. I experience my own intellect as the product of liberatory learning in various forms and contexts, some transposing and some clearly drawing on Freirian philosophy—women's studies, African American studies, labor studies, and most recently, lesbian and gay studies. Unfortunately, lesbian and gay studies, in my experience—and perhaps it's because it's still relatively new—has seemed the least interested in connecting its theoretical work and research with issues of pedagogy and student consciousness. This is a connection I hope it will make. The writing class, with all its self-consciousness about the conditions that foster the creation of meaning, seems like a promising place to begin.

Part Three

The Lesbian-
and
Gay-Themed
Writing Class

Chapter Six

Construing and Constructing Knowledge as a Lesbian or Gay Student Writer
Reflections on an Identity-Based Course

An analogy for one of the overarching difficulties lesbian and gay student writers face came to me some time ago while I was watching a *60 Minutes* piece on the singer/songwriter Paul Simon. In his interview Simon said that years ago, when the song "Mrs. Robinson"—which included the line, "Where have you gone, Joe DiMaggio?"—first came out, DiMaggio wanted to sue him. "What do you mean, where have I gone?" DiMaggio asked him angrily. "I'm very much here; I do Mr. Coffee commercials." Paul Simon commented wryly to the interviewer, "Obviously, he hadn't begun to think of himself as a metaphor." Sports idols and movie stars are the revered and privileged Others of American society; but less respected Others, too, however greatly they may desire to experience themselves simply as subjects, are continually brought back to awareness of their simultaneous existence as social metaphors.

Lesbian and gay students in mainstream writing classes who wish to write from a position of acknowledged lesbian or gay subjectivity must inevitably confront the ways that they function as social metaphors for their audience—their audience being, presumably, class peers and teacher. It is hard for them to forget that they have been—and the emphasis shifts depending on place and time period—metaphors for sin, sickness, criminality, bourgeois decadence, and the demise of the family. Homosexuality popularly signifies that which transgresses on

111

virtually all the institutions of our society: the law, the government, religion, the family, the police, the medical and psychiatric establishments. Institutional violence against lesbians and gays from these sources has included capital punishment, police brutality (or indifferent neglect during assaults on gays), administration of involuntary electroshock or drug therapy, beatings and other forms of violence perpetrated by family members, and imprisonment. In the context of a society that so sweepingly condones this sort of violence and so forcefully blames its victims, it is hardly surprising that peer gay bashing among high school and college-age students—and nearly half the perpetrators in gay-bashing incidents are twenty-one years old or younger, with the great majority being under twenty-eight (Comstock 1991, 59)—would take on, in one former perpetrator's words, the heroic stature of "'a kind of holy war'" in which the warriors are "'doing the world a favor'" (19). In a survey, one quarter of the victims of antigay/antilesbian violence reported school itself (college, senior, or junior high) as the site of the assault, and lesbians and gays report almost three times as many incidents of crimes against them in school settings as do victims of crime in general (48, 51). And contrary to the simple optimistic belief that "things are changing now" in some linear, unidirectional way—i.e., that increased visibility for lesbians and gay men is ushering in a new era of acceptance—political gains have been accompanied by a dramatic rise in antilesbian and antigay violence. The growth of institutions serving the community and the development of gay neighborhoods have created easily identifiable hunting grounds to which perpetrators have said they are glad to travel, and assaults are focused on those known or believed to be gay or lesbian (25, 61–62; Weston 1991, 46–47). Within this context, for lesbian or gay students to write about their experience in a classroom is to put themselves at great risk—not only socially and psychically, but physically as well.

A few years ago I began to conceive of a course in which some of the prohibitive forms of "danger" that exist for lesbian and gay student writers might be reduced. I also wanted it to be a course that acknowledged how various sorts of danger make the experience of construing and constructing knowledge particularly convoluted for lesbian and gay students, wreaking a special kind of epistemological trouble. At the same time, I knew that the danger had a certain kind of perverse usefulness, too. An awareness of it always hovering at the borders of one's speech inspires resistance to it, and the dance of this danger and this resistance can lead to a multivoiced discourse that subjects writing from zones of relative "safety" lack. So I didn't want my class to be a place in which students would entirely forget about the danger, but rather to be a place in which they could, from something like the provisionally protected space of an embassy in a hostile country, peer out at it and examine what it was in their relationship to the danger that invigorated—not just stifled—their literacy acts.

Jerome Bruner (1986) has described a process that he calls *subjunctivizing reality,* which he principally applies to readers of fiction (26, 31–37, 159). For Bruner, subjunctivizing means thinking hypothetically in order to engage with the reality of a character. The illusion of reality arrives via an *as if* transposition that the reader makes. The reader mentally *rewrites* a text as she reads it, rendering what Bruner calls a *virtual text:* an interpretive re-creation of an actual written text. This virtual text, Bruner says, is the only one that will ever be accessible to us, since all of our thinking is subjective.

I would like to borrow Bruner's concept of subjunctivizing and use it here to describe a discursive process that denizens of nondominant groups undergo when they use language in dominant communities. Heterosexual discourse, for instance, has many qualities of a canonized work of fiction. It is an epic romance that successive generations of readers inherit and retell, and it carries all the prestige and unassailability of a classic. One way that the cognitive distance traveled in coming out could be described would be to say that closeted gays are fixed as eternally subjunctivizing readers of this romance, while the movement toward outness means becoming a writer—using language to inscribe *alternative* actual texts that *others* must reciprocally subjunctivize their way into. In a large sense, the politics of subjunctivizing are related to the politics of publishing: texts that reinscribe dominant discourses have an easier time achieving a public life, inasmuch as their emergence is facilitated by the well-connected agents of dominant discourses; and what is "public" is that culturally visible space toward which those in the darkened hall of the audience must strain if they want to be in on the social conversation. Only when the presses are seized and the textual economy reapportioned will the members of diverse communities be forced to make comparable subjunctivizing leaps across discursive boundaries—and engage in what Bruner calls "joint culture creating" (127, 132).[1]

Since a joint culture was not yet in the offing in 1991, however, I decided that what I really wanted to do in creating a writing class based on lesbian and gay experience was to find a way of, in Nancy K. Miller's (1986) words, "changing the subject." Though Miller's "subject" is women, her "subject" and mine are closely aligned enough (and of course, considerably overlap) through the politics of gender and sexuality to warrant a bit of adaptation. Writes Miller, "Because the female [read alternatively: lesbian or gay] subject has juridically been exluded from the polis, and hence decentered, 'disoriginated,' deinstitutionalized, etc., her relation to integrity and textuality, desire and authority, is structurally different" (106). I wanted this structural difference, conceptually embedded in the reasons Miller gives for this difference, to be the basis of a writing class. It didn't have to mean that everyone in the class was lesbian or gay. It did have to mean, though, that the class's collective gaze would shift as the spotlight fell on the very "decentered" zone of queer critical subjectivity, rendering it the focal point of inquiry. It would mean that everyone would have to consider what it would mean to read the world from a queer interpretive stance. It would mean that everyone would have to problematize the seemingly generic concept of heterosexuality, and consider the ways that, in Sedgwick's terms, "homosexual panic" infuses everyday discourse. With these as organizing assumptions of the course, I hoped to create what I would (privately) call a "lesbian and gay discourse community."

There were also emotional reasons for wanting to design a course like this. I knew that lesbian and gay students had most likely never had the chance to read, write, and think about their lives in this way before—certainly not in school. It wasn't only that most of them would have been influenced in some way by feeling unsafe, or by being actively discouraged from writing about their experience in other school environments; it was also that they would not have had access to the kind of information and texts that they would encounter in this course. The whole movement toward multiculturalism in education has been rooted in the notion that there are diverse cultural histories that matter, and that we need to discover how meanings have become inscribed upon different sorts of bodies occupying different social spaces. At its most basic level, this course would start to fill a curricular gap that virtually all lesbians and gay men—and heterosexuals, too—in this society have experienced, whether or not they are conscious of it or even imagine that a lesbian and gay studies curriculum could exist. I thought that the course would be meaningful to these students, and also that it would be exciting and fun.

I also thought that the course would be an ideal vehicle through which to enact some of the principal goals of contemporary writing pedagogy. I thought that lesbian and gay people's function as social metaphors would have much to teach students about systems of signification. Examining one's relationship to heterosexist thought must almost inevitably lead into a questioning of one's epistemological processes, of the ways one makes—and can reconstitute—meaning. Because merely raising the subject of lesbian/gay existence demands that we think about identity and power, to write about it jolts us into rhetorical considerations of voice, position, audience, perspective, relation, and authority. Inviting students into the world of academic discourse involves helping them to make the familiar strange and to decenter their reflexive assumptions. It seemed to me that a writing course that would raise the themes I was planning to raise and ask students to write about them, workshop them, revise them, share them, and ultimately carry them in some form into the rest of their academic and professional thinking would both contribute in important ways to the writing program in which the course was housed, and, at the same time, push the boundaries of that program by experimenting with new frameworks within which these goals might be achieved.

Finally, I did want the course to be "liberatory." The liberatory goal was really the sum of the other goals I have just described. I wanted it to help "liberate" the students from the experience of being, at least in part, tangential to the subjects of their studies; from not being able to use an important part of their subjectivity in academic work; from the millions of ways that both homophobia and internalized homophobia stunt one's growth and impinge on one's well-being; and from having to undermine one's potential strength as a writer. I wanted it to liberate them from being vulnerable to a constant onslaught of homophobic information about themselves from countless regions of their lives. I wanted them to have queer classmates, a queer teacher, a queer syllabus, queer textbooks, queer homework. And yes, I did hope that the course would make them activists, and if they were already activists, then better, more reflective activists. I wanted it to help them fight back.

The "Liberatory" Dimension

As it turned out, I taught two different, though very similar, courses in the spring 1992 term. One took place at a large, urban, private university that I will call Cosmopolitan University. The other took place at a large, urban, public college that I will call Municipal College. The two classes, along with interviews that I conducted with selected students after the courses ended, provided the context for the study that will inform the remainder of this book.[2]

Some aspects of liberatory learning were manifested in the lesbian- and gay-themed writing classes in ways that I hadn't planned or anticipated. In each class there were a number of students who were quite politicized and politically active, while others weren't. For some of those who weren't, examining the cultural machinery that produces homophobia and reflecting upon the ways that heterosexist society negated and suppressed their human potential propelled them toward activism. The ones who were more active often brought in announcements of new legal decisions, boycotts, and demonstrations affecting the lesbian and gay community, including information related to AIDS. Some of the less active students were emboldened to attend demonstrations or meetings of organizations for the first time. When one student announced at the end of one class that she would be late for the next class meeting because she would be coming from an ACT UP demonstration (blithely adding that she would not be there at all if she got arrested), we anticipated that part of our next class would be spent hearing her first-person report of the experience and collectively analyzing it. In addition, students reported that the class was giving them a necessary context in which to come out, they brought issues we discussed in class to their dorms, friends, and families, they challenged professors in other courses when lesbian and gay perspectives were ignored, and some of them brought these perspectives into the workplace—such as one student who successfully pushed for the inclusion of lesbian and gay issues at a large civil liberties organization where she worked in an administrative support position.

One student commented at a certain point that it was "hard to tell whether this is a class or a political meeting at the [Lesbian and Gay Community] Center." On another occasion, a student similarly remarked that it was hard to tell whether it was a class or group therapy. In response to both comments, I asked them, "What *is* the difference?"—a question which led to reflection on the ways that the boundaries between all of these were in fact blurred. They agreed that both political work and therapy were most effective when they incorporated certain features of progressive education—encounters with new ideas, critical reflection, charged and respectful discussion, and production of new knowledge—and that education was most effective when it utilized their rational and affective, public and private selves, touching upon parts of their lives that were deeply important to them and helping them to think, feel, and act in the world with creativity, transformative power, and integrity.[3]

They were conscious and vocal, then, about the energy and commitment they chose to invest in their work because they saw the significance of that work extending beyond the walls of the classroom. It was a kind of energy and commitment not unique to that course, but the kind that classes in women's studies programs, for instance, frequently elicit. In an article called "Class Conflicts: A Vindication of the Rights of Women's Studies" (1993), Ann Powers writes of how the creators of women's studies

> encouraged students to take the practices they developed outside the classroom. Doing so, they extended the boundaries of the text they were writing on each other's consciousness, in pursuit of that mythical revolution. It was a naïve move, to think that this new vision would spread so easily. But it operated on another level, building a notion of intertextuality of which French theorists should have been envious. Women, viewing themselves as texts composed by society, turned their new notion of authorship back on the world. Activism

> was viewed as rewriting the world through the self. Written texts were viewed as part of the process, constructed simultaneously by self and world. (11)

Powers half-facetiously compares the high theory of graduate school—poststructuralism "for the strong-stomached thinkers, the *real* thinkers"—with the "warm-fuzzy area of autobiography and personal 'dialogue'" (10) that, according to its detractors, is the province of women's studies. She argues, though, that the two realms are closer than they seem, that poststructuralist theory deconstructs the world "by digging at the roots of the order of things, and women's studies showed how those roots ran through my own backyard" (10). Because women's studies uses personal experience to identify asymmetrical power arrangements and the insidious workings of false consciousness in patriarchal culture, in it "the postmodern notion of the decentered self finds its natural meeting point with the most radical notion of identity politics: that of the individual as a work-in-progress, witnessing its own construction" (12).

In my lesbian- and gay-themed writing classes, students expressed a similar sense that in shifting and, sometimes, lifting the boundaries between "public" and "private" spheres, between life inside and outside the classroom, they were composing new forms of both consciousness and agency for themselves. Excerpts from reflective essays that three different students wrote at the end of the term suggest the forms this agency might take and the unpredictable kinds of significance such a course can have for students. The first:

> What I have discovered [in this course] is that what was holding me back was internalized homophobia, manifesting itself in my fear that others would not take me as anything other than just a gay man once they knew I was gay. I was not proud of who I was, I was afraid. But this course has given me a vocabulary, a history, and a greater sense of the community where I belong—"where I belong"—it's even given me the courage to stop trying to fit into the "us" that was never really mine, and make what I always thought of as "them" my "us."

The second:

> If we learned anything this semester, it was how our writing puts us in a position to be an activist of a sort, queer defenders with powerful pens. . . . I have written about queer topics before coming to this class but I have never felt as empowered by my writing as I have come to feel in this class. Through my writing for this class I found that I was able to go beyond simply having and feeling my identities to utilizing them as instruments of creation. I don't think that I have ever felt as compelled to work as hard as I did in this class.

And, painfully, the third:

> This writing course came at just the right time. My life had been
> falling apart, at least at the time it felt that way when I found out I
> was HIV positive. I thought that life was over (although the reader
> does not know this, it took me 5 minutes to type 3 simple letters).
> This was why I had a hard time writing in my journal. I was afraid,
> for myself and anyone who might discover the terrible truth. For a
> long time I felt that I would not have long to live. . . . That was
> why I was so desperate to be in this class and do all the things I felt
> I would not be able to do since I felt that soon my time would be up
> and I could never again be in a writing class with gay and lesbian
> issues.

I have to admit that I was shocked when the message in this
student's essay sank in the day after classes were finished and I sat
wading through the stack of final portfolios on my desk. Mostly, I was
shocked by a surge of grief for the young man who was himself still
reeling from the news—shocked the way you are in the first seconds
when someone you know is ejected from the happy, humdrum cocoon
of immortality and becomes that marked Other whose existence clearly
has a beginning, a middle, and an end. But I was also shocked at my
own naïveté. It occurred to me for the first time that no student in
either of the classes had ever discussed his or her HIV status—even
though we had read, written, and talked about AIDS activism. Every
single participant in both classes had been (voluntarily) out about her
or his sexual identity, but I suddenly realized that there had been
another closet present that I had been in complete denial about, informing the process of the class in ways I hadn't thought of. I asked a
student that I interviewed a few weeks later what he thought about
the existence of this other closet. He was a little older than the others,
an active member of the gay community. "I obviously had the same
denial as you," he told me, "because I was able to convince myself that
anyone here who was HIV positive and wanted to come out, would.
Among the people I know, the HIV closet is not about people like us.
The people I know who are HIV positive come out with it all the
time—in very casual ways, and to people they've just met." He added
that the class had certainly been "supportive" enough for anyone who
wanted to to come out in.

Yet the student who wrote this text was obviously looking for
something beyond "support," which, he wrote in his reflective piece,
he got from his friends. For his third paper he had written, as per the
assignment, an analysis of a piece of AIDS activist art. He had chosen
to write about the appropriated version of the American flag in Douglas

Crimp and Adam Rolston's *AIDS Demo Graphics* (see Chapter 3 and Appendix), and he had described the way the "flag" tricks the eye, sending from a distance a message of patriotism which upon closer inspection it punctures with its message of governmental depraved indifference. His analysis was laced with anger, militance, moral outrage—yet no more so, in my first reading, than the analyses of many of the other students. After I had read his final reflective essay, though, I went back and saw it differently. It was like experiencing John Berger's demonstration, in his book *Ways of Seeing* (1972), of how a written caption can change one's response to an image. On the bottom of a page is a picture of Van Gogh's painting *Wheatfield with Crows*. Berger invites the reader to turn the page. On the next page is the same picture, but this time beneath it are the words, "This is the last picture that Van Gogh painted before he killed himself" (27–28). Similarly, this student's essay hit me in the stomach when I went back and read it captioned with the new information he had given me. When I read his interpretation of the motivation behind the poster—that it was, in his view, intended to enrage its viewers so that they would "fight back, fight AIDS" (ACT UP's trademark chant)—I got a sense of how high the stakes of reading and writing must have been for him in the course.

What most of the students wrote, in some sense, was: "This class was more than just a class." Creating classes that are more than "just" classes—"just" obligatory rites of passage toward credentialing of one sort or another, occasions for passing on the baton of received knowledge, theatres for performing the scripts of the status quo, or in composition, the ritual of alienated labor that Jasper Neel (1988) calls "anti-writing," by which he means constructing formulaic paragraph arrangements filled with arbitrary content—has been the long-standing plan of liberatory pedagogy.

Inside/Outside the Classroom

At the beginning of each class there was a series of announcements of news and events relevant to the class—including theatre and dance events and literary readings in which students were participating; legal decisions that had just been handed down on lesbian and gay rights cases; city council, board of education, and other legislative or civic decisions that were pending and required the writing of letters; boycotts; demonstrations; and conferences. These announcements occasionally dovetailed with a topic we were reading or writing about at the moment, and sometimes led to heated discussions. For example, when someone brought in an article headlined "Levi Strauss OKs Benefits for Unmarried Partners" (Associated Press 1992), an argument ensued about whether heterosexuals "who could choose to get married anyway" should be included in these benefits, or whether diminishing the privileges of marriage was of social benefit to everyone, gay and straight, and should unite these groups in common interest. Was it worth worrying about the rights of straights when "they" had never worried themselves about the rights of gays? On the other hand, was it retrogressive to perpetuate this division of "us" and "them"? Some students on each side were incredulous that even in a room full of *queers,* so many disagreed with them. These sorts of issues were confronted again when we read "I Hate Straights," a broadside "published anonymously by queers" that had been distributed at the New York Lesbian and Gay Pride March in June 1990, and generated a major controversy that ran through the gay community and press for months. Employing the traditional inflammatory rhetoric of separatism and signaling an incipient movement of "queer nationalism," "I Hate Straights" was the kind of propaganda piece that moved or enraged people to think about how they wanted to identify or position themselves—if for no other reason than that they didn't want to be identified with *it.* In our class, lesbians and gays in different ideological locations, as well as straight people, took positions in writing and put their texts into conversation with each other.

Students didn't only bring their experiences with activism *into* the class; some of them became participants in community events, carpooling together to the April 1992 abortion rights demonstration in Washington and to the OutWrite [Lesbian and Gay Writers] conference in Boston. For some of them, activism had functioned as an introduction to lesbian and gay studies; this course both built on that knowledge and at times deconstructed it as activist premises and strategies were subjected to theoretical review. Students brought lesbian and gay issues up at work, into their creative work, and to their friends and families. One heterosexual student named Jennifer told the class that an old friend had come to her dorm room and seen the books for our course spread out on her bed. When the friend asked, with obvious apprehension, why she was reading the books, Jennifer opened her mouth to answer but then changed her reply—which would have been the simple truth that she was taking the course—as it occurred to her how much her friend needed her reassurance that she wasn't a lesbian. Instead, she answered evasively that she was "just reading them because she wanted to." Jennifer made it clear to us that she wasn't deliberately trying to fool her friend; but she had been hearing enough of the experiences of the lesbian and gay students in the class and thinking enough about homophobia to reject claiming social redemption by affirming her membership in the privileged group.

Another instance where forms of knowledge produced inside and outside the classroom collaborated with one another was when we discussed race and gender difference. The students occasionally reacted to writers they read in the course with feelings that their own identity was being ignored, marginalized, trivialized, or vilified. Some male students, for example, felt this when they read Adrienne Rich or Paula Gunn Allen—writers whose concept of lesbian identity is based more on gender solidarity and resistance to patriarchal structures than on genital experience or physical desire; one older lesbian feminist felt strongly, though, that gender, not sexuality, created the ultimate basis for human bonding; some people of color felt that queer theory was falsely generic and naïvely assumed *white* queerness; and some white students felt that queer writers of color made sweeping judgments about *all* white people that were unfair. These views were, of course, not exclusive to these classrooms, but manifestations of discussions that have taken place in the wider lesbian and gay community—and in other politicized communities—for years. Here, students responded to course readings partly by writing about the conflicts they had experienced in the community. A gay white male student, for example, wrote about trying to organize a "diverse" group of volunteers to work on the garden committee of a building housing lesbian and gay groups, and his lack of success in mobilizing anyone but other gay white men. In responding to his text, students used their own experiences of organizing and of being organized as particular gendered, racialized selves to elucidate, from a number of angles simultaneously, some of the complex, sensitive, and subtle factors involved in such an enterprise. Other students wrote about the ways that their sexual and race or gender identity informed each other. One male student wrote that he identified more as a lesbian than as a gay man; one wrote that the course made him realize why it was harder for him to come out as Hispanic than as gay; and one wrote that his feelings of Otherness in both the gay and Black communities coalesced in him so that he identified neither as "Black" nor as "gay," but as the new hybrid identity "gay Black man."

Finally, the realm of theatre inevitably permeated the borders of our class, where a number of the younger students were majoring in the dramatic arts. Gary, an acting student, was the first to write about interpreting dramatic texts from a gay perspective, prompting other students, as one put it, to "start thinking how sexuality affects what you're doing in theatre." The text he wrote and read to the class at the very beginning of the term is a good example of how a course in writing and reading can interact with interpretive events in everyday life outside the classroom. It reads in part:

> As an actor, I am constantly told to think about all aspects of a character, specifically the ones which are not mentioned in the script. As an example, sometimes I think about what that character would do in the kitchen—what he or she would eat, how he or she would make a sandwich, what would he or she put on it, that sort of thing. I also think about what kinds of things the character would read—comic books, literature, or pornographic magazines. This last choice leads me to a more specific question—what kind of magazine, male or female. Is it possible that the Man of La Mancha enjoyed looking at pictures of naked men? Why not?
>
> When I approach a role, I find this to be a big problem because I feel like I am the only one who sees a gay side in a character. Every time I read a character's lines, I wonder about his or her sexual orientation. Recently, I have acquired a role in the musical *Grease*. The character who I am currently playing, Doody, is described as the "youngest of the guys." When I read through Doody's lines, I see a lot of myself. To me, Doody is somewhat of a tag-along who may even have a semi-crush on the guys. I say this because when I was a kid, I always looked up to older guys in a worshipping way that I could not understand because it was more than just a friendly admiration. I enjoyed being in their company, but deep down, I felt that I wanted more than that even though I didn't know exactly what it was that I wanted. I am not saying that Doody is a gay character. Contrarily, I am merely illustrating that Doody is assumed to be heterosexual, but because I am homosexual, I can see another side to Doody in his dialogue.

One thing I particularly enjoyed about this text was its blithe "death-of-the-author" assumption—that is, its implicit premise that just as characters have so often been de-gayed, they can also be "gayed" by a reader's or actor's interaction with them, regardless of the author's intention. But more specifically, this text made explicit the ways that the realm of the "possible" could be enlarged; human variety encompassed, after all, more than different things to eat and wear. This is important because although vegetarianism and carnivorousness, casual and formal wear, urbanity and provincialism, and other vagaries of taste, style, and temperament are all generally admitted as characteristics a real or fictional character might have, sexuality is usually considered a closed set in public and dramatic discourse, with one manifestation of it—heterosexuality—generically eclipsing all alternative possibilities. Gary's queer reading of characters from Doody to the Man of La Mancha suggests that theatre, or literature in general, not only requires the production of new gay characters; it also requires the production of new gay readers who can reinterpret old creations in new ways.

Praxis

Each of the courses was divided into four thematic units—lesbian and gay theory, history, politics, and culture. Attached to the theory unit was a subunit on coming-out narratives; the idea here was to use the theory we had just read to consider the interpretive frameworks lesbians and gay men use in constructing stories about their lives. In addition, as I will describe in Chapter 7, there was a short introductory period where we read, wrote, and talked about what it meant to read and write from the location of a particular sexual identity. My intention was to get students thinking about lesbian and gay existence not simply as material or "content" for a writing class, but as material which involved them in particular rhetorical activities. I believed that becoming self-conscious about their rhetorical positioning as lesbian, gay, bisexual, or heterosexual writers and articulating what they noticed would make them stronger readers and writers because they could make more intentional and less ingenuous use of their subjectivity.

As conceived, there wasn't one overarching "purpose" to each unit, but each one did suggest a particular benefit. The unit on theory gave the students new conceptual material to work with, particularly the notion of identity as a social construction. The history unit located the concept of socially constructed identity in particular times and places, and suggested that who people (or narrators in texts) "are" has something to do with who is reading their lives, from what perspective, and for what purposes. The unit on politics brought the classes back to some of the gritty, immediate community issues and debates with which they had been familiar before the class started, except that by now they had some new terms with which to compose their opinions. The unit on culture, which was devoted solely to AIDS activist art, brought up issues of representation and the ways that the relationship between language, form, audience, and purpose can be creatively manipulated to force debilitating social practices and institutions to change.

It was important to me that my own authority as class creator, facilitator, and evaluator leave room for the authority of students to determine certain aspects of course structure, design, and procedure. This impulse toward democracy was challenged the very first night at Municipal when the ten students who had signed on to the course waiting list showed up along with the twenty-five who had enrolled, and everyone looked uneasily around the converted gym that was our classroom, wondering who was in and who was out. In most classes, this wouldn't be a particularly momentous decision; certainly those not at the top of the waiting list would have to go. But this was different; the course had never been offered before, and it might not be offered again. I hoped to be leaving the following term for a full-time position somewhere else. As the students introduced themselves, it became clear that some of those who were "in" had only a casual interest in the subject, while many of those who were "out" looked desperate for a place in the class.

Was it insane to contemplate running a writing class with thirty-five people in it? Definitely. It was certainly done all the time in overenrolled, underfunded and understaffed inner-city basic writing programs, but we knew that that bargain-basement level of personal attention and involvement shouldn't be our model. The only other choice, though, was to turn people away. Splitting the class into two groups wasn't possible because of the logistics of scheduling. I told the class that they as a group would have to decide what to do. I pointed out that if we accepted everybody, I wouldn't have time to conference with them the way I would like to, they would in general receive less individualized attention from me, people who had fears of reading their work publicly would have a larger crowd to worry about, each person would have less air time in full-group discussions, and the class atmosphere would be less intimate. In fact, I saw very little benefit to the individuals who were already enrolled in permitting everyone who was there that night to enter (as well as little benefit to myself, who could look forward to being overwhelmed with work). On the other hand, what did it mean to turn away people for whom this course represented much more than merely an academic experience? (I would find out, for instance, that the student who had found out he was HIV positive and worried that he wouldn't have another chance like this was on the waiting list.)

In what essentially became a "town meeting," the students spent that first class debating the merits of different solutions to the problem, suggesting alternative ways of operating as a group that would help them receive more attention from each other so as not to completely overburden me, toying with innovative ideas about class scheduling, asserting their conflicting desires for personal focus and fairness to others in an unusual situation, examining the problem from ethical, political, academic, and "purely selfish" standpoints, and ultimately voting unanimously to let everyone stay. (A few people who clearly *didn't* want to be there but were apparently not comfortable saying so in that atmosphere simply vanished after that night, making the class size more manageable; after the usual attrition due to a variety of causes, the class stabilized at the originally prescribed size of twenty-five.)

The pedagogical design of the course was dialogical and constructionist. It was "dialogical" first in the literal sense that virtually everything that happened in the class involved interchanges: among students, between students and myself, between students and texts, among students' texts, and between students and the wider lesbian and gay community. All of the students' papers were workshopped either in groups or in gatherings of the entire class; often they ended up in some way responding to issues others had raised, or to ideological arguments that had arisen in class. The students also wrote journal entries in response to everything they read, and these journals both initiated class discussion of those texts and, on many occasions, sustained the discussion throughout the class session. Often we would have a "conversation between journals," where each reader would seize upon what someone else had just read aloud as the relevant moment for her to enter the conversation. The content of journals was open, but guidelines that I called "Possible Ways of Using Journals," adapted from suggestions by Toby Fulwiler (1987, 3), were provided that suggested various modes of response: writing observations, questions, speculations, affective response, drawing connections to other texts, ideas, and experiences, exploring issues of self-awareness raised by readings, and revising earlier ideas, written and unwritten, in the light of current reading. Often, when a topic felt particularly charged or slippery, we would interrupt our discussion for an impromptu interlude of freewriting. Much of the time freewriting would be used for matters of definition or value clarification. For example, the terms "lesbian" and "gay" might have been used indefinitely as if we were all talking about the same thing had we not started to suspect otherwise, and then freewritten definitions which we shared. I particularly stressed generating questions, even though many students, at least initially, felt uncomfortable raising questions they couldn't answer. I urged them to use rather than avoid their discomfort, since it helped in moving them away from closure, and the further we moved from expecting absolute answers the wider the conceptual landscape could open up before us. When students felt immobilized from contemplating questions that seemed unanswerable to them, I would suggest that they speculate about possible answers and test these answers out provisionally. Sometimes, it seemed, the sheer unanswerability of a question was the answer; it was at moments like this, when some question that seemed absolutely fundamental—such as "What does it mean to be gay?"—eluded definition, that the indeterminacy of meaning *had* meaning for them. That is, if they couldn't attach any specific definition to gayness,

that lack of fixture in itself could affect the ways they identified themselves and others, made alliances, fought homophobia, and conceptu-
alized community.

Revision sometimes involved "re-envisioning" in ways that were
potentially threatening, since the material of the course asked students
to reconsider old premises and maxims from the arena of gay politics
and elsewhere which had sustained them in important ways. One
student, for example, a twenty-seven-year-old African American woman
at Municipal named Tina who had been politically active for some time,
wrote a very "in-your-face" style piece for the first open topic essay.
Taking what she and many others call a "pro-sex" position against
feminist antiporn activists, thereby inserting herself into one of the two
established camps of what have been known as the "feminist sex wars"
of the 1980s, Tina launched a vitriolic attack against the "Sex Police"
who have "disregarded positive sexual images" such as those found in
contemporary performance art that "have helped many stay sex-posi-
tive in a sexually repressed time."

When she showed me her essay in a conference, I told her that I
thought she did a competent job of arguing her position, but pointed
out that this position had been competently argued by others for at
least a decade—as had the opposing position. What had made her want
to write it? Was it to echo and confirm a stance that had impressed her
with its importance? To vent? To knock the opposing side on the floor?
To take the conversation to a new place that might break the painfully
prolonged polarity of the fight? She seemed torn between purposes.
As the conversation continued, she remarked that in gay male porn,
Black men are usually "tops" while white men are usually "bottoms."
I asked her why she thought that was, and she answered, "Because it's
written from the white men's perspective. They get off on it because
they consider that the ultimate degradation—to be dominated by a
Black man." When I asked her how she felt about the use of racism
for titillation, she laughed and observed that much of what she spent
her life fighting politically she found sexually stimulating. I told her I
thought she had identified a fascinating contradiction—one I imagined
many others felt but rarely admitted. What does it mean, I wondered,
to take a side in a political split when you actually feel split within
yourself? In what ways do the exigencies of political alignment blur
the paradoxes we carry around inside us that offer potentially useful
metaphors for political analysis? Tina and I discussed what it would
mean to explore such a paradox in her writing rather than avoid
it—what it would mean to her, and what the insertion of such a
perspective could mean within the larger context of the deadlocked
debate. In our interview after the course, Tina referred to that conversation, saying, "I fight against dyadic sorts of composition, but usually

it's the easiest way to write. An either/or dyad—a yes or no sort of thing. But there's that challenge now for me to really figure out a different way to approach this topic."

Behind my desire to literally generate dialogue in the class was the notion that Bakhtin (1981) famously explored—that a discourse's vitality, perhaps its sheer existence, depends on its recognition and incorporation of other discourses. This is related to what many writing theorists mean when they say that writing is a social act. Karen Burke Lefevre (1987), for instance, has countered the Platonic view of an atomized self generating ideas in contemplative solitude with the idea that social forces have *already* constructed the inventing "I." Any writing act, she says, is inescapably structured by an audience made up in part of "social collectives, such as institutions, bureaucracies, and governments" (2) which not only receives, but also delivers the premises that guide the writer. Douglas B. Park (1988, 160) has pointed out that "audience," a central concern in rhetorical acts and writing pedagogy, is often imagined to signify only actual people external to a text; yet it is also "a set of suggested or evoked attitudes, interests, reactions, conditions of knowledge" which are implied in the text and shape its rhetorical structure. Much contemporary writing theory on the social nature of writing and language can be traced back to Vygotsky ([1934] 1986), who challenged Piaget's idea that the primary thought and speech of children is "egocentric" or "autistic" and resists the encroachment of social forces (to which it nonetheless must eventually capitulate). Vygotsky's clinical studies led him to take exactly the opposite view—that "[e]gocentric speech emerges when the child transfers social, collaborative forms of behavior to the sphere of inner-personal psychic functions" (35). He concluded that "the true direction of the development of thinking is not from the individual to the social, but from the social to the individual" (36).

Bakhtinian dialogics hold that language is not a construct of individual consciousness, but "exists in other people's mouths, in other people's contexts, serving other people's intentions: it is from there that one must take the word, and make it one's own" (294). For Bakhtin, making discourse is inherently collaborative; linguistic theories which perceive language as unitary fail to recognize the ideologies that fill it and the assimilation of Otherness that gives it substance. Bakhtin calls this nervous coalition of ideologies and perspectives which push and pull at each other within a discourse *heteroglossia*. In recent years, some feminist theorists have applied Bakhtinian dialogics to questions of gendered discourse, seeing in his work the potential for a "feminist dialogics" that resists cultural domination by insisting on the polyvocality of all legitimate structures (Bauer and McKinstry 1991, 4). As Patricia Yaeger (1991, 245) puts it, "Both feminist praxis and dialogic thinking emphasize the political struggles of our texts and our lives, insisting that there should be no reign of normative speech without revolt, protest, challenge, invective—in short, without trouble."

In my classes, I didn't want to simply remove the "trouble" of the homophobic world and replace it with a monologically untroubled environment. Such an environment constitutes that mythological land known as "safe space." Like the fantasy of the "world made safe for democracy" (achievable by killing whatever forces stand in the way of democracy), the dream of "safe space"—safe for, presumably, the return of the repressed parts of hegemonic culture—usually involves trying to evacuate anything that might distress whatever is being protected. Yet nothing breathes in a vacuum. Historian/musician Bernice Johnson Reagon has addressed this issue in her essay "Coalition Politics: Turning the Century" (1983) by noting that coalitions are dangerous places where would-be enemies team up in order to accomplish something important to them. Expecting coalitions to be warm, nurturing havens of like-minded people is preposterous, she says, because out in the world, people are different; the place to look for the comfort of people like yourself is home. But home is also the place you have to leave to have agency in the world. Similarly, agoraphobic discourse, by definition, has no place in school.

The classes I taught weren't really in danger of such insularity, since it became clear after a certain point in the term that gendered, raced, classed, politicked, aged, majored, and regioned subjectivities sliced at infinite angles through the identity category "lesbian and gay." But the existence of a minority of heterosexuals in the classroom—who were also complexly constituted—made the scene richer, dialogically speaking, since their presence raised the implicit question, "What is *heterosexual* subjectivity?" Neither mainstream culture nor the lesbian and gay community had ever shown much interest in such a question. Mainstream heterosexual culture was too busy dehumanizing lesbians and gays through its own monologism to look beyond its presumed unmarkedness and perceive that it *had* any particularity; lesbians and gays were too angry at heterosexuals for that and for their entitlement to seemingly endless air time to ask such a thing. But in our class, heterosexual subjectivity took on a different form; it saw itself. Seeing itself, it could recognize the Other—a fact which implicitly restructured the Other's Otherness. The heterosexuals in the class were not, by and large, radically enlightened heterosexuals, but they were curious and polite and wanted to get something out of their education. They expressed no sensational fantasies about lesbians and gays that anyone had to waste time refuting. They were eager to be properly "supportive." If anything, their initial deference and willingness to consign themselves to the margins of class discussion was the problem. Many of them spoke of themselves in the beginning as "observers" in the course, "outsiders" who could "listen and learn something." I had to establish quickly that their full, active participation was expected and that material from their own lives was relevant, not only because heterosexuality *was* a generally unremarked-upon, unanalyzed identity, but also because our subject, homosexuality, had in fact no meaning or existence apart from its binary complement; it was the confluence of our identities as subject matter that would help us understand sexual identity as a social phenomenon in more profound ways. After this, the dialogical possibilities opened up. Some of the boundary lines that ostensibly distinguished the queers from the straights even turned out to be infirm in certain ways. "A language is revealed in all its distinctiveness only when it is brought into relationship with other languages, entering with them into one single heteroglot unity of societal becoming," wrote Bakhtin (411). The distinctive languages revealed in the class permitted a discursive ecology characterized by, in pyschoanalyst Jessica Benjamin's (1988) terms, an "intersubjective" exchange—one in which it is mutually understood that "the other whom the self meets is also a self, a subject in his or her own right" (20). With all sexual identities and their attendant discourses resituated outside of their natural habitats, so to speak, homophobia itself was denaturalized, and thus available for critical examination and dialogue.

Related to the course's reliance on dialogism was its constructionist orientation. Discussions of phenomena in the queer world were always brought back to questions of how language and context construct meaning, and how we as a community constructed meaning through language. In other words, we didn't talk about "issues" or "experiences" as events that simply existed in the world or in ourselves about which we only needed to "express" opinions in writing. Instead, the emphasis was on the discourses that made these events take on particular meanings for us. When students talked, for instance, about their desires to come out to their parents, we might explore the chasms that gaped between their language and their parents' language that would have to be negotiated in order for the "coming-out" event to promote the hoped-for result. Similarly, we might discuss the very different meanings that lesbian or gay identity took on for them as they moved from one context to another, such as from our class to a long-distance telephone conversation with their parents, or from being in New York City to being home for spring break in a rural upstate town.

Perhaps one of the most important purposes that the constructionist orientation of the class served was its addressing a truism that the vast majority of the students came in firmly insisting upon: that "people are just people." For them, homophobia had to do with difference, and difference was associated with prejudice and disharmony; their response, then, was to pretend to erase their awareness of difference. Yet, paradoxically, that erasure would mean forfeiting the project that had brought them to the class in the first place. If we could immediately dispense with difference, and say, "OK, we're all the same," what were we to read, write, and talk about? Why would the experience of sexual identity matter? It clearly did matter, and part of what we did was to upgrade that "mattering" from the status of "problem" to that of a rich subject of critical inquiry. People came to the course, or chose to stay in it, to learn about themselves—as lesbians, as gay men, as bisexuals, or as heterosexuals implicated in the machinery of homophobic culture. From all that they said and wrote, this was clearly their prime motivator.

Yet given that identity is complex, fractured, composite, what do we privilege and what do we marginalize or ignore when we turn to that fascinating exploration of "ourselves"? How do totalizing "I's" function here to reduce our complexity, make us choose one part to represent who "we" are? Several students expressed the feeling at the beginning of the term that writing about lesbian and gay experience was "self-indulgent" or "self-serving" or "not legitimate"—in the sense that it was too much about "themselves," too "personal," to count as a source of knowledge in the rational, public world of the academy. Some of them were consumed with questions such as, "Am I a 'gay' writer? Or just a writer who happens to be gay?" They were struggling to locate their gay identities within their identities as writers, afraid that the gay part, so overloaded with cultural meaning, would drown out the other parts, render them invisible. Yet they also said that it was the gay part that had always before been suppressed in their writing and that they longed to express. When one, wrestling with feelings of guilt about devoting a whole writing course to "himself," commented in a text, "Writing is a self-oriented form of creation, it is a dialogue with our self," I wrote back, "Yet so much of what you write here seems to have to do with the voice of a homophobic society creeping in, infiltrating that dialogue with yourself. Isn't the whole world kind of in our heads every time we write—even if it's private journal writing? Aren't some of the issues you write about—the desire for affirmation, the fear of repercussions from your writing—issues that imply that writing is some form of social exchange?" One of the things that we had to address in the early part of the course was simply what made the identity-marker of sexuality so much more significant, at least in some people's view, than others. Likewise, we needed to examine the sources of their fear that to focus on their sexual identity would enforce the obliteration of their other identities and the disconnection of themselves as writers from public discourse.

"The Audience I Have Waited My Entire Life For"

When I talk with lesbian and gay colleagues and students about the problems lesbian and gay student writers face in mainstream writing classes, I most commonly hear references to "voice"—or, to be more accurate, "voicelessness." Facing an audience of their peers and teacher, students feel afraid—afraid that they won't be listened to, that they will be ridiculed, beaten up, punished, ostracized, that their expression will be curtailed, that they will be relegated to the remove of Other, that they will be denied, either explicitly or implicitly, the opportunity to articulate their "real" thoughts. Their stories about the expression of lesbian and gay existence in relation to school are narratives of suppression, repression, and omission. Lesbian and gay students lack an audience of their peers, a group whose "reading schema" line up with their own.

In *Facts, Artifacts, and Counterfacts* (1986), David Bartholomae and Anthony Petrosky describe a writer's task as one of location within the givens or conventions of what they call "our" culture. For the writer, they say,

> the "text" is the text of our common culture. The rhetoric of the controlling idea requires writers who are not only able, but also willing to work with common examples or to take common truths as their own. It presents special problems, then, for marginal students, students outside what we take to be our "common" culture, students without easy access to that stock of commonplaces or routines for their presentation. (10)

The distinction between students "able" and "willing" to employ the stock of commonplaces is an important one for the purposes of my discussion, since lesbian and gay students have usually been immersed from birth in heterosexual commonplaces and are adept at using them. The "common culture" is, simply, the dominant culture, one in which subordinate groups speak by virtue of a kind of bilingualism (while possessors of dominant subjectivities are limited to knowledge only of their own language). Like Mitterrand in his dialogue with the mono-lingual Reagan, it is the queer voice that must both speak the alien language and at the same time suppress its heteroglossic knowledge. At the same time, as with any marginalized group, alternative "common truths" are available to queer writers that, cordoned off from the sphere of "public" knowledge, describe the "private" and familiar commonplace experience of their marginalization. This means—though this is something that Bartholomae and Petrosky don't discuss, certainly not within the context of the academy—that if you change the "we," if the culture at the margin becomes the culture at the center, the privileged stock of commonplaces shifts, and the writer suddenly has a host of formerly underutilized "conventions" at her disposal. At this point she is able to recuperate what is alien and cast it in *her own* terms—that is, install it at the nucleus of her own field of queerly inflected epistemic operations—though possibly rendering it unintelligible to the monolingual speakers of the so-called common culture (thus revealing what is limited and parochial about that culture). This is what can happen in a queer discourse community.

One night in the class at Municipal, a student volunteered to read an informal draft to the gathered circle of listeners. Although the assignment had been to write an analysis of several coming-out narratives that they had read, Dennis, like a number of others, ignored it and appropriated the subject to tell his own story. When he announced to us that the title of his text was "The Audience I Have Waited My Entire Life For," a responsive murmur went around the room. The text he read was rhythmic and incantatory, each sentence taking the reader a chronological step further in the story of his development as a gender-bending child. An abridged version of his full text is as follows:

> Perhaps it was when I was in nursery school and put on a wig to do a show for my peers as they ate their cookies and drank their Kool-Aid during snack time? Perhaps it was another day in nursery school, when I consciously decided that I was supposed to play with toy cars and trucks and took a miniature black Volkswagen and pushed it in a circle around me for a minute before deciding that it was very boring? Perhaps it was in the first grade when I offered to assist Katherine, Katherine the Kissing Girl in her self-prescribed duty to chase down and kiss boys during recess? . . . Perhaps it was when I was seven or eight and my mother asked me why her pajama top was on the living room floor—I would put her shoes on, take one of her pajama tops and fashion it into a skirt, add her jewelry and parade back-n-forth on the coffee table, watching myself in the mirror above the sofa when no one was home? . . . Perhaps it was in the second grade when I made a macramé belt and wore it to school? . . . Perhaps it was all those . . . days in the third grade, when during story time, Eddie Horrigan and I would draw on each other's backs with our fingers, first I would do it to him, then he would do it to me? Perhaps it was when I was eight or nine and suggested to my cousin Kevin that we wrestle in the nude? Perhaps it was the summer of 1976 or 1977 that I was forced to play little league and was called the Statue of Liberty because I refused to swing at the ball? Perhaps it was in the fourth grade when I was called gay for the first time and I thought that it was just part of the passing slang and would, like all other slang, soon die out of use? . . . Perhaps it was when I was ten or so and Bo Derek was in fashion and I filled my hair with multicolored

clothespins and looked at myself in the bathroom mirror? . . . Perhaps it was in the eighth grade when Brad Stevens, who was the most popular boy in school, called me to exchange notes on a chemistry project we were working on and I shook on the other end of the phone? Perhaps it was when my mother explained to me about sex and I was already worried about the man getting cum on the sheets—how did it stay in there, I asked? Perhaps alongside the agony of growing up gay, there were some things that were very funny?

When I interviewed students after the course ended, several from the Municipal class spontaneously mentioned this text of Dennis's as something that had been memorable to them. One student, who cited it as his favorite of the student texts he had heard, said, "I thought that summed up the experience of this class. Because all the writing that we did, we were doing to be read in this class, and to be seen by people in this class, where you could finally feel acceptance. And I have to agree, it's the forum I've always wanted to express myself in." Another concurred: "What Dennis wrote—that was really the perfect phrase to describe what I got in that class—the audience I've always wanted. The audience who knows what questions to ask. The audience who knows the background material and who accepts it as valid and important and relevant, and they can see the missing pieces in the logic." Still another student mentioned Dennis's reading of this text when she commented, "To hear people's stories about how their writing in other classes had compared to writing in this class—it was definitely a three-hanky event."

I would hypothesize that part of the reason that Dennis's reading touched such a nerve in his listeners was that his subject still pushed at the border of taboo, since, as Sedgwick remarks in her essay "How to Bring Your Kids Up Gay" (1991), "effeminophobia" reigns even within gay communities and particular stigmas regarding nonmasculine gay men are still institutionalized. Sedgwick points out that, although it is well known that gay activists were successful in getting the American Psychiatric Association to remove homosexuality from its Diagnostic and Statistical Manual (DSM-III) list of pathological disorders in 1973, it is little known that another disorder was subsequently added: "Gender Identity Disorder of Childhood," which transfers the onus of maladjustment from sexuality to gender-appropriateness. Though disentangling the often radically different matters of sexuality and gender has been a progressive move in recent lesbian and gay thought, says Sedgwick, "There is a danger . . . that that advance may leave the effeminate boy once more in the position of the haunting abject—this time the haunting abject of gay thought itself" (20).

That considered, it shouldn't be assumed that Dennis's reading of his text was easy or altogether "safe" in the context of our class. Had it been, it probably wouldn't have moved people the way it did. Yet our class no doubt provided the first context in which the distance that such a text had to transgress would be thinkable and bearable. Like students in mainstream writing classes who, encouraged to be "honest," push the limits of safety in measured amounts and experience the exhilaration of moving one fencepost beyond what is comfortable, Dennis too had a reasonable starting point from which to chart the length of his course.

Nobody, to my knowledge, ever remarked that Dennis's title hardly seemed to correspond to his subject. I believe it was a function of our class as an interpretive community to understand that the audience was as much the subject of the text as his growing-up was, even if we were never mentioned explicitly after the title. Just as arrival at the threshold of intimacy is often signalled by a lover through the revelation of vulnerabilities, Dennis's medium was his message. Yet the audience he had waited all his life for was not *only* "accepting"; it was also an audience uniquely situated to receive a particular "stock of commonplaces" along with particular "routines for their presentation." This audience could respond to those things about growing up gay that Dennis suggested were "very funny" with laughter because they could hear, in Bakhtinian terms, the "double-voicedness" of Dennis's discourse. That is, they could hear in it the voice of his pleasure along with the refracted disapprobation of the dominant culture which reconstitutes such pleasure as calamitous transgression.

In our two classes, there was also a sense that texts produced could have a place in the world outside the writing class. Several students said at the end of the course that they planned to start writing for the queer press, and saw the audience inside the class as a microcosm of the audience they would be writing for outside. For many of them, writing for the audience of our class suggested the possibility of writing in the "real [public] world" where there hadn't seemed to be such a possibility before—since "public" had signified only the domain of the dominant heterosexual culture, with the gay world seemingly consigned to a "private" back room. Writing about being gay had, for some of them, seemed to necessitate writing across a gulf of misunderstanding, requiring that they "explain" or "justify" their existence before they could engage in discussing it with any complexity. Their coming out in the class as gay writers had much to do with the simultaneous coming out in the class of a body of visibly present, available gay readers. At the same time, their own experience there as gay readers of the work of writers they had never met told them that there *was* a community of gay writers who were already published, and that gay ideas were already circulating in print. They learned from their experience of being an audience that they could have an audience—that there was a community they could join which, like other discourse communities, had its own ongoing conversations, debates, themes, ways of trying to figure life out.

The Out Lesbian as Teacher/The Teacher as Out Lesbian

Certainly another important factor in constructing a new sense of audience for the students was my own role as an out lesbian teacher. One gay male student said to me in his interview, "The fact that you yourself used 'dyke' and 'queer' said something to me—that you identified with a lot of the things going on outside. It made me less inhibited. And it wasn't a barrier, like 'gay and lesbian class'—sweet-voiced—it was very out and strong." A lesbian student called having an out lesbian teacher "a great kind of modeling experience," and explained, "I have this whole background of twenty English classes, or something, and generally it's been a real straight male kind of thing. And I've tried to be like them. It's a great thing to have, as a lesbian student, an out lesbian teacher. It gives me a little more confidence in my perspective meaning anything." Another gay man said about my being an out lesbian teacher, "I don't have to defensively or offensively acknowledge my sexuality, or even include my sexuality. It can just be taken as a given." He would have been uncomfortable, he said, had he known I was a lesbian but if I weren't out to the whole class, as had been his experience with another teacher. In our class, he said, "I felt much more comfortable discussing gay- and lesbian-themed things, without feeling that I was either putting someone on the spot that didn't want to be on the spot, or forcing my views about sexuality on someone else." A lesbian student said my being out made her start to think about teachers from the past, "how their silence affects you and makes you silent. And just the fact that some of my teachers might have been gay, and they might have been really closeted and feeling like they had to be. And how they didn't talk about gay history and stuff, and how I never could write about it before—or never did. I suppose I could have. I don't know what the reaction would have been." The gay male student who said that on some level he felt more like a lesbian than a gay man said, "In a way, I identified with you." A gay man in his late thirties said that my being an out lesbian teacher made him care more about my response to his writing: "I'm more interested in the dialogue with other gay people than I am with educating straight people."

Interestingly, one heterosexual student who was a young, Jewish woman had, in her apprehension that she would be an outsider in the class, focused on my name as a basis for identification before the first class meeting. "I was like, OK, she's Jewish, just because—you know, it's like a Jewish thing, you try to figure out who is and who isn't." Still, she said, before the first class met "I guess I was just a little bit concerned that I didn't know what your views were, or if you were just going to bond with the gay people. Or if you were going to be someone who was like, 'Oh, come on, you're not straight, nobody's straight.' I worried that the teacher would be someone like that—you know, 'But don't you think that maybe you're gay?'" When class started, though, she said, "I was glad that you were open, because it made me feel more comfortable. And I know that coming out is not something that's always easy, and it's a process that people go through. You were just very comfortable with it, and open with it, and I wanted that to be the atmosphere of the class. You know, no playing around about it."

In addition to being an out lesbian teacher, I was one who was going to write about our class and make information about it public. Students eagerly volunteered to be part of my study, expressing the conviction that it was an important enterprise and the hope that its message would reach other writing teachers who would act upon it. Throughout the term, then, there was a heightened sense of excitement about being in an experiment, a pilot program of sorts whose results would be reported and whose influence would be felt in the world beyond our classroom.

A Few More Words About Heterosexuals in the Queer Classroom

"Uncommon sense" learning, says John Mayher (1990), "is based on learning as the result of intentional or purposeful action," in which the learner is motivated by a sense of personal investment in what is learned. "This can be seen both in the importance of contextualized as opposed to disembodied learning and in the recognition that learning in school and out of school involves fundamentally similar processes" (104). The lesbian and gay students who enrolled in my classes came in the hope of having an uncommon need fulfilled. The heterosexual students, to varying lesser degrees, did, too. For some of them, the need was not exactly burning, but simply rooted in a desire to understand people different from themselves and so, contingently, themselves. For others, the need was more complex, as in the case of the student who was afraid she would be an "outsider" in the class because she was straight, but easily connected with the course content and other students because she had been raised in a lesbian household. For her final project she did a family ethnography, interviewing her siblings (two of whom were stepsiblings) and including her own autobiographical reflections.

> I was about six when my mother told me that she loved other women. I didn't really grasp what that meant, it seemed very natural to me. After all, my mother loved me, and I was a girl. Why couldn't she love other girls, even grown-up ones? I knew, however, that many others didn't agree.

When her brother did not understand the importance of keeping this information from their father, she admonished him, "Don't you get it? People will think that just because Mom is gay, we'll be gay, too." She observes later, "People greatly overestimate the risk of children being teased or harangued for having a gay parent. If they think back, the sexuality of parents is not a hot topic among teenagers." As a result of having been raised in a lesbian household, she writes,

> I feel as though I am a stronger individual and more willing to believe in my own ideas and feelings. Society has told me that gays are inferior to heterosexuals. I know in my heart that is not true. It therefore makes me distrustful of other things my society would have me believe, and has forced me to think for myself.

Another heterosexual student wrote at the beginning of the term:

> I hope we can address the issue of heterophobia in this class. As a "straight" person, I often feel discriminated against by my gay friends.

By midterm, however, she wrote:

> I'm so glad to have this course right now. I feel really lost in this heterosexist society, and I need this environment to nurture my needs as a bisexual human being. I can hardly even write that word. It's too scary. For so long, I've preached to all of my friends about how great it is to be whoever you really are. But, when it comes to me, I feel lost in states of confusion and denial. . . . I can't just say I'm "questioning" anymore. I need to answer some of these questions.

For this student, the writing class—interestingly, rather even than the Lesbian and Gay Community Center, her theatre studio workshop, or a campus lesbian and gay organization—was a place to come out, perhaps because "identity" was "uncommonly" posited here as fluid and changeable, whereas community-based groups may suggest in the minds of newcomers the idea that one's identity is or should be "declared" by membership or attendance. Another heterosexual student, Jennifer, illustrates another sort of "burning" need that might propel a heterosexual to take a course such as this. She wrote at the beginning of the course:

> I am not gay and I am not homophobic—of these two facts I am sure. However, when I was looking through the course selections for Writing Workshop and I saw the description for this class, I immediately disregarded it and decided it just wasn't for me. I went on to decide that I would be the only person who wasn't gay in the class and that if I took it, other people would think I was gay and I didn't want that. Well, it only took another moment for me to really hear and begin to hate the thoughts that had just run through my so-called open mind. I couldn't believe how uncomfortable I felt just by reading the course description. Immediately, I knew I wanted and I needed to take the class.

At midterm, having read lesbian and gay theory, history, and coming-out narratives, and having listened to the coming-out narratives of members of the class, she wrote:

> I've been doing a lot of looking back on my past recently, at my home life, my education, and my friends, and I can see clearly the places and times that there was pressure to be a certain way. I can see now that there was simply no room made to be homosexual. So how much have my values and who I am now been socially constructed? . . . As a writer, I now fully appreciate the freedom I always had to write about my exiences fully without fear of someone finding out something. Most homosexuals have had to censor things and that makes me especially upset being a writer. . . . I've also wondered about my own family. . . . I've really been wondering how my open-minded liberal parents who support us in whatever we do would have felt had I been a lesbian. Part of me knows for sure that they wouldn't have been so open about it—especially my mom. That has been a very interesting and difficult thing for me to find out.

An interesting postscript to this text came up in my interview with Jennifer some time after the course had ended. Her experience in the class had prompted her to initiate a talk with her father over the summer in which she asked him if he and her mother had ever thought that they might have a child who was gay. "I was surprised because he said yes, they had thought about it," she reported. "It was something I had never talked about with my parents. And he was saying that when he was younger, maybe in early college, he wasn't really sure of—he told me quite openly that he didn't know what he was. And that being gay wasn't something he was sure he wasn't. It was a unique conversation to have with your parent."

What happened inside our class, then, overran curricular borders to make "uncommon sense" even within that most commonsensical of social institutions, the nuclear family. Convinced that the discourse of our class was utterly extraneous to the discourse of home, Jennifer found to her surprise that (to paraphrase Dorothy Gale from Kansas) if she wanted to discover signs of "homosexual panic"'s conspicuous silence she need look no further than her own backyard. In her father's unexpectedly unearthed revelation was an illustration of Sedgwick's point: that homosexual consciousness, rather than being absent from heterosexual culture, is a fully incorporated part of its structure and an ostensibly "silent" partner which in truth wields a powerful—though desperately camouflaged—interest in its production of knowledge.

Notes

1. It must be noted that when Bruner refers to "joint culture creating"—something he sees as "an object of schooling and . . . an appropriate step en route to becoming a member of the adult society in which one lives out one's life" (127), he is referring to a collaboration of generic individuals; he does not discuss the significance of "joint culture" for the membership of particular social groups.

2. I will describe the study in detail in Chapter 7.

3. Martin Duberman, in his autobiographical psycho/social history, *Cures,* writes about his teaching experiments at Princeton in the 1960s, which produced similar confusion over the exact demarcation line between education and therapy. "Rather than advocating that education and therapy should . . . become interchangeable processes, I was working instead to undermine the simplistic dualism which pretended that education is concerned solely with informing the mind, and therapy with understanding the emotions. Such neat categories falsify our everyday experience, for our emotions . . . always color our intellectual views and our minds are continually 'ordering' our emotional responses. Even in a university seminar, purportedly devoted to a high-level exchange of ideas, passion and irrationality inevitably color that exchange (and are in turn influenced by it)—and it was precisely that fact which traditional education, to its detriment, ignored or evaded" (111).

Chapter Seven

The Course of Study/Study of the Course

When I was a teenager, I went to see the musical *Hair* on Broadway. While waiting for it to begin, I noticed a shirtless man sitting high on the back of a nearby seat. Just as his inappropriateness struck me, I noticed someone else's legs dangling from one of the box seats tiered on the wall. Suddenly, it seemed there were other strange people scattered about the audience. Individually, they started to move, and then it seemed that all of them were in movement, and then they were singing "Age of Aquarius" and swinging from the lighting equipment and sprinting onto the stage and I never did know exactly when the show had actually begun.

It's hard to pinpoint the dawn of any particular consciousness. Isolated events happen quietly and coalesce subtly, warming knowledge and bringing it slowly to a boil. Until a few years ago, it never occurred to me that sexual identity had anything to do with composition. The oversight is notable, since I knew—and frequently proclaimed—that race, gender, and class had a lot to do with it. Furthermore, I was a lesbian, angry like lots of other lesbians about always being obliterated from public discourse. (This was before lesbians were chic.) But, probably because there was virtually no suggestion in the composition literature that pedagogical issues of sexual identity existed, my mind wasn't organized to notice the obvious. (Cognitively speaking, my academic training hadn't equipped me with that reading schema.)

Isolated events happened and coalesced. At the annual NCTE convention, one person out of hundreds of presenters gave a paper on teaching gay literature. In New York, record numbers of gay bashings were reported and demands mounted in the lesbian and gay commu-

140

nity for the state senate to pass a Hate Crimes Bill. I wrote a paper on gays and lesbians and multiculturalism for a conference on writing programs. Queer Nation was formed. Little bits of militant, inflammatory rhetoric began to creep into my academic writing. I came upon *The Lesbian in Front of the Classroom* (Parmeter and Reti 1988), a small volume of essays by lesbian teachers published by one of those obscure feminist presses from prechicness days. It wasn't something you'd read in a doctoral program in composition. Yet in this book I found Ellen Louise Hart's "Literacy and the Lesbian/Gay Learner." I read it lying on a couch, and afterward I continued to lie there, having an epiphany. "[T]here is another level of literacy that moves beyond the performance of concrete tasks to the creation of self, world, and identity," wrote Hart. "Homophobia advises our students not to write clearly" (31, 35). I decided to write a dissertation about it.

My epiphany charged me, it seemed, with a very clear and simple mission—to show that composition debilitated lesbian and gay students as writers by ignoring their experience. I would argue that including them in composition's professed intention to address "diverse" perspectives and take seriously the social contexts in which students write would wrest them from the benumbment and social inertia of those consigned to silence on the margins. To support the argument that I already had fully constructed in my mind, I would interview some lesbian and gay students, all of whom, I was certain, would corroborate my thesis that writing courses annihilated their expression. They would say that because they couldn't write what they really thought and felt they were epistemologically straightjacketed and therefore deprived of a full, meaningful education.

That fall, I found out that proposals I had submitted to teach lesbian- and gay-themed writing courses at two New York City colleges had been approved. Suddenly, I had a unique setting in which to conduct a qualitative research project based on case studies, and so I switched my methodology. I still, however, expected these case studies to give me information that would support my preconceived thesis (since I couldn't conceive of any alternatives to it).

Meanwhile, I had started to immerse myself in postmodern queer theory, and all the premises I had constructed based on my concept of lesbians and gays as a unified identity category with common concerns collapsed. In the spring of 1992 I taught the two courses, and what happened there eroded whatever was left of my illusions that lesbian and gay students shared a distinct pedagogical plight. As I described in my introduction, I discovered that though many students did indeed feel silenced by homophobia, others felt that it *invigorated* their writing. I had simply ignored in my analysis the strength one can draw from living on the margins, the special acuity that comes from viewing the world from a decentered spot. In fact, a well-known story in the lesbian and gay community is that of Karen Thompson (1988), whose lover, Sharon Kowalski, was forcibly remanded by a court to the guardianship of her parents after she was severely brain injured in a car accident. The fight to gain custody—which would have been granted automatically to a heterosexually married partner in such a situation—politicized Thompson, who ultimately tapped the strength not only of the lesbian and gay movement, but of the disabilities rights movement as well in her successful legal battle for Kowalski's return. She learned to speak in public, to navigate the legal system, to identify and activate the forces that would bring her case to national attention, and to mobilize mass resistance to homophobic injustice. She brought information about the importance of executing power of attorney to millions of people who were potentially vulnerable to the same situation she faced. Her landmark case also produced precedent-setting legal language when the court of appeals said that Thompson and Kowalski were "a family of affinity." She certainly wasn't "silenced" by homophobia—nor were the thousands of supporters who cheered and openly wept as she and Kowalski led the 1992 Lesbian and Gay Pride March down Fifth Avenue as its Grand Marshals.

Aside from being either silenced or stimulated to write by homophobia, the students in my classes were struggling with questions of where their queerness fit in among their other identities and how that would work itself out in their writing. Many of them were trying to decide whether the lesbian and gay community (which some found "ghettoized") or the mainstream world (with all its homophobia) was their optimal audience; figuring this out had a lot to do with how they would rhetorically position themselves. Some of them *had* had writing classes in which lesbian and gay issues were discussed and in which they had written about sexual identity; theirs, however, were by no means uniformly upbeat stories. Some had felt that even in classes of liberal, well-meaning people, everything about them was homosexualized after the coming-out moment and they lacked an audience that was able to hear their complexity. Others felt galvanized by adversity, finding in their role as corrector of homophobic myths and misconceptions their raison d'être. Some had screwed up all their courage to write papers about being gay, only to receive the paper back from the teacher with nothing on it but a grade.

After the courses ended, I interviewed selected students. Over the summer, as I reviewed the transcripts of those interviews and began to analyze them along with the students' texts, I felt utterly confounded about how to file and code the complex subjectivities of these lesbian and gay people. Resisting the project, I instead began to construct preliminary portraits of each of them based on close readings of their self-descriptions and written texts. I used the commentary from the interviews to contextualize what the students were saying in their written texts, and concomitantly used their written texts as interpretive frameworks for their orally recorded observations. As I became engrossed in interpreting the ways that students used language to construct self, community, and relation of self to community, and as I started to mentally chart the ways they did this as if with dots on a screen that could be connected in different patterns, I realized that, at least in part, I was doing what is known as "hermeneutical" research.

Kurt Spellmeyer (1993) has broadly described hermeneutics as "the study of meanings and contexts" (9) and hermeutically driven rhetorical research as the study of "the different dialects spoken by students outside the classroom, as reflections of different cultural 'scripts'— widely different visions of a life worth living" (26). Such an approach to learning about our students' discourses would, he says,

> make explicit the connections (and the disconnections) between formal knowledge and day-to-day experience. For teachers of writing, however, this project must take a complicating turn, since they will need to become more adept not only at pursuing the connections for themselves but also assisting student writers in their progress toward the same hermeneutic sophistication. Aristotle, I suspect, would be the first to agree that until our students have begun to consider knowledge in its relation to specific forms of life—their own first of all—they will remain the passive recipients of our "treatments," instead of playing their rightful parts as reflective, socially critical practitioners, the closest modern-day equivalents to the free citizens of the polis.[1] (26)

Hermeneutical inquiry also acts as a check on teachers' and researchers' partial, professionally situated perspectives on their students, according to Spellmeyer, because

> those who conduct interpretive research on writing would be obliged to test, as often and as thoroughly as possible, their determinations (from case studies, statistical samplings, and participant surveys) against what student writers have to say for themselves on the page. While the self-understanding of novice writers is no more definitive than anyone else's, their voices, heard in counterpoint to ours, can challenge methods, assumptions, and hidden agendas that have hitherto authorized profoundly disabling—and profoundly dishonest—"constructions" of the student and the student's language. (27)

I think that Spellmeyer captures something of what I ultimately tried to do. I thought that by creating composite portraits of lesbian and gay students responding in speech and writing to the semiosis of their lives—their lives in writing classes, in other parts of school, in families, in communities, in their metropolitan world—I could help to bring into focus for myself and for other writing teachers their needs and something of the nature of their existence as literate beings. For reasons that I think will become much clearer in the next four chapters when the students get to speak for themselves, this sort of inquiry could not have been done with lesbian and gay students in a mainstream writing class. Suffice it for now to say simply that these same students in mainstream classes would have written different texts, been different sorts of readers, would have been differently constituted as audiences, had different sorts of intertextual relationships with their peers' writing, and in the end would have inevitably reflected back upon the whole experience quite differently. I am not saying that they wouldn't have written about lesbian or gay issues, or used their queer subjectivities to write about virtually any topic; I'm just saying it would have been significantly different. I believe there are unique things to be learned about queer people—largely because of what queer people learn about *themselves*—in a queer discourse community.

I am not offering this study as an exemplum of how to run a lesbian- and gay-themed writing class—though I hope others will attempt similar experiments (and some already have).[2] I present it rather as a way for interested teachers of writing to begin, if they haven't already, to learn about lesbian and gay students. If they are truly interested, I trust that they will continue to pursue the project in other ways. One way that they can start is to read some of the texts students read in our classes which I will describe in this chapter.

In the rest of this chapter I will explain the design of the two courses upon which this study is based as well as the logistical bases of my research. Chapters 8–11 consist of what I call "interpretive portraits" of four lesbian and gay students from those courses.

The Two Courses

As I explained in Chapter 6, two different, but closely related, courses provide the context for this study.

Writing About Lesbian and Gay Experience was offered at Cosmopolitan University in the spring 1992 semester as one of eighteen "special topics" sections that honors writing students could elect to take for the second term of the required freshman writing workshop. All instructors (who are primarily graduate assistants) in the expository writing program are invited each year to submit proposals for these courses in any area of their interest, and the program directors make the selection. Students become eligible for honors sections upon recommendation by their first-term writing instructors, and are then free to choose from a list of course descriptions. The class size is limited to fifteen students. The description of Writing About Lesbian and Gay Experience read:

> We will read lesbian/gay theory, history, politics, and culture, and explore in writing what it all means to us. What effect does homophobia have on our lives and on us as writers—lesbian, gay, bi, or straight? What do we mean when we use the word "out"—to "come out," to "be out," to "out" someone? Is there such a thing as a "lesbian/gay culture"? What do gender, race, class, age, and able-bodiedness have to do with sexual identity? What is the relationship of "private" to "public" life? How is the lesbian/gay movement changing our thinking about the world? What does it mean to be gay in the Age of AIDS? What does it mean if you're not gay? What images of lesbians and gays do we see in art and the media? We will explore these and related ideas through intensive writing. All students welcome.

The course at Municipal College, where I had taught for several years as an adjunct lecturer, was offered the same term as the one at Cosmopolitan and was a "special topics" section of an advanced essay writing course. Its title was amended to Writing About Lesbian and Gay Issues because of the department chair's concern that "experience" too strongly implied one's own. This, he felt, might discourage students who didn't identify as lesbian or gay from enrolling, just as it might discourage lesbian or gay students who were not yet ready to publicly identify themselves. (This seemed reasonable to me, though ironically, the proportion of heterosexual students who took the Cosmopolitan course with "Experience" turned out to be considerably greater.) As an adjunct unsure of how to establish the candidacy of a course like mine for adoption, I had asked the chair informally one day about the chances of running it. He was extremely supportive, encouraged me to submit a written proposal, and sped the approval process through so that I was able to teach it the following term. I printed flyers to publicize the course, using a description almost identitical to the one I used at Cosmopolitan, which I posted in hallways and left in the offices of the Lesbian, Gay, and Bisexual Alliance and the women's studies program. The Municipal course had two prerequisites—one term of freshman composition and an introductory literature course—and it could be taken as an elective or it could fulfill a requirement for writing majors. The class met in the evening, and was officially limited to twenty-five students.

The Students

The students in the Cosmopolitan class were all eighteen to nineteen years old, freshmen, and from varied white ethnic backgrounds except for one Hispanic man. The majority were from middle-class families, had come to New York from other parts of the country and were living in the dorms, and were majoring in the arts. Forty-five percent of the class was male, 55 percent female; 63 percent identified themselves as "queer" in some form (gay or bisexual), 37 percent as heterosexual. All of the heterosexual students were women.

All of the queer students and one of the heterosexual students had enrolled in the course specifically because of its theme. The remaining heterosexual women said that they had registered for it because it was the only honors section that fit their schedule, or because they hadn't read the course descriptions and had simply trusted to luck. They all, however, said that they were interested in the subject and wanted to stay. Several men who did not disclose their sexual identity appeared on the first day and were never seen again. One man told me that he was heterosexual and "a right-winger" and asked that I help him transfer to another section "for everyone's sake." The result was that everybody who stayed in the class, even if they had arrived arbitrarily, made a choice at least by the end of the first day to engage with the material.

The Municipal course contained a much more diverse spectrum of students, ranging from those who were of traditional college age to two in their fifties. The majority were white, from varied ethnic backgrounds, but there were several African American and Hispanic students and one Filipino student. Most of them were from working- to lower-middle-class backgrounds, worked full-time in addition to being in school, commuted to school from home, and had grown up in the New York area. Unlike the Cosmopolitan students, they did not "choose" New York as a place to go to college because of its diverse, plentiful, and unconventional attractions, communities, and ideologies; for most of them, local public education was the only affordable and accessible source of higher education, and Municipal one of the highest-quality choices for the money.

Municipal is, in fact, in many ways a plum of urban public higher education, as it attracts a high-quality faculty, offers challenging interdisciplinary curricula as well as a solid groundwork in the traditional liberal disciplines, and has a reputation as a site from which the children of immigrants rise to achievement and its attendant assimilation. Despite being a commuter school, it has a vibrant atmosphere; the corridors are full of posters and leaflets about special events, student-staffed educational tables about AIDS and apartheid, video displays of student arts projects, and impromptu rallies convened for various causes by an active student government. At the same time, by the spring of 1992, tuition hikes and budget cuts were starting to take a serious toll on many students' ability to continue their education.

Fifty-four percent of the class at Municipal was male, 46 percent female; 87.5 percent identified as lesbian or gay, 12.5 percent heterosexual. One of the heterosexual students specifically identified herself as the daughter of a lesbian mother. Just as at Cosmopolitan, none of the students who remained in the class after the first night were heterosexual men.

Most students in both classes were motivated by their excitement at the novel theme of the course. Some squeezed the course into an already-full schedule because of fears that it would not be offered again. Others—primarily at Cosmopolitan—took it *only* because it fit into their schedule, yet found it sufficiently "different"—and therefore stimulating—to give it a large proportion of their academic attention. The students in both classes were unusually prolific, based on my prior experiences teaching writing courses at various levels for ten years, and—also highly unusual—they requested, consumed, responded to, and even took responsibility for photocopying greater volumes of reading material that I initially suggested. Some—though far from all— were active in lesbian/gay organizations on campus or in the community. While a number of them came into the class with ideas at least partially drawn from contact with, or knowledge of, the lesbian/gay political movement (often via the lesbian/gay press), virtually no one was familiar with lesbian/gay theory or history, or used to thinking about issues of sexual identity within critical or analytical frameworks. Virtually everyone came into the class with some feelings of homophobia, projected toward others and/or internalized. This last observation is not only mine, but their own; many of them mentioned it near midterm, reflecting back on their beliefs at the time of their entrance into the class with what they felt to be new critical insight. Various students also expressed, with a sense of urgency, their conviction that courses "like this" needed to be available to many more lesbian and gay students insofar as such curricula—which subject lesbian and gay reality to rigorous intellectual inquiry and imbue it with a sense of academic legitimacy—provide important institutional sources of self-esteem.

Course Texts

Students in both courses received a lengthy and detailed syllabus on the first day. In addition to describing the course texts, goals, methods, requirements, and method of evaluation, the syllabus listed numerous questions that were grouped according to thematic areas the class might want to consider. These thematic areas included the intersection of sexual identity with reading and writing, sexual identity and the politics of education, the meanings of "coming out," the social construction of sexual identity, the philosophy of "private life," the role of AIDS and AIDS activism in shaping consciousness, notions of lesbian/gay politics, and the creation of a lesbian/gay culture. The syllabus also contained a bibliography in four sections: lesbian and gay theory, history, politics, and culture, from which I told the students that they could select many of the specific texts we would read in each of these units. They were also invited to extend the bibliography with their own suggestions.

The course goals were presented as follows:[3]

> In this course you will be asked to read and think about lesbian and gay experience and to write critically about the politics and representation of multiple sexualities. Using that as a thematic framework, the goal of this course is to help you develop the ability to write essays in which you explore issues, interpret texts and other sources, and present a point of view based on your reading, research, and reflections over a period of time. We will be conducting various sorts of inquiries into the nature of our own thinking: how we decide what we believe, what counts for us as "truth," on what sorts of evidence and belief systems we base our opinions, and what uses of language can help us to articulate our ideas effectively. This honors section is an experiment; it's the first time I'm teaching this course, and lesbian and gay studies is a field that's just starting to explode across the country. So I guess I would say that another "goal" of the course is simply to find out what can happen when lesbian and gay experience becomes the content of a writing class.

The required texts listed were:

- Ann Snitow, Christine Stansell & Sharon Thompson, eds., *Powers of Desire: The Politics of Sexuality*
- Martin Duberman, Martha Vicinus & George Chauncey, Jr., eds., *Hidden from History: Reclaiming the Gay and Lesbian Past*
- Douglas Crimp with Adam Rolston, *AIDS Demo Graphics*
- Photocopied handouts to be distributed
- A writer's handbook and a college dictionary

Also recommended and stocked in the bookstore were Audre Lorde's essay collection *Sister Outsider* (1984) and John D'Emilio's social history, *Sexual Politics, Sexual Communities: The Making of a Homosexual Minority in the United States 1940–1970* (1983b).

Powers of Desire is an anthology of writings that explore social, historical, pyschological, institutional, and controversial aspects of sexuality from feminist and gay perspectives. Allan Bérubé's essay "Marching to a Different Drummer: Lesbian and Gay GIs in World War II" documents the treatment of lesbians and gays in the military both during the war and during the McCarthyite interrogations and purges which followed. John D'Emilio's "Capitalism and Gay Identity" illustrates how the rise of industrial capitalism both made possible and suppressed the notion of lesbian and gay identity; the essay provides an excellent example and explication of what it means to view sexual identity as a social construction. Adrienne Rich's "Compulsory Heterosexuality and Lesbian Existence" is a canonical and controversial analysis of lesbianism as a continuum of female identities resisting the patriarchal institution of heterosexuality. Amber Hollibaugh and Cherríe Moraga's "What We're Rollin Around in Bed With: Sexual Silences in Feminism" is a dialogue about butch-femme identity that was considered revolutionary when it first appeared in 1981 because of the blatant challenge it posed to lesbian feminist ideas about lesbian sexuality.

Hidden from History features a range of essays that together comprise a portrait of contemporary work being done in lesbian and gay history. The essays cut across cultures and represent a variety of theoretical perspectives and methodological approaches, including archival research, oral history interviews, and social constructionist interpretation. In our classes we began our unit on history by reading and discussing the introduction to the book, which presents an overview of the kinds of questions and issues current lesbian and gay historians are working with, and the essay "Revolutions, Universals, and Sexual Categories" by John Boswell, which continues this discussion but focuses it more specifically on competing views of how to frame categories of sexual identity and how those views are used as contexts for interpreting the past. In addition, we read Paula Gunn Allen's "Lesbians in American Indian Cultures," Eric Garber's "A Spectacle in Color: The Lesbian and Gay Subculture of Jazz Age Harlem," Erwin J. Haeberle's "Swastika, Pink Triangle, and Yellow Star: The Destruction of Sexology and the Persecution of Homosexuals in Nazi Germany," and Lourdes Arguelles and B. Ruby Rich's "Homosexuality, Homophobia, and Revolution: Notes Toward an Understanding of the Cuban Lesbian and Gay Male Experience." These selections not only provided a range of cultural constructs within which to consider questions of sexual identity; they also raised questions about the perspective of the writer in constructing the contexts within which "history" is understood to occur. Some students, for example, were disturbed by Garber's focus on cultural luminaries and artists in his description of lesbians and gays during the Harlem Renaissance period; they wanted to know, as social historians often do, how "ordinary people" further away from the public eye were thinking and behaving at that time. Others were interested in the ways these accounts differed from other accounts they had heard or read of events like the Holocaust or the treatment of lesbians and gays in Cuba.

AIDS Demo Graphics demonstrates how AIDS activists have appropriated the techniques of advertising to create graphic art that confronts the forces in our society that have permitted AIDS to escalate to epidemic scale. Targets include presidents and mayors, health commissioners, religious leaders, the medical establishment, corporations, prisons, school systems, media, local and national budgets, as well as the bigotry, mythologies, and indifference they have promulgated that have allowed HIV infection to spread at dizzying rates. The book features many reproductions of AIDS activist art, discusses the uses of art as propaganda and education, and provides accounts of specific actions in which the art was used—including the notorious "Stop the Church" action at St. Patrick's Cathedral and the Wall Street action which led to a speedup in the FDA's drug approval process and Burroughs-Wellcome's lowering of the price of AZT. The book also suggests interesting ways of looking at the roles that language and images play in the shaping of social events—whether the "event" is as large as allocation of government funds or television airtime, or as small as the entrance of a virus into a bodily fluid.

The first readings I assigned in each course were about the relationship between sexual identity and reading and writing. The classes read Amber Hollibaugh's "Writers as Activists" (1990), in which she discusses her experience coming from a working-class family that used language in primarily oral ways and her movement into activism, in which reading and writing played essential roles. They also read Ellen Louise Hart's "Literacy and the Lesbian/Gay Learner" (1988), written from the perspective of a writing teacher but raising many issues regarding their experiences as students, and Jeffrey Weeks's "Writing About Sex" (1991) in which the author describes the issues involved in writing about "the complex relationship between history, sexuality, and identity" (1).

Next, I assigned (with their input regarding specific selections, based on my descriptions) some theoretical pieces that I hoped would create contexts for future discussion: Gayle Rubin's "Thinking Sex: Notes for a Radical Theory of the Politics of Sexuality" (1989), Diana Fuss's introductory essay to *Inside/Out* (1991), and several Audre Lorde essays from *Sister Outsider* (the Lorde selections were different for each of the two classes). All of these essays are, in some sense, about the constitution of insiderhood and outsiderhood as a social epistemic phenomenon. Rubin attempts to sketch the political economy of sexuality in the United States and literally diagrams what she calls "a general version of the sexual value system" (280). Using the graphic image of a circle within a circle, the two cross-cut into pieces like a pie, she explains that the slices of the charmed inner circle constitute "good, normal, natural, blessed sexuality," which she identifies as

> heterosexual, marital, monogamous, reproductive, and noncommercial. It should be coupled, relational, within the same generation, and occur at home. It should not involve pornography, fetish objects, sex toys of any sort, or roles other than male and female.

The pieces of the pie that Rubin says lie on "the outer limits" are the ones which constitute "bad, abnormal, unnatural, damned sexuality," which

> may be homosexual, unmarried, promiscuous, nonprocreative, or commercial. It may be masturbatory or take place at orgies, may be casual, may cross generational lines, and may take place in "public," or at least in the bushes or the baths. It may involve the use of pornography, fetish objects, sex toys, or unusual roles. (280–81)

It is standard social practice, Rubin says, to "draw the line" at a clear point among sexual practices that will "stand between sexual order and chaos" so that we may avoid "a domino theory of sexual peril" (282). She points out that the precise location of the line does change, and that in recent years "unmarried couples living together, masturbation, and some forms of homosexuality are moving in the direction of respectability. Most homosexuality is still on the bad side of the line. But if it is coupled and monogamous, the society is beginning to recognize that it includes the full range of human interaction" (282–83). Granting those who engage in certain sexual behavior a degree of moral complexity that is denied others has, says Rubin, "more in common with ideologies of racism than with true ethics. It grants virtue to the dominant groups, and relegates vice to the underprivileged" (283).

Diana Fuss writes about the different sorts of spaces that are designated by the categories "inside" and "outside." Repudiating the idea that social identity is naturally bifurcated according to "the structural symmetry of these seemingly fundamental distinctions" (1), she raises questions about the construction of sexual borders, the psychosocial forces that demand and enact that construction, and the identifications (e.g., bisexual, transsexual) that are rendered unimaginable within this "rigid polar logic" (2). She says, "The problem . . . with the inside/outside rhetoric, if it remains undeconstructed, is that such polemics disguise the fact that most of us are both inside and outside at the same time" (5). Disguising that fact is, though, essential to the maintenance of sexual power arrangements, since, "[t]he difference between the hetero and the homo . . . is that the homo becomes identified with the very mechanism necessary to define and to defend any sexual border" (3). Fuss concludes that "[c]hange may well happen by working on the insides of our inherited sexual vocabularies and turning them inside out, giving them a new face" (7).

Audre Lorde, who died in 1992, was for many years a primary force in inspiring both the women's and lesbian and gay communities to think about the nature and politics of difference. She was also the author of numerous statements that have achieved axiomatic status in the feminist community (particularly in literary circles, among women of color, and among others involved with issues of race) and in the lesbian (and to a lesser extent, gay) community. Certain Lorde lines have come to be invoked at conferences, forums, readings, and in women's studies courses almost in the manner of sound bites—for instance, "The master's tools will never dismantle the master's house," "Your silence will not protect you," and "Poetry is not a luxury." Others appear epigrammatically in countless papers, articles, and speeches: "[O]ur place was the very house of difference rather than the security of any one particular difference"; "Difference must not be merely tolerated, but seen as a fund of necessary polarities between which our creativity can spark like a dialectic." Lorde, who frequently introduced herself or was introduced by others as "a Black lesbian feminist socialist poet warrior" (sometimes adding additional descriptors such as "mother of two, including one boy, and a member of an interracial couple," her age, or her status as cancer patient and veteran of a mastectomy), consistently used her multifaceted identity to disrupt simple schisms of unified insides and outsides, oppressed and oppressors. The central theses of the essays collected in *Sister Outsider* might (quite inadequately) be summed up as: Difference exists; don't deny it, misuse it, misjudge it, or undervalue it [my words]; and, It is crucial to bring about "the transformation of silence into language and action" (Lorde's words).

I also had the classes read D'Emilio's "Capitalism and Gay Identity" at this time so that they would have a concrete reference point for understanding what it means when we say that sexual identity is a construction, and homosexuality not necessarily a transhistorical experience.

These texts, then, gave the class some new theoretical vocabulary with which they could approach other texts, issues, and ideas. The next thing they read was a series of coming-out narratives that I culled from *The Coming Out Stories* (Penelope and Wolfe [1980] 1989) and Kath Weston's *Families We Choose: Lesbians, Gays, Kinship* (1991). After that came the unit on lesbian and gay history. The unit on lesbian and gay politics was the only one in which the choices of the two classes significantly differed. The class at Municipal chose to read articles on outing, lesbian and gay nationalism and separatism, and race and ethnicity issues in the lesbian and gay community. The class at Cosmopolitan also chose to read about nationalism and separatism, but in addition read articles on bisexuality and did a close reading of Adrienne Rich's "Compulsory Heterosexuality" from the perspective of gender differences within the lesbian and gay community. Both classes read *AIDS Demo Graphics* in the final unit of the course.

Course Assignments

There was considerable overlap in the student writing projects assigned in each of the two classes, but because of certain logistical differences between the classes, the assignments were structured somewhat differently. Writing projects at Cosmopolitan consisted of:

1. First-week letter to me responding to the syllabus, explaining personal history as a writer, and describing what brought student to the class (expectations, hopes, fears, goals, suggestions)
2. Informal essay (ungraded) on the relationship between sexual identity and students as readers and writers
3. Formal essay using lesbian/gay theory to analyze patterns in coming-out narratives (3–6 pages)
4. Formal essay on (either): (a) The factors that serve to construct the sexual identity of someone like you, or (b) Analysis of a particular institution, law, practice, or concept related to the notion of sexual identity (e.g. stag parties, prohibition against lesbians/gays serving in the military, compulsory heterosexuality, spousal health insurance benefits, "family" restaurants) (3–6 pages)
5. Cultural criticism (formal essay): Analysis of a piece of AIDS activist graphic art (3–6 pages)
6. Final project: Open topic, based on area of individual interest (8–10 pages)
7. Revision of essay from first week on relationship between sexual identity and reading/writing, from perspective of having completed course
8. Midterm and endterm reflective pieces
9. Much informal writing: journals, freewriting, metatexts.

Writing projects at Municipal consisted of:

1. First-week letter to me (same as Cosmopolitan)
2. Informal essay (ungraded) on sexual identity and students as readers and writers

3. Formal essay: Open topic, based on lesbian and gay theory
4. Informal draft: In what ways do coming-out narratives puncture, recast, or affirm popular notions of biological family?
5. Informal draft: Choice of "construction of sexual identity of some-one like you" or analysis of institution, law, practice, or concept (see Cosmopolitan)
6. Informal draft: Position paper on *one* of three issues in lesbian/gay politics: (a) outing, (b) race and ethnicity, (c) queer separatism
7. Formal essay: Revised and developed version of one of the three informal drafts
8. Formal essay: Cultural criticism: Analysis of a piece of AIDS activist graphic art
9. Final project: Open topic, based on area of individual interest (8–10 pages)
10. Revision of essay from first week on relationship between sexual identity and reading/writing, from perspective of having completed course
11. Midterm and endterm reflective pieces
12. Much informal writing: journals, freewriting, metatexts.

The informal essays were treated in various ways. For instance, I used the first informal essay on the relationship of sexual identity to reading and writing to get them to start thinking about the ways particular identities interpretively and rhetorically position us. Each student read her essay out loud, and everyone else wrote one question in response. The questions were read to the entire group (the writer was not to answer), and then the slips of paper with the questions were passed to the writer. The questions sat with the writer all term, to be used when the writer revised the piece at the end of the course from whatever perspective she had arrived at by that point.

Another use of informal drafts came up in the course at Municipal, where they wanted to do more reading on politics than could reason-ably be connected to any one writing assignment. The solution I came up with was for them to choose one of the three political topics we were reading about and to write a position paper on it. The nights that we discussed each of those topics, we sat in a circle and the students who had written on that topic read their essays out loud, one after the other. The point here was not to workshop the pieces, but to use the series of papers much as one uses a panel at a conference, so that different perspectives would be aired and starting points for discussion could be generated. Later on, the students turned the drafts into formal essays, using the discussion to inform revision.

All of the student texts generated in response to these assignments were considered relevant data in my study.

Selection of Students for Study

I originally selected fourteen students from the two courses I taught at Cosmopolitan and Municipal to interview for this study. Of those, eleven were lesbian or gay, and three were heterosexual. Students who identified as "bisexual" but who called themselves, in cultural parlance, "queers" or "dykes" were included in the misleadingly rigid-sounding category "lesbian or gay." One of the three heterosexual students missed several appointments for an interview, and so of necessity I eliminated her.

At the time, I envisioned not only the method but also the scope of this study somewhat differently than I did later, in that I originally planned to give much more attention to the experience of heterosexual students writing about sexual identity. Later on, I decided that it would be more feasible for the purposes of this study to concentrate predominately on the experience of lesbian and gay students. I selected four of the lesbian and gay students I interviewed for extensive treatment in the form of individual profiles; interview commentary and texts from the others do, however, appear throughout this book.

An initial survey of students who might volunteer to be part of this study showed me that there was a more than ample pool to choose from. Among those, I attempted to select students who represented a somewhat diverse sample of the class populations—particularly in regard to gender, race, age, and socioeconomic class. Diversity of interviewees was important to me because features of identity intersect in ways that can produce extremely different perceptions across social/demographic realities. For example, gay white men often feel that "we all" have a "common enemy" that we should unite to fight against—the "we" being the lesbian and gay community, the "enemy" being the homophobic heterosexual world. Lesbians and gays of color, however, frequently find that "we" and "them" are untenably simple formulations, as their experiences of oppression and allegiance have simultaneously been structured by racial identifications. Many lesbians, likewise, have historically looked for solidarity based on shared gender experience with heterosexual women rather than on shared sexual orientation with gay men because of sexism in the gay, as well as straight, world. Lesbians and gays of more affluent backgrounds have often escaped the homophobia of their families and communities by going away to college in liberal or cosmopolitan locations, while working-class lesbians and gays have traditionally found the military to be the only way out—and that route has been a paradoxical one, since the military has been both a likely and, as the nation's furor around the issue of gays in the military illustrates, also a forbidden place for homosexuals to find others like themselves, and the penalties for being discovered have been great. Lastly, the Stonewall rebellion in 1969 that marked the beginning of a mass liberation movement and the onset of the AIDS crisis in 1981 are two crucial moments that demarcate the consciousness of people in the lesbian/gay community. Those who came to sexual awareness pre-Stonewall as opposed to the 1970s or later, and those who came out pre-AIDS as opposed to in the 1980s or 1990s, often have vastly different notions of affiliation, pride, appropriate behavior, and the significance of politics, among other things. These, then, are some of the reasons why diversity in my student sample was so important.

Of the eleven lesbian and gay students I interviewed, six are female and five are male; six are white, two are African American, and three are Hispanic; six are twenty years old or younger, five are between twenty-five and thirty-eight years old; six are from Municipal College, five are from Cosmopolitan University. The socioeconomic class backgrounds of my participants are harder to summarize, since many of my participants were unsure of how to categorize themselves, and described class mobility between the time that they were growing up in their parents' homes and the present independence of their young adulthood. They do, though, range from working class to middle class.

The heterosexual students I interviewed were both white women, one of whom was Jewish; were aged eighteen and twenty, respectively; and one was from Cosmopolitan and one from Municipal. A young Filipino heterosexual woman was to have been part of the study but unofficially withdrew.

The students I interviewed were at varying levels of writing proficiency, but all in what I would classify as a fair-to-high range. Because the Cosmopolitan students had each been selected to participate in an honors seminar, they tended to be in the upper ranks of proficiency for college freshmen. The Municipal course was a higher-level course but drew a greater range of students; a surprising number of them, though, were highly skilled writers.

The four students I selected for in-depth presentation were chosen partly to maintain a diverse sample, and partly because their interviews and texts illustrated themes that seemed to me to be representative of themes that many of my students had been engaged with. They were also chosen in part for the richness of their oral and written expression, and for what I felt was their effectiveness in communicating the nature of issues that, from my experience with these two classes, I had come to believe affected many lesbian and gay student writers.

Data

Primary data are student texts, including formal and informal writing, and audiotaped interviews that I conducted with students after the courses ended. The interviews were intended to elicit narratives about the students' experiences in mainstream writing classes, in our lesbian-and gay-themed writing class, and in other academic contexts relevant to the subject under study. In the interviews I also asked the students for metacommentary about texts that they had produced in my writing course and, when possible, in prior writing courses, and about the process of producing them. In addition, there were questions that sought information on the student's history as a writer, on coming out, on relevant personal history (e.g., socioeconomic class, religion, parents, siblings, community) and on the student's perception of his/her sexual identity and its meaning.

The student texts that I examined included formal, revised writing, informal drafts, journals, introductory letters that students wrote to me, and reflective writing. (See Course Assignments for detailed lists.) I have used these in four ways: (1) as primary texts that provide information about students' thoughts, perceptions, feelings, and experiences in these and other writing classes; (2) as primary texts for my own analysis—i.e., I have looked for assumptions, constraints, and conceptual frameworks that appeared to inform the creation of particular texts, and for evidence of rhetorical and epistemological change from draft to draft and from one part of the term to another; (3) as reference points for the reader in conjunction with students' taped discussions of particular pieces of writing that were produced; and (4) as illustrations of what can happen to lesbian and gay students when they are in a nontraditional writing class that is centered on their experience.

I required all students to keep all of the semester's work in a portfolio to be submitted at the end of the term for a grade. In addition, I asked students I interviewed, where possible, for copies of assignments and texts from earlier writing courses so that the work they produced in my class could be compared to their work in a mainstream environment. This was easier for the students at Cosmopolitan, who had just taken the first of their required two-term writing workshop sequence the term before, than it was for the students at Municipal, some of whom had taken freshman composition several years earlier or at other institutions.

Interpretive Portraiture

In each of Chapters 8–11 I present what I will call an "interpretive portrait" of one of the students I interviewed. Probably best classified as hermeneutical analysis, these portraits are part biographical narrative, part literacy narrative, part textual analysis, part an inquiry into epistemology, and part cultural theory. They are my attempts to capture issues that I perceive, based on my work with a number of lesbian and gay students, to be relevant to larger numbers of lesbian and gay student writers. Of course, no student is ever really representative, in any holistic or generic sense, of masses of people, no matter what his or her social identification; but as I read some of the surprising and unsurprising, familiar and idiosyncratic thinking of my students as reflected in these pages, I sensed that there was much that others could relate to and learn from.

In each portrait I give contextual information about the student, usually related to the student's growing up, coming out, academic experience, and perceptions of what happened for him or her in our class. The first section of each portrait includes introductory matter about the student's life and schooling; the second section focuses on the student's experience in our class; and in the last section of each portrait I look closely at selected pieces of student writing and rhetorical issues that have emerged, examining them within interpretive frameworks suggested by the student's oral account, lesbian and gay theory, and the social contexts within which the student is operating. These frameworks are not strictly ordered here; I am simply citing them to give some sense of the lenses through which I analyze the students' work.

In each portrait there is a greater amount of biographical information than might ordinarily be considered relevant to an analysis of student textual work and classroom experience. The reason for this is that this information isn't really meant to be read as "background." I have foregrounded it because it describes the circumstances that frame, and in many ways, serve to construct, the part of these students' textual experience that I call "lesbian or gay." Because of their everyday experience of living as lesbians and gay men in homophobic culture, what happens outside the classroom provides crucial rhetorical lessons that can have a large effect on what happens inside the writing classroom. I am therefore including information about the students' lives—particularly their coming out, their prior experiences in school and as writers, their relationships to their families and communities, and the experiences that gave them their sense of the meanings and values attached to being lesbian or gay—as primary material of these narratives.

Notes

1. It is somewhat ironic, especially in light of my purposes here, that Spellmeyer uses this analogy, since most inhabitants of the polis *weren't* free. Women, slaves, and foreigners did not have access to what Spellmeyer describes as the "all-inclusive, unrestricted debate" of the polis. Because of this, many contem-

porary scholars see familiar forms of exclusion and disenfranchisement rather than ideal democracy as the polis's governing principle, and are unconvinced that they can benefit from its example. For instance, while it is well known that male homoerotic activity was a social norm in classical Greece, almost nothing is known about lesbianism—partly due to an absence of sources describing activities other than those of men, and partly because women, cut off from the public sphere, lived secluded with female relatives and children and probably had little opportunity for homoerotic relationships (Pomeroy 1975). Even Sappho's erotic orientation is completely unknown except for what one infers from the surviving fragments of her poetry.

2. Courses that I know of include Sarah-Hope Parmeter's intermediate composition course, "Writing About Queer Controversies," at the University of California at Santa Cruz; Jan Cooper's special topics composition section, "Issues of Sexuality and Language," at Oberlin; and Paula Ressler's freshman writing workshop, "Lesbian, Gay, Bisexual, and Transgender Experience: Rewriting Our Education," at New York University.

3. The course goals were presented in substantially the same way in the syllabi for both classes, with only minor changes made in the Municipal version to address the difference in course name and description.

Part Four

Portraits of Four Student Writers

Chapter Eight

Adrian O'Connor
"It's a Social World"

Adrian O'Connor[1] is nineteen years old and has just finished his freshman year at Cosmopolitan University. After high school, he took continuing education courses for a year at a state university near his home; the year before that, he had been an exchange student in Germany. With his major still undecided, he's leaning toward "something along the lines of sociology" that will allow him to focus on issues of gender and sexuality. He is also considering transferring into a school within the university that allows students to follow an individualized course of study.

Of mostly Irish background, Adrian grew up in an eastern college town with a large, visible lesbian population. Both his parents have master's degrees; his father is a professor of English and journalism at a community college and his mother is a librarian. Adrian describes them both as heterosexual and his family's socioeconomic stratum as "middle-middle-class." The child of a Protestant Baptist and a "non-practicing Catholic," he grew up going to church once a week but felt no strong sense of religion at home, and he stopped going to church when he reached adolescence.

Though his grades have always been adequate in English classes, he says, "I never really felt like I was accomplishing anything," and he rarely participated in those courses or felt much interest in writing until he came to college. "I never really saw writing as any kind of medium for me." His disengagement from his subject matter—which he feels was at the root of his alienation—was briefly challenged in his junior year of high school when he responded to an open assignment for a research paper (for which "I didn't feel necessarily that I needed to do any research") with a piece on homosexuality. "Of course, I was very interested, but at the same time, I was distancing myself from it completely. I put in a great amount of, like, 'This is interesting, but I don't tie into this in any way.' I talked about inequality, and homophobia, and I thought that was really too bad. And how there have always been gays and lesbians. And I was really kind of nervous to hand it in, because certainly my school was not a place where there was any representation of gay or lesbian students. But my teacher just kind of read it like any other paper. For me, it was a big event. For him, I think it was just kind of like—there. We never talked about it or anything like that. Maybe I was relieved, because I would have been scared if he had. But at the same time, I think I would have liked to have gotten more feedback."

Adrian says that he vaguely gathered that his topic was "inappropriate" for a class assignment. "In high school, any kind of sexual knowledge is not encouraged. Or even knowledge about your body in general. So I was really hesitant to write it. That was a period when I felt my personal life couldn't come into my writing. And this was really personal. And not only that, it was a taboo subject. And because the topic of being queer was never in any way approached in anything in high school, to take that initiative, to take that step, was kind of scary. And like I said, he didn't give it much response at all."

His feelings about writing changed in his first college freshman writing course. He was inspired by an instructor who gave him "a lot of feedback, both positive and critical. I started seeing myself more as an individual writer rather than lost amongst a class of people, and I started getting out of my fear and mode of nonwriter status." The instructor gave them "a lot of leeway" in terms of subject matter, and encouraged them to write about their "real interests." Adrian "started not worrying about grades any more" as he enjoyed "getting feedback on what I was saying." He wrote about his "first encounter with personal violence" in sixth grade, a work experience "in a really homophobic situation," several pieces of social commentary, and "some really neat freewriting, where we were just encouraged to tell someone off, and then write a response by that person to our telling them off. It was really like, if you want, go inside yourself and see what you find."

"The incident that I wrote about in the workplace was all about kind of like my being gay. And the incident when I was in the sixth grade, when this guy punched me in the face, was dealing with, I'd say, my not measuring up masculinity-wise. These were the things that really interested me. Finally it was like, my God, I can write about these things. These are things that have had an impact on me. And reading it, it was like, wow, that's my life. Just as other people have written about their lives, I can write about my life."

Adrian remembers taking "a really strong plunge" on the first day of that class. During a fifteen-minute freewriting exercise he wrote about attending Wigstock, an annual downtown New York drag festival, on one of the first days after his arrival in the city. He even read it out loud to the class because he "had gotten a very good sense from the instructor in the first half of the class. He was putting forth this idea of writing as a real personal tool that can sculpt what you as a writer want to do. I certainly didn't feel a hundred percent safe. I was scared about his reaction and the class's reaction. But I definitely did feel more safe than I ever had." As the course progressed, the instructor occasionally referred to gay issues—"When we'd talk about racism and sexism, he would include homophobia in that"—and that encouraged Adrian to risk writing the gay-themed texts that he did.

The students, following the instructor's lead, responded well to these texts in workshops, but in an anonymous writing situation something else happened. ""We had a thing in our class called 'Hot Topics,' and we had a computer class, so there would be these hot topics that Mike often wrote up—and we could write up ones if we wanted to—pertaining to different hot issues of the day, like last semester Anita Hill, or the Gulf War. I would do it once a week, and I'd find out what had been written since the last time I'd been there. It was very informal. It could be very screamy or in-your-face. One of them was about some man who was getting involved with some other man, and they wanted to get married, and should they be allowed to get married. And of course, then you responded to it. We all had pseudonyms, so we never knew who anybody was. And I went into that one, and I was really surprised, because there was a lot of homophobia in there. There was all this, 'Well, I think homosexual relations are OK just as long as they're not in my face and just as long as I don't have to see them,' and 'God created Adam and Eve, not Adam and Steve, let's not forget that.' And I was like, 'Who is this? Who is writing this shit?' I told Mike that that really pissed me off, and he said, 'Well, write something to it. Create your own hot topic.' And I said, 'Maybe I will!' And I responded to it. I wrote, 'It's time to get over this fear. As long as we perpetuate this kind of homophobia, nothing's going to change. Would you ever think of telling a straight couple that they shouldn't show any kind of affection in front of you?' Meanwhile, Mike had written this absolutely kick-ass comment. It was something like, 'God did create Adam and Eve, but just because we have fingernails doesn't mean we have to clip them. And we have chicken that we can eat but we can also eat marmalade and lamb. We have decisions. Just because there's a volcano doesn't mean we have to dive into it.' And I read that, and I was like, 'Go, Mike, go, yeah!' The person never responded again. And it was the first time Mike wrote his real name, without a pseudonym.

"Earlier, it had seemed like sexuality was something that couldn't really be approached in a school setting, a writing setting. It's always been something that's private, and that you restrict to a bedroom. It's not a public topic. I didn't feel that writing classes were for personal things. Maybe for 'chosen' personal things that were OK, like a child-hood experience on your bicycle or something like that. But certainly not something that was pertinent to all of us, like sexuality. Which made this class this [second] semester really intriguing, because it was taking all that stuff that's been put into you about sexuality *as* a private thing, and pouring it out, and here I am taking it at school. And it's great. I've never had such an opportunity. In high school we're still, in adults' eyes, budding children, and they don't want to ever imprint any ideas that may be objected to by parents. Classes that were saying, on the surface, go in and look at yourself, really didn't reflect that. The one place where you could really explore continued to be a place that was just—not there." Adrian feels that his experience in Mike's class, and then later in our gay-themed writing class, made "the utter ab-sence of any kind of discussion about sexuality [in earlier schooling] even more pronounced. I just realized how much I had had to keep quiet."

Adrian remembers becoming conscious that sexual identity existed in seventh grade, when peers began to taunt another student and himself by calling them "fag" and "queer." "It's funny, because now we're both gay. It's almost like, damn, I couldn't prove them wrong. It was really upsetting because on some level I knew that what they were calling me was in actuality not that wrong, and yet it was used so violently and viciously. I identified with it. I didn't identify with me being ridiculed. But if you took away all the bad connotations and just left the 'gay' part, then I identified with that. But very deep inside. I didn't let it out or explore it."

In high school, Adrian worked in a local bagel shop largely staffed by very out lesbians. "I just remember as individuals, they were really happy with who they were. They weren't afraid to show their sexual-ity. It was really inspirational for me." He spent his senior year studying in Germany, reading James Baldwin and "really identifying a lot with what he was writing about." He began to tentatively come out by talking with a few friends there and with his host family, whom he describes as a support system and perhaps surrogates for his own family at home. Upon his return to the United States, he spent time with a lesbian friend and decided to just "make the leap" from "intellectualizing" and "distancing" himself from his sexuality to actually coming out. He began to date a man, and came out to his family, with whom he was living while he took continuing education courses. His mother and two older sisters were "really supportive," while his father's reaction, he says, was simply, "Oh, OK. I kind of thought so." He describes himself currently as a "ten" on a one-to-ten outness scale.

Adrian describes himself as "both a gay man and a fag—it depends on whatever comes out of my mouth, or on my mood." He defines "fag" by raising his fist in a proud and militant gesture, and explains, "It's a really in-your-face term. It means if you've got a problem with it, that's your problem, and you go deal with it. It's such a nasty term, always thrown viciously in your face, and I'm taking their most ultimately harsh weapon, other than their fists, and making my own connotation out of it." He adds, "But that's not what first comes into my head [to describe myself]. I think of myself first as just a man, maybe just a person. And a gay identity doesn't always fit in, though it's certainly a large part of me." The reason he calls himself "gay" is "maybe to explain all the shit I've gotten in my life—in terms of being 'other' or different, or in terms of not adhering to social mores and rules, and being your typical masculine person. By taking on the identity of 'gay' or 'queer,' I'm acknowledging that difference within me, a difference I've always felt. It's empowering to know that I'm no longer going to just pretend the difference isn't there and hope that it goes away. I'm acknowledging it. I'm saying yeah, it is there."

When asked what makes him ascribe the "difference" specifically to his gayness, he describes ways that he differs from culturally prototypical (or stereotypical) masculine gender characteristics—which he portrays negatively—and identifies with positively valued feminine ones. "The difference is that I'm not big and strong, and I'm not constantly grabbing my crotch, and I'm not calling women bitches, and I'm not demeaning people in different ways. And that I am sensitive, I do consider myself to be a very emotional person, I express my emotions, and I try not to suppress things, I look for companionship with people, I look for meaningful relationships with both men and women—although I usually find it more so with women—and I'm not an island in the sea. I'm not this unapproachable rock or loner, or the Marlboro man." It is only when I mention to him that the qualities he has listed are generally associated with gendered behavior, rather than sexuality per se, that he adds to his definition, "the fact that I like men, that I'm attracted to men."

Having said this, though, he immediately veers away from the "attraction" component of his definition to resume his discussion of exploring difference. "Acknowledging myself and identifying myself as gay maybe gives me more leeway to explore different parts of me. I've already said that yes, I am different than what is socially acceptable, that I accept that in me, that I explore that in me—and once I've made that differentiation and that distinction, further self-exploration comes much more easily, and is more approachable. It's not such a difficult thing to look inside of myself. I've already done a lot of self-introspection. Some people are so adamantly against it, they're freaked out by what they might find. And I'm thrilled with what I'll find. It might be scary, but I want to find it. And identifying myself as gay in a way gives me the leeway to do that. Because I think straight men *don't* have a lot of leeway within our society to really look within themselves. I don't think they're really encouraged to do so. And by saying that I'm gay, it's almost like, Ah, whew! Now I don't have to pretend anything, and it gives me room to really explore more. More so than I would have if I were still closeted, and not living it and accepting it."

Adrian also embraces the word "queer" as a broader appellation that signifies choosing to be different. "You don't have to be gay or lesbian to identify as queer. It's much more inclusive, it allows for a lot more diversity. You just have to be self-identified as different. If you're going to take the responsibility for using the word 'queer' for yourself, then that says a lot about you. 'Queer' is like my mother identity."

Writing in a Queer Class: The Personal Goes Public

Adrian's first response when I ask about his experience in our class is, "Really where classes begin is with the student-teacher relationship. You let us explore." He explains that my use of language demonstrated from the start my membership in the lesbian and gay community, and that this was important to him as a writer. "It said something about your outer life, not only as a teacher, but as a person. So for me it was an immediately personalized class."

He feels that the student-student relationships were also very important. "After the first couple of weeks, people really began to express themselves, and to expose a lot. And were very honest. It's not that I'm alienated from a class where I feel I'm the only gay person. But there definitely is a strong differentiation between the two. It was really good to have people I could identify with on a sexual orientation basis. We all have our different stories, but there are commonalities between us. And the fact that we were all interested in taking this class said a lot. I didn't feel the straight students had any negative effect on things. There were a couple of times maybe when I would get frustrated—where I just wanted to throw in the entire bag because I didn't think there was any point, where we could just go around and argue forever. But I guess that only encouraged me to find my voice. Because I realized that we're never going to find the common voice, the totally common voice. We'll find common points, but we'll never find a totally unified one. So I've got to continue to strive to find my own.

"At first I thought it was pretty self-indulgent to take this class. I thought, why should I write about this type of thing? This is a thing that is supposed to be private. Aren't I just whining, or just griping about inequality? And while I *wanted* to think of it as a worthy topic, there was so much in me that was battling against that, and putting it down. But the readings—it was really inspirational to read people's work, to see that this was what they were writing, this was completely valid, it was completely appropriate, and really strong. Hearing lesbian and gay voices not justifying themselves, and not excusing themselves to anyone—it was like they were saying, 'I have as much validation to write about this as this other person has to write about European monarchies.' Those writers were so confident in what they were saying. They weren't apologetic in any way. Their writing that stuff was justification in itself. It just served to reinforce and reassure me that these are very important topics, they're very worthy. And to show that it's only the individual who's going to decide what is worthy. Those readings really acted as catalysts—within this whole queer, sexual spectrum—for me to find out what I relate to, what I identify with, and what maybe I want to express on my own.

"That very positive environment made everything much more interesting for me. I asked for extension after extension on my papers because it was becoming very personal. Even more so than last semester. It was a time really to express myself, a very personal part of myself. That's not something where I can just put my brain into action and go. It required a lot of thought, and looking inside. And I liked that a lot. I felt it gave me more of a voice. It gave me a place to express that which I kind of thought wasn't supposed to be expressed publicly. Or certainly not in writing. For people who don't consider themselves fully as writers, to give them an opportunity like that in an educational setting I think is really spectacular. Giving a voice to that part of me—to my sexuality, to my being queer—I'm sure I could have found it in other places, too, in going out to community organizations, but it would have been different. There wouldn't have been the same amount of structure. It wouldn't have been so official—it would have been a very on-the-side type of thing. Whereas this was very much in the forefront of what I'm doing. I mean, I am going to school, I'm getting an education—and with the connotation that school has had for me, classes like this really serve to restructure—or I'll use the phrase, to *deconstruct* my perceptions of school, and what school is. It makes it much more of a place than ever before where I, the individual, have a place. Where I'm not just there because it's required of me, but because I want to be there, I learn what I want to learn. School was never a place where I was personally challenged, where I brought myself into it. This class incorporated education, politics, personal stuff, experience—in a way that's very hard to come by in classes. I think for a writing class that's really important. Because writing is *about* finding a voice. I've learned so much in this class because of how things were personalized. Learning really starts to take off for me when it transcends just the traditional academic setting. Where my personal stuff starts to come into the class, that's where it really accelerates for me."

Adrian feels that the bits and pieces he learned in the course of deconstruction and social construction theories were particularly useful. "It's served to make me know that there is no answer to anything. The way I see the world is going to be different from the way the next person sees the world. And we can have common ground on some things, but there are definitely going to be things that we don't agree about. And it's folly to believe that we will agree."

The notion that divergent perspectives can claim validity in different ways leads, for Adrian, back to his quest to locate the "personal" in a new sphere of value. "This class has taken things that are very personal for me, and I'm realizing that though they may be personal to me, they may not be to other people. And it's taught me not to let that hinder me from exploring them. Not to let someone else's power in any way get on top of mine. That's not to say that I want to exercise power—but I do want to have a sense of self-determination. So I'd say this class has been very conducive to further self-determination. It let me see that issues of identity and sexuality are very valid. That questions that I'd asked myself for a long time about my sexuality, about my gender, are very relevant, and deserve a voice. *Need* a voice. They've gone without a voice for too long. Because let's face it—I'm not an independent entity in this world. I'm affected by what other people say to me, and their perspectives, and I look for support in what I do."

Reflecting on the difference a gay-positive discourse in a class makes for him, Adrian mentions once again the time he wrote about homosexuality in high school. "If it had been a gay-positive class, it probably wouldn't have been such a trauma for me, or such a trial to actually come to this decision to write about it. It wouldn't have been that inner self-struggle to debate whether I should do it or not, and I wouldn't have been so alone in that struggle. Even last semester, writing about that homophobic incident—I really wanted to, but it took a lot of strength to write a paper about me as a gay man. I felt I had to justify myself in different ways. Unlike in this class, I had to give a whole introduction about me being gay, and what being gay was like and meant. And that homophobic situation needed a background. Maybe I just wasn't quite as out. I didn't feel quite as justified about writing what I wanted to write. It had a lot to do with audience. My papers now are not so consumed with audience. I mean, I'm aware of it, but it doesn't exercise as huge an amount of control over me as it used to. Maybe there isn't that sense of friction. But there also isn't that sense of me trying to justify myself. Now I feel that what I do write about *is* justified, and I don't have to struggle to make someone believe that it's justified. I definitely want to reach my audience. But I think I'll be more effective in reaching them if I don't spend a page and a half trying to justify what I want to write. That justification doesn't just have to do with my audience. It has to do with me justifying myself and what I'm writing this for."

Adrian thinks it would be a good idea to have more classes like ours—or, more generally, classes that are "conducive to people that are not approached in traditional academia. Or regarded. Or dealt with. Or acknowledged." He feels that those classes are important because they can deal with "topics that are important to people, and show that education can be open to diverse kinds of interests." He feels that a responsive university would "open its eyes to reality and say, 'Wow! There's a growing queer movement! Maybe we should open the ivory towers to it!'" Otherwise, he says, "I don't think people are really going to learn. People aren't going to be challenged. And people aren't going to be inspired. And people aren't going to be encouraged to really explore. Education is about challenging yourself. And if you're not interested in what you're learning, then why are you going to challenge yourself? Issues of race and class and ethnicity and gender have gotten the foot in the door, and I think it's about time queer issues got a foot in the door, also." He feels that it will be useful for heterosexual students "just to open their minds further to the concerns of gays and lesbians. Just as I think it's important for me to have my mind be open to experiences of people of color. Having experienced my own kind of discrimination, I see homophobia and sexism and racism as all interconnected in different ways. I think homophobia and sexism, while they're different, stem from similar fears and root causes. Being gay doesn't let me understand everything else, but it gives me more of a *fathomness* of it. I think that happened with the straight people in this class. I don't know how much they changed, but they were definitely open to it. Their eyes *were* open and their eyes *did* open. I think they probably did go through a lot of change. I think there really is a good learning opportunity for heterosexuals, just as there's a good learning opportunity for me to go into classes that deal with issues that don't directly pertain to me. I would only hope that more straight men would take such a class."

Reconstituting the Personal

Several themes emerge repeatedly in Adrian's interview. One is his concern with what he calls "personal" experience and the various constraints within which he operates as he seeks to relocate the articulation of this experience from private to public realms. He never specifically explains what, for him, qualifies any subject matter for membership in the categories "personal," "private," or "public," but his commentary does indicate that he views these categories as somewhat unstable, with borders that shift within variable interpretive contexts. For instance, there seems to be a recurrent insistence in his account that sexuality is "personal," that this personal matter has in the past been forcibly repressed to a private sphere (in which, due to the constraints of privacy, it had no "voice"), and that his experiences in college writing classes and his encounter with lesbian and gay studies have in a sense released the subject of sexuality from its confinement in private space to a place in legitimate public discourse. He says early on in the interview, speaking of his time in high school, "That was a period when I felt my personal life couldn't come into my writing. And [homosexuality] was really personal." He remembers that "it had seemed like sexuality was something that couldn't really be approached in a school setting, a writing setting. It's always been something that's private, and that you restrict to a bedroom. It's not a public topic." Later, though, he felt good about his first college writing instructor because "he was putting forth this idea of writing as a real personal tool that can sculpt what you as a writer want to do."

At this point, the boundary between private and public discourse seems to have started to erode: a "personal tool" was revealed to be the instrument of choice in a public "writing setting." Later still, in his lesbian- and gay-themed writing class, the instructor's use of words like "dyke" and "queer" signaled a further erosion of that boundary, as the colloquial and sexualized "outer life" and the work of the classroom converged, creating for Adrian the sense of "an immediately personalized class." As he perceived the usual constraints to be lifted, he began to spend unprecedented amounts of time on his papers, asking for "extension after extension" in order to fully capitalize upon this "time really to express myself, a very personal part of myself." Finally, now, feeling that he has grown as a writer, he rereads his earlier experiences with education through the lens of his new perspective of the personal as heuristically valuable: "School was never a place where I was personally challenged, where I brought myself into it. . . . I've learned so much in this class because of how things were personalized. Learning really starts to take off for me when it transcends just the traditional academic setting. Where my personal stuff starts to come into the class, that's where it really accelerates for me."

Adrian's reassignment of "personal" material from a private realm in which it is "taboo" and silenced to a public realm in which it figures prominently in the making of history, politics, education, social knowledge, and intertextual academic conversations parallels the reassignment of that material in the making of contemporary queer politics and culture. As I pointed out in Chapter 1, a major project of the gay rights movement has been to problematize old, liberal chestnuts—such as "I don't care who you sleep with" or "What I do in my personal life is my own business"—which aimed to defuse the potential social explosiveness of gay information by making it seem irrelevant to public discourse and social ethics. Resting its case largely on the sort of thinking popularized by the feminist maxim "The personal is political," different strands of the movement have variously contended (a) that homosexuality involves a person's entire life, not simply his or her sexual activities, (b) that institutional prohibitions against homosexuality—such as sodomy laws in roughly half the states, immigration laws banning the entrance of gays into the country, lack of civil rights protections including custody rights, health care benefits under partners' policies, discrimination in housing and employment, the ban on gays in the military—illustrate that sexuality is very much a matter of public policy, and (c) that gay liberation implies sexual liberation for all people—liberation from the tyranny of compulsory heterosexuality, repressive religious dogma, sexism, and the rigid mores that have been used to maintain the nuclear family unit under capitalism—and that in repressing gays, straight society is really trying to squelch the public representation of something it deeply fears in itself.

In all of these cases, the schism "private/public" has been challenged, even sharply dividing the movement at times (as in, for example, the debate over the practice of "outing"; opponents of the practice have attacked it as an invasion of "the right to privacy," while others have contended that the secrecy surrounding being gay is a matter of being held hostage in the closet by the repercussions of exposure, not of freely chosen "privacy"). Thus it seems not too surprising, and consistent with concerns that have evolved in the mass lesbian and gay liberation movement, that much of Adrian's metacommentary on his own history as a writer is about the importance, for him, of moving the "personal" matter of sexuality out of the private and into the public sphere. What may be more surprising, though, is to discover that the texts he produced in the gay-themed class had almost no "personal" content in them—if one interprets the word "personal" to mean writing that is confessional, autobiographical, self-revelatory, or first-person experiential. With only one exception, his formal writing is typically academic, expository, and rooted in observations and analyses of phenomena in "society" rather than in himself—even where other options were available or the language of the assignment invited the inclusion of some sort of autobiographical data. Here, for instance, is an assignment given about halfway through the term:

> Now that you have read a number of accounts of lesbian and gay experience in social and historical context, write an essay in which you explain the factors that serve to socially construct the sexual identity of a person like you. By "like you" I mean someone of your age, historical time, place—not you specifically. In other words, what does "sexual identity" mean now, and what are the social forces that have given shape to that meaning?

In class I amplified upon this orally by saying that though I wrote "not you specifically," it *would* be helpful for them to consider the particular towns in which they grew up, especially factors such as the size, demographics, and values of those towns, as well as the media they encountered in those settings (e.g., Was cable TV available? "Alternative" newspapers and bookstores? Art film houses? Were "televangelists" frequently on the air?) Many students did choose to pursue those avenues of exploration, and some inevitably veered into autobiography. Adrian, however, wrote a text that left scant factual clues as to the identity or background of the writer (though his ideology was clearly inscribed upon it). Entitled "Where Do We Learn?," the essay focuses specifically on the contested appropriateness of school as a site of sexual knowledge and the role of school as a place which, in his view, is most often used to reproduce restrictive sexual values. Although his "personal" experience is omitted from the text, his concern with attempts to erase "personal" (once again, specifically, sexual) experience from social discourse and public policy is manifested in "objective" terms. In one early section he writes:

> Among [the social forces] that have a strong effect [on the formation of sexual identity] is the interrelationship between family and school, particularly the role played by parents in influencing and regulating what the school can and cannot teach their children. Long an institution whose purpose is to reflect social mores and create individuals who uphold social standards, schools have been primary places that influence the growth and development of youth. Because schools have little agenda of their own other than to educate, the regulation of what is to be taught lies greatly in the hands of those who have a direct interest in youth, namely parents, and who have primary access to financial funds, such as the government. The role of school is a large one in that they have the task of undertaking the responsibility of youth. What the school teaches and particularly what individual

teachers teach must be socially acceptable, otherwise they run the risk of condemnation and a threat to their livelihood, be it renouncing of funds or the loss of a position. In this way, those who are in the teaching profession are on some level aware of the tremendous responsibility bestowed upon themselves by taking on the role of educator. What they teach must not only be acceptable by the school board, which monitors their performance, but also by parents, influential members of the community, religious leaders and governmental leaders. In this light it is clear that schools are not entities that continue on their own basis, but rather by the assessment of outside forces on their performance.

He goes on to discuss how these "outside forces"—particularly parents—influence sex education in school and the current debate over condom distribution. Maintaining sexuality as a "traditionally hushed topic" and "not an issue to be discussed with their youth," parents' desires to "regulate the development of sexuality in children" can have lethal consequences in the age of AIDS.

The need for condoms in a time when sexual diseases, particularly HIV infection, pose a strong threat to everyones' lives is being pushed aside to accommodate adults' fears and uneasiness when it comes to accepting sexual activity in youth. . . . No longer is it an issue of "proper" sexual mores, refusing to take the role of educator inhibits children's learning how to protect themselves from possibly life-threatening situations. . . . The image of the youth as immature and incapable of making wise decisions is a picture created by adults, not by youth themselves, and serves to reflect the extent to which youth are still in the hands of adults. . . . This debate on condom distribution in the schools serves to reflect parents' desire to keep sexual discussion out of the public sphere of the school and restrain it to the private home, thus keeping control over it. . . . For many, the media may serve to "educate" about sexuality when other areas remain off limits. Sexuality as portrayed in images may serve to give a picture of something exotic and exciting, but cannot serve as a substitute for a topic that receives inadequate attention from more personal sources. In this sense, learning about sexuality has been transferred from a personal resource to an impersonal one, the media, where questions cannot be asked and direct dialogue remains impossible. In my mind, this replacement from a personal sphere to an impersonal one leaves many questions unanswered and renders the development of sexual identity yet again something we must seek out ourselves with little expected support.

There are two rhetorical issues that especially interest me about this text. One is that in detailing the ways that sexual discourse is controlled, withheld, and monologically supplied, the author either consciously or unwittingly detours around the actual question he has been asked: What sort of identity is produced as a result of these factors? The second is that a hint at the answer sneaks in almost surreptitiously at the very end, where developing a sexual identity is suddenly something *"we* must seek out *ourselves* with little expected support" (emphasis added). For the first and only time in the essay we are informed, albeit obliquely, that the author has a personal stake in this mess—as one of that mass of youth who has been controlled and thus been let down. It is our only clue that he has any direct investment in his subject besides social and ideological concern. At the same time, Adrian's interview suggests that this sort of writing *did* meet his need for "personal" expression.

As teachers of writing, what may be valuable for us to consider here are the complex meanings of a writer's sense of "personal" connection to his material, and the ways that different invocations of the "personal" enable writing. By extrapolating from Adrian's oral account, we might hypothesize that whatever felt implicitly "personal" to Adrian in this essay—one that most readers would be unlikely to judge "personal"—permitted him to have a different kind of engagement with his work than he had had in the past with work that might be more generally characterized as "personal," yet which he wearily characterizes as "like a childhood experience on your bicycle or something like that." Although his interview alone might lead us to believe that his desire is to write about individual experience (that is, if we interpret "personal" in certain conventional terms—as I initially did), we find in his formal texts that he never detaches the "personal" from the public and the social. It seems that perhaps his understanding of the personal *as* social was what liberated him to write the text. Ironically, the problem with his prior writing experiences may have been that his "I," even when not explicitly articulated, seemed to have no social, public place, and thus no room in public discourse. Perhaps one constraint that exists for many of our students is their inability to imagine some crucial part of their identity having a public existence. Without public representations of their "selves" to assure them that such an existence is possible, the uses and possibilities of language must seem very limited. This is, after all, a lot of the basis for current arguments for multicultural curricula.

Justification and Its Discontents

Another theme that appears in Adrian's interview is his perceived need to "justify" himself and queer issues in a world of hostile or insufficiently knowledgeable others. He cites course readings written by political and academic queers as an important source of inspiration.

"Hearing lesbian and gay voices not justifying themselves, and not excusing themselves to anyone—it was like they were saying, 'I have as much validation to write about this as this other person has to write about European monarchies.' Those writers were so confident in what they were saying. They weren't apologetic in any way. Their writing that stuff was justification in itself." Even in his fairly supportive first writing workshop, he says, "I felt I had to justify myself in different ways. Unlike in this class, I had to give a whole introduction about me being gay, and what being gay was like and meant. And that homophobic situation needed a background." After taking our class, he says, "Now I feel that what I do write about *is* justified, and I don't have to struggle to make someone believe that it's justified. I definitely want to reach my audience. But I think I'll be more effective in reaching them if I don't spend a page and a half trying to justify what I want to write. That justification doesn't just have to do with my audience. It has to do with me justifying myself and what I'm writing this for."

It sounds as if what Adrian calls "justification" may be an umbrella term for several issues that figure prominently in rhetorical theory. One that I am thinking of is the issue of authority. What authorizes a writer to use language at all? And then what authorizes the writer to offer that linguistic product to the public world? If authority involves, as David Bartholomae suggests, a sense that one can reasonably imitate, and thereby enter into, the language of the privileged community, what happens if one wants to use language *against* that community? (What if that community, by virtue of its privilege, is the very thing that has kept the writer from speaking in the first place?) How does a writer's knowledge that the community he addresses is predisposed to powerfully resist his message on multiple fronts leave room for him to find a way of addressing that community? What words can a writer marshall to communicate to that community the existence and authority of a new community (or perhaps, to adapt Halliday's terms, an "anti-community") with, in some sense, alternative uses of language, a different epistemology, ontology, psychology? Patricia Bizzell (1982) has written, "Producing text within a discourse community . . . cannot take place unless the writer can define her goals in terms of the community's interpretive conventions. Writing is always already writing for some purpose that can only be understood in its community context" (227). This leads her to conclude that "Composition studies should focus upon practice within interpretive communities—exactly how conventions work in the world and how they are transmitted" (239). When the "conventions" of particular communities are informed by deep prejudice and "moral" or religious conviction, the work of composition and communication—and of the individual rhetor—enters a new key.

The issue of authority is bound up with the issue of audience. If any argument or analysis comes into existence through resistance to a familiar point of departure, then the proximity or remoteness of that point in relation to the rhetor will render the rhetor's work less or more difficult. As Lester Faigley (1989) has pointed out, the student essays that teachers most often applaud are those they deem most "honest" or perceive to possess an "authentic voice" or "integrity"; yet such response often depends on the fact that "the truths 'exposed' and 'revealed' in the essay are a series of recognitions for a college English teacher" (408). It seems that for Adrian, the work of "justifying" himself has something to do with having to travel an inordinately long discursive distance in order to establish initial contact with a homo-phobic—or simply ignorant—audience. When he can, conversely, as-sume an informed and sympathetic audience—one that might, for instance, share a "personal" sense of the relevance and importance of his topics—his point of departure can be one that is equivalently significant and familiar to him as it is to them. Going the extra distance, although an occasionally necessary choice that a writer must make in the context of certain goals, becomes exhausting when it is always a prerequisite to the movement one desires to make from one's *own* point of departure—which is usually, after all, the impetus toward writing. Adrian is describing, in a sense, being condemned to always write about what he already knows, rather than being permitted the intel-lectual excitement of writing himself into some new epistemological place. That he didn't feel the exhaustion of having to "justify" himself in our class indicates that the perceived need to "justify" depends on the knowledge and understanding one can expect of one's audience, not on their necessarily sharing the writer's identity, since over a third of the members of our class identified as heterosexual. What counted was that as the course progressed the heterosexual students did be-come quite conversant, if not fluent, with queer vernacular and dis-course.

When I look at two conventionally "personal" texts that Adrian showed me from his first-semester writing workshop, I see two differ-ent approaches he took to the need to "justify" himself. In an essay near the beginning of the term called "The First Hit" (his "first encoun-ter with personal violence"), he avoids the imperative to "justify" altogether by simply de-gaying himself. Because he is writing about himself in the sixth grade, it is easy for him to blur the distinctions between not living up to an ideal of masculinity because he is gay and not doing so because he is preadolescent. He writes near the beginning:

> I was, like many other sixth graders my age, already going out with
> a girlfriend, if I may so describe our relationship. I liked having a

girlfriend, and enjoyed the newfound status that came with being involved with someone. No doubt it meant that I was an okay person, and someone worth accepting. At this age, at least in my eyes, acceptance was important, and the more the better. Her name was Pamela, and she had been a good friend before we started going out. The time we spent together was fun, and we both enjoyed the excitement of telling how we loved one another. Once she had even given me a cloth with the words "I love you" ironed on. Needless to say, even at my young age of eleven I had strong feelings for her, and although I didn't know it then, instilled much trust in our relationship. I think that's why it hurt so much when things started to change between the two of us.

As the narrative continues, Pamela starts to hang out with the tough kids from the projects, to whom she confesses her dissatisfaction with Adrian's lack of sexual advances. ("Whew!" he writes. "In the sixth grade I was hardly even thinking about sex!") She breaks off the relationship. Adrian writes:

> This of course was not cool in the eyes of many, and in retrospect, was interpreted as a failure of my masculinity. The fact that I wasn't even interested in sex meant that I was less than a man, and that I was therefore weak. I think that it is around this age that boys become more concerned with proving themselves, and this often translates into physical strength and sexual prowess. I lacked both of these, and this made me a target.

Finally, the toughs corner him one day at recess, and while hurling verbal taunts (which are not specified) the gang leader punches Adrian in the face. Adrian concludes by stating his mystification regarding physical force as a solution to conflict and his current belief in nonviolence.

There is no evidence that the story is being narrated by an out, self-aware adult gay man. In fact, little additives like the "Needless to say" that prefaces the statement "even at my young age of eleven I had strong feelings for her" suggest that he, like his presumed audience, cannot conceive of any but heterosexual feelings. His expletive "Whew!" before "In the sixth grade I was hardly even thinking about sex!" (his teacher wrote in the margin, "At all?") adamantly forecloses upon any explanations for his sexual passivity other than his lack of maturity. Yet paradoxically, he never accounts for why his peers—boys his own age—would target him for his "failure of . . . masculinity" if being prepubescent were the real cause of his plight, nor does he seem to feel that the inherent contradiction requires explanation. The narrator presents himself as frank, honest, and willing to supply any information that will help to explain the incident, even if it makes him vulnerable—and thus he comes across as reliable. Because of that narrator's own failure to imagine alternative explanations, the reader is seduced into similarly bracketing out those possibilities. Why would he tell us a story if he wanted us to miss the point of it? I believe him.

Adrian deals with the pressure to "justify" himself as a gay man in "The First Hit" by simply eliminating his gayness from the narrative. Considering that the buried theme is youthful gay bashing—an activity that draws moral approval from a frighteningly large percentage of teenage males—the "justification" required here might have indeed been enormous, and could conceivably have included a section persuading the readers not to automatically identify the basher as the hero. In his next paper, though, written just a few weeks later, Adrian decides to come out. "Holding Back" is another personal narrative, this one consciously explicating the missed cues that occur among acquaintances when one of them is closeted and is thus interpreted as being heterosexually available. It is the story of Adrian at a summer job in a pizza delivery outlet, working under a female supervisor who hurts his feelings by constantly commenting on his deficit of physical strength, yet who also tries to fix him up on a date with her female friend. Adrian, swallowing her insults and dodging her matchmaking, feels badly about "playing a game" by not coming out, but doesn't feel comfortable enough to do so, and eventually leaves the job. He prefaces his narrative with this bit of contextualization:

> As a gay man, I often must face the decision of whether or not to reveal my sexuality when in new situations. We live in a world that assumes everyone is heterosexual, and for eighteen years of my life I tried to believe that I was also. Although I have come out to myself, my family, and many people around me, coming out is a continual process. It can be a difficult thing to do, as I am not always aware of the consequences that may follow. I am proud of my sexuality, but nonetheless our world is predominantly intolerant of my life-style, and this is a factor that I have to consider when coming out.
>
> I am not known for living in the closet, but it is something I found myself doing last spring at a job I had in a pizza restaurant. . . .

Once again, I remember Adrian's comment about writing in the first-term writing class—the very class in which he *did* feel encouraged to be out and to write about his sexuality: "I felt I had to justify myself in different ways. Unlike in this class, I had to give a whole introduction about me being gay, and what being gay was like and meant. And that homophobic situation needed a background." That this introduction is so strikingly unlike anything he wrote in our gay-themed class is hardly surprising, since it is clearly addressed to an audience of heterosexuals whose sympathy may be gained, but of whose prior reflection about gay reality the author has very low expectations. Why else would he backtrack from his own point of departure in analyzing this experience to inform his readers that "we live in a world that everyone assumes is heterosexual," that coming out "can be a difficult thing to do," and that "our world is predominantly intolerant of my life-style"? Yet, anchored in such elementary truisms, how far can he go in the space of an essay? Does a point exist here at which he can leave the responsibilities of reportage behind, and go on to the work of deciphering the far more complex meanings of becoming a gay adult in a heterosexist society? What resources exist to help him in that work, and what access does he have to them within mainstream academia?

By sharp contrast, he begins his final project for our class—which was the one conventionally "personal" text he produced and in which he analyzes the way his sexuality makes him feel "different" even among gay men—with a stream-of-consciousness, syntactically unconventional rumination about the meaning of sex and gender roles within gay male culture, punctuated with questions about his own confused identifications. The presumed audience here is obviously different. In this introduction, his gayness is assumed, as is a familiarity with queer jargon, gay male culture, and popularly conceived gay male behavior from a vantage point that is not that of mainstream culture with its judgments about "promiscuity."

> Me I Sex Men Where do I fit in? What is sex for me like? What is sex for other men like? Me as playing the role of the female, but not in a butch-femme sense, more like I feel that in sex I transcend myself out of it, disregarding or distrusting my own pleasure. I concentrate on the pleasure of the other, the other man. I am not meant to feel pleasure—that desire and fulfillment is someone else's—I fulfill that desire in someone else, but I don't have it myself. Somewhat like in writing. It's only now more so that I feel that I write for myself, that I find satisfaction in writing.

> Sex. Of course it's satisfying, of course it's exciting, and of course I enjoy it, but how much am I there? And how much do I desire it? I've seemed to relegate sex to a sort of secondary status for me. It is not accorded the same kind of input and energy that other aspects of myself are, such as my emotional and intellectual selves. But I'm a man—I'm male, and I'm not supposed to do that. I'm supposed to want sex twenty-four hours a day, at all times. What's more I'm a gay man, and so it's expected almost more that I'll have tons of sex, because all men want sex, especially sex without commitment, and what better place to find that than with other men. . . . These are self-exposing questions that make me feel a bit vulnerable and weary, but no, it's interesting to get it out on paper, in a public sense. So am I repressing something pertaining to sex, and if so isn't that odd for a man? Where does this come from? Where is its origin in my life? Is it social or psychological, or can this be determined? Nature nurture,

nature nurture. Dislocation. From sex, from my gender. I expect it to
subside, or do I?

In this, Adrian's first overtly autobiographical piece since "Holding
Back" the term before, he seems to have made a huge leap from
explaining the basics of gay existence to an audience of outsiders to
directly entering the internecine debates of gay culture itself—debates
in which matters and meanings of sexuality are continually examined.
Though the issues raised here are certainly more "taboo" (his word
from the interview) in mainstream culture, certainly far more removed
from what is largely considered acceptable public discourse, and thus
would seem to lend themselves more easily to making the author feel
"vulnerable and weary," they hardly give him pause because overriding
those objections is his feeling that "it's interesting to get it out on paper,
in a public sense." Sex may be a matter of fulfilling someone else's
desire, but as he says in that very poignant analogy, writing is no longer
that for him: "now . . . I find satisfaction in writing." As a writer, Adrian
has rolled off his back, so to speak, and learned to take his own
pleasure.

In doing this, he positions his text within a queer discourse community and enters into dialogue with queer theory. His principal object
of textual interchange is Judith Butler's essay, "Imitation and Gender
Insubordination," which appeared in the anthology of lesbian and
gay theory, Inside/Out (1991). Butler disputes the notion that gendered mannerisms and behavior are inherent qualities, their outer
manifestations springing from an inner core; instead, she sees gender
as a performance, and "appropriate" gender behavior as a panicked
attempt to imitate a socially constructed ideal. Adrian responds to
Butler:

> From this standpoint, for there to exist a proper gender presentation
> there must inevitably be an improper one as well. In discussing the
> politics of drag, Butler makes this point. "Drag constitutes the mun-
> dane way in which genders are appropriated, theatricalized, worn,
> and done; it implies that all gendering is a kind of impersonation and
> approximation. If this is true, it seems, there is no original or primary
> gender that drag imitates, but gender is a kind of imitation for which
> there is no original . . ." (21) From this theory, then, if there is no
> original, then what is the notion of a proper gender and proper gender
> representation? If there is no original, or so to say inherent gender,
> how can we place a label with the connotation of either acceptable
> or not on something that really has no real, "natural" basis? Were
> gender to be such a "natural," inherent aspect of our being, then it
> would follow that there would be no need to pass judgment and
> reinforce proper ideals of what it means to be male and female. So I
> ask myself, if there is no such thing as "true" gender, what has made

me so confused and given me the feeling of detachment and non-identifiability with my own gender here in our culture? If I'm at the hand of my own representation and self presentation, should I not be able to be whoever I want and strive to be?

He continues to return to passages from Butler's text and to wade through their implications for his own dilemma:

I suppose my question now is how might I break this pattern of trying to fill the gap between the ideal male, and the man that I actually am? Is there in fact any real gap, or is the breach something socially constructed that I've taken to be the real?. . .

. . . To view oneself as "better" requires that you have something or someone else in mind with whom you're making a comparison. This "other" is of necessity to support your own theory, for if the other didn't exist, a comparison could not be made. In terms of gender, a heterosexual ideal requires something against which to be juxtaposed, for how can there be an ideal if there is not something that occurs that counters that ideal? For every ideal there must be something that doesn't meet that ideal, creating, as mentioned before, a kind of hierarchy. . . . The idealization of heterosexuality depends upon this power structure for its continuation, and thus it depends on its opposite, homosexuality, for its survival as the original and superior. The risk of heterosexuality losing its dominant status depends upon its subordinating homosexuality. . . .

From this it seems that I, as a gay man, am that very factor that enables the heterosexual ideal to continue on this basis of a hierarchy. If I didn't exist, then there would be one less person against which this ideal could be measured. The dislocation I feel is then, in a sense, reflective of my not meeting the standards of the so-called inherent aspects of maleness, particularly the drive to seek sexual satisfaction and fulfillment when and wherever possible. It sounds crazy, for this really entrenches one in a nature-based perception of life, ignoring what we as humans create and develop to give ourselves a sense of comprehension and security in this world. Amidst a conglomeration of diversity of attitudes and life-styles, there inevitably is going to be dispute over which one is the "proper" one, and against which all others will be measured. In terms of sexuality and gender, heterosexuality serves this purpose of setting the standards that serve as guidelines for human actions. I've succumbed and fallen under it, and it has only been through this kind of deconstruction of gender and sexuality that I've been able to recognize its very construction as human induced, not necessarily one that is "natural" and inherent.

I should mention that Adrian does add near the end, almost as a rueful postscript, "Just because I've come to recognize how I've been influenced does not mean that I'm free from this point on from further influence. . . . It is a social world. . . ."

It *is* a social world, and deconstructing our culture doesn't necessarily enable us to transcend all its pressures. Yet it seems that something important happens for Adrian as a result of his encounter with theory that addresses his "personal" needs. The point from which his thinking departs moves to a new latitude, in tandem with his sense of audience and academic enterprise shifting to a new site. The writer who just a semester earlier had only vague, humanistic arguments based on a general notion of "fairness" to offer the anonymous homophobe of the "Hot Topics" polemic ("Would you ever think of telling a straight couple that they shouldn't show any kind of affection in front of you?"—"Of course not," the homophobe could just as easily answer back, "because they're not sick and immoral like you.") now has a sense of roots and causes, a social theory to *explain* homophobia—which is an indispensable prerequisite to fighting it. In retrospect, it seems that the supportive instructor of the first writing workshop mainly supported the "justification" of gay existence, in effect raising his voice (by including his real name with his emphatic counterattack, thereby throwing the weight of his authority as teacher into the debate) to bolster Adrian's assertion, as unsupported as the homophobe's own, that "gay is OK." While I in no way mean to detract from the value of that teacher's act of solidarity—an act which far surpasses what most teachers would have done under those circumstances, and by which I feel extremely moved—I think it is important to consider, from the perspective of Adrian's work the second term, whether it was enough. I would contend that Adrian needed—and the rest of the class, also readers of the anonymous outburst, needed—tools to make sense of a statement like "God created Adam and Eve, not Adam and Steve, let's not forget that." This is *not* simply the raving of one misguided individual; it is a popular cliché with millenia of accrued religious philosophy and fervor inscribed upon it, to say nothing of centuries of juridical condemnation, decades of psychoanalytic theory, and a society currently caught up in a panicked backlash to a vocal gay rights movement. An act of resistance requires more than simply punching someone back in the face. It requires radical recognition and reorganization of the forces that left you vulnerable to being punched in the first place. For Adrian, theory becomes a source of authority offering previously inaccessible forms of rhetorical mobility. By the end of the second term, he has begun to arm himself with new ways of knowing about sexual oppression, and is preparing himself to effectively resist. New ways of using language and of probing the language of others are pivotal in this enterprise.

My knowledge of Adrian and his writing stops here. It remains to be seen how, and for whom, and for what, his textual work will be produced in the future. I don't expect—nor do I hope—that he, or any gay writer, will write *only* and *always* for gay audiences. My intention in designing a lesbian- and gay-themed writing course was not simply to make student writers feel comfortable by removing the tension of the straight, or even just the homophobic, world. But judging from Adrian's experience, without *some* experience of writing from within a queer discourse community it's not clear how a queer writer can learn how to move beyond the need to "justify." Our class was a place where a writer like Adrian could analyze his experience, not simply argue for its validity. Importantly, it wasn't a queer-only place, but rather a community forged by a coalition of discourses in which queerness claimed a visibility and authority it doesn't ordinarily enjoy in the world. The heterosexual students in the class became skilled at launching their acts of reading and writing from more advanced points of departure when it came to queer topics; the queer students learned that by articulating the complexity of the world from their own vantage points they could create the audience that they needed.

Though Adrian acknowledges that such a group—any group—is "never going to find the totally common voice," he says of the class: "It let me see that . . . questions that I'd asked myself for a long time about my sexuality, about my gender, are very relevant and deserve a voice. *Need* a voice. They've gone without a voice for too long. Because let's face it—I'm not an independent entity in this world. I'm affected by what other people say to me. . . ." It would seem that finding a "voice" for Adrian involves the resolution of two paramount issues: relocating the "personal" in the public realm, and moving beyond the need to "justify." When these issues are resolved, "voice" emerges as the product of a community's dialogic—one that under normal academic circumstances would not get the chance to exist.

Note

1. All names of participants in this study, as well as names referred to in their texts and commentary, are pseudonyms.

Chapter Nine

Isabel Serrano
"Setting the Record Straight"

Isabel is a thirty-two-year-old English major at Municipal College, a first-generation U. S. mainland-born Puerto Rican returning student, who grew up in New York City in a devout family of Jehovah's Witnesses. She is close to completing a B.A. in the traditional four years, though she has worked full-time all along as a booking agent for musicians. She envisions no career benefits to her college degree and says that she is doing it "just for herself."

Till age eleven, Isabel grew up in the housing projects of upper Manhattan. Then her family moved to a neighborhood in one of the outer boroughs of the city where they were the first Hispanics, a place she describes as "a very narrow, bigoted environment." Her father was an elder in the church; as a child Isabel went to Witness meetings five times a week, took a review-like exam every five weeks, and canvassed door-to-door on weekends. Though both her parents had only grade-school educations, Isabel says that they were "self-taught" due to "reading and writing constantly because of the religion." Isabel feels that "religion was an addiction" for her parents, though she herself felt ambivalent about it even in childhood, frequently challenging her father's accounts of things with her own "close" readings of Bible passages and calling him a hypocrite. She says that the subjection of women always seemed wrong to her, and that the religion—which proscribed smoking, drugs, and fornication before marriage, and deemed homosexuality "unnatural" and therefore sinful—never felt fair. At the same time, though, she recalls being frightened enough at the idea of being separated from her brothers and sisters after death, of being excommunicated or marked (which would mean not being allowed to

186

associate with followers), and of losing the approval of her parents to stay within the church until she reached the age of twenty-one. At that point, while she was practicing as a Bible teacher to youth, the combination of recognizing her sexual orientation and realizing that women who were being abused had no rights within church doctrine to fight back led her to unofficially break with the Witnesses by ceasing to attend meetings. She says that she still values certain humanistic religious principles, but that she now credits "the unique conscience of the individual to monitor behavior" as the guiding moral force in people's lives, and calls herself an agnostic.

Growing up, Isabel kept journals and she took several creative writing courses in school. She's not sure that she sees any sustained relationship between her lesbian identity and her writing—"I don't know that I write thinking I'm a lesbian"—though connections have appeared in unexpected circumstances, such as in a course where she was asked to write a paper about "how the music industry could cater to a person like me. So of course I have to mention it." She says that when it does come up, "I focus more on being gay *and* lesbian. Like the injustice, what we have to go through as a community, rather than just focus solely on *my* experience as a lesbian." She took her first college writing courses at another campus which she attended for a year, a technically oriented school where "everyone was outspokenly homophobic" and where she feels that more generally "I didn't have the freedom to voice what I think I voice at Municipal." She produced little there that felt of value to her, and she says that because of the much freer environment at Municipal "my writing changed drastically when I came here."

At Municipal, discussion of lesbian and gay existence arose in several courses; she cites a Virginia Woolf course, a course on women and the law, and a communications course as examples. Within this new social context, she found herself responding to individual homophobic remarks as stimuli rather than as restraints. "Nowadays what's happening is that when I find that people are uncomfortable with lesbian issues or gay issues, it makes me want to write about it. That's been happening in the past year." She finds that she is much more inspired to write about lesbian and gay issues when people express discomfort about them than when there is either an absence of such discussion at all or blatantly outspoken homophobia. The reason, she feels, is "because I'm getting really angry. I'm just getting really upset and tired of people misconstruing what is." When she feels the need to address lesbian or gay existence in a course, she says, "My first thought is always, should I say this? Then I say, the hell with it, and then I write it. But there's always been that question, thus far—do I *want* to say this?" She is always moved to actually write by realizing "of course I want to say it. I look at what I really want to say, and this is what I really *want* to say, and I say it. Because it should be said."

Isabel feels that often when she does take the plunge of writing or speaking about lesbian and gay issues, the response is "silence. Everybody stares." Yet she finds herself driven by a desire to "set the record straight" each time she encounters "the inaccurate perception, the *limited* perception, of what it is to be gay." In her communications class, she was part of a panel discussion in which her topic was "declaring Madonna a saint." She spoke about Madonna's celebration of sexuality and showed the performer's controversial "Justify My Love" video. When the instructor commented that the lesbian and gay community was angry at Madonna because she had not come out as a lesbian—an observation that Isabel felt to be false—she found it impossible to counter the charge without identifying herself. "I started saying I know a lot of lesbians. Well, of course I wasn't going to say I know a lot of lesbians and not say I was one! So I said it very casually. I just came out like I was talking about ice cream. I said, 'Well, I know a lot of lesbians, myself included. And we don't feel that way.' And then, you know, you feel that silence—like everyone cannot believe you just said that."

"I have three things going that I have to contend with," Isabel says. "I'm a woman, I'm Puerto Rican, and I'm a lesbian." One time in a class she announced these three facets of her identity as preface to further commentary in which, she says, "I just went in on a soapbox." Yet she emphasizes repeatedly that in response to the "stereotyping" and "stigma" that she feels is inscribed upon her by numerous others, "I find that I have to set the record straight."

Her first awareness of gayness came from her brother's caricatured imitations of gay men, her father's derogatory remarks, and frightening references to the "unnaturalness" of homosexuality in the Bible. Yet, she says, "I never viewed gays and lesbians as disgusting, as people in my religion did. I never had that sentiment at all. To me they were people. They were like me. The few people that I did know through school, and the ones at school that I did not know, I was always intrigued with the fact that they were so open about it." When I comment on the irony of her appropriation of the liberal tenet "They were people; they were like me"—expressions usually employed to reveal the discovery of an amazing similarity despite huge perceived differences, while she is talking about a group of which she literally *is* a part—Isabel says that until she was twenty-one, she simply didn't identify as a lesbian. "Whenever I had crushes on someone, I would fantasize that I was a boy in order for it to be OK." She also mentions "a little escapade" with an older woman during her teens that she "literally blocked out"—a curiously anomalous coping strategy for someone who, despite having been surrounded by negative discourses of homophobia, is sure that she "never had that sentiment at all."

Coming out began for Isabel through an act of writing. "I went to my sister's apartment; she was out of town, and I fed the dog. And I was staying there that night, and I was writing. This very quiet neighborhood in Queens was very conducive to writing. And then I just wrote about being a lesbian. And I remember that I just cried—not because I was sad, but because this was such a great realization." She realized that she was attracted to women, but was "still kind of lingering in and out of the religion. Not being an active member, but still being associated with it. Basically I kind of weaned myself out of it, till one day, probably a month or two after, I decided that there was no way I could be part of this." She still didn't come out to anyone else or act on her attractions to women, but she made lesbian friends and went with them to lesbian social spots such as Provincetown. A year later, she had her first lesbian relationship. Though she says "I was definitely ready," she also comments, "I felt as uncomfortable at the beginning saying I was a lesbian as I did saying I was a Jehovah's Witness to people that weren't Witnesses." She has never come out to her parents. Though they feel close to her lover of three years and have been to the one-bedroom apartment which the two women share, everyone has tacitly chosen to preserve the myth that Isabel and Julia are "friends." "My mom discounts [my not being married] by saying I'm very independent. The reason [she does this] is because I was officially baptized in the religion, and I was not excommunicated. Because it's not like they caught me sleeping with a woman. I just kind of disassociated myself by not attending. If they excommunicated me, that would mean that my parents would have to keep limited association with me. And I don't know that I could deal with it. It's not that I'm ashamed. It's simply that I don't know if I could take not talking to my parents."

Isabel rates herself "anywhere between seven to eight" on an "outness" scale of one to ten "because it fluctuates, depending on where I am. With my family I'm out in a sense even not talking about the relationship, because Julia's always, for the most part, there with me. At work I'm totally out. In the street I'm careful because I don't like being harassed."

When asked what it means for her to call herself a lesbian, her first response is to reflect on the instructive dimension of self-definition, casting the act in terms similar to that of her wish to "set the record straight": "The first thing that comes to mind is the word 'specific.' I want to be specific. Because I think lesbians are still very much a minority, and people don't know we exist, so I notice that lately I do say it sooner than I would a few years back. Because I want to let it be known that we exist." When pressed further—"But what makes you *consider* yourself a lesbian?"—she says, "It's because I really do have a strong identification with women—like emotionally, spiritually, physically. I understand a woman much better than I do a man. And vice versa. Many things need not be explained. There's a common ground there that's very strong."

The Joy of Discomfort

"Our class just made me think more of myself as a lesbian," says Isabel. "I was surprised at the class that being gay was an issue for a lot of people. It hadn't been for me—but I've realized that it is. I mean, I don't live a real closeted life. So I never came to terms with my anger. And there is some there, and I think this class kind of made me angry. I also think writing the paper on how 'out' a lesbian can be—it just occurred to me then that no matter how 'out' I strive to be, I can never be truly out. There will always be instances when I do have to conceal my sexual identity. And that realization, although it's a very simple one and probably everyone knew that in coming to the class, I was not dealing with it, or thinking about it. I think I'm really *thinking* about gay now, where before I was just *being* gay."

The first class meeting, in which the debate about overenrollment took place, scared her "because it was so polemical. I thought this was going to be a very *positive* class, and we were going to talk about the *good* stuff." A very outspoken lesbian feminist in the class initially alienated her—"I picked up on her anger right away, and thought, I'm not going to like this"—yet Isabel feels that ultimately she "understood" her and concluded "that she's right. She's right about women not being taken seriously. I understood what I considered her fanatical need to always be around women. In the end I was glad that there [are] Veronicas in this world, because we need them. They're constantly reminding us that we still have a struggle. I've always had a very difficult time being around negative people. But I now understand that their experience is different, and this is the way they deal with it, and it's not necessarily bad." By the end, Isabel says, she not only accepted Veronica's difference, but also came to see her as not so different; she felt that she actually identified with her.

More broadly, Isabel's first take on the class was that "everyone was uptight about being gay. Being gay was an issue in their lives. It was something that they dealt with constantly, day to day. And I felt—I'm not like that." Yet as time went by, she felt "enlightened": "I feel now that I have the same thoughts, except I may not express them in such a vehement manner. But I have them, and what remains to be seen is how I'm going to deal with them." She says that being in the class she felt, for the first time, the need to come out to her parents, even while realizing that she doesn't have the courage to do it yet. As a result of the class, she says, "I feel that I'm tired of the misunderstanding that people have toward gays and lesbians. And I've become outspoken in all my classes. Not that I haven't been in the last semesters, but this semester it just came very naturally to me without any thought." She noticed that in those classes where she brought up the subject of lesbian and gay existence, "I was very emotional. I probably sounded like some students in our class." She acknowledges that in these classes, as in some earlier classes, the discomfort of the other students and sometimes of the teachers produced a responsive discomfort in her that she is on some level appreciative of, and which propelled her toward speech. She tries to account for the strange pleasure of her own discomfort: "It's forcing me to think about an issue that involves me, and that involves a lot of my friends, a lot of people I know, my community. And it's forcing me in a direction that I can't pinpoint at this point in time, but I think if I had to say it in one sentence, it's forcing me to set the record straight. And I suspect that it will come out in writing—in creative writing, articles. I have that need now—whereas before, it wasn't a compelling need. This class has made me more focused. It gave me the impetus, the clarity, to just go for it." She also says, "I feel I now give more deliberate thought to being gay, because I'm being asked to think about being gay. In another class, I wouldn't have been asked to think about that."

Certain course readings particularly shaped Isabel's focus. She credits Adrienne Rich's essay "Compulsory Heterosexuality" for jolting her from a habitual stance of conceptualizing "women as a whole" to recognizing the "more specific category" of lesbians. "In my other [women's studies] classes I never wrote about lesbianism. I wrote about women's rights. So that article was the beginning of a process that was subconsciously making me zoom in on lesbians." She also cites Amber Hollibaugh's "Writers as Activists" as an important influence because it suggests possibilities for human change. Hollibaugh writes of the use of the "oral tradition" in her working-class family, in which "you convince people with the power of your body and your voice." Hollibaugh opens by saying,

> Writing is the most difficult thing that I do, and activism is the easiest. The first four or five years that I wrote anything at all, I constantly

told everybody that I just put it down on a piece of paper—but I wasn't really a writer. . . . I didn't know how to see that identity—of being a writer—in combination with the way that I had constructed my politics. (69)

"I identified with that," says Isabel, "because to this day I don't consider myself to be a writer. And she went from not being political at all to being so political. And I was wondering, how does one do that?"

Isabel describes with particular relish reading the assigned series of coming-out narratives. "What I really enjoyed was the level of discomfort that gays and lesbians feel about being gay. It comes back to my not dealing with that aspect. That there *is* discomfort. And this is what I was feeling now—discomfort. Not with being gay—but with the fact that I can't be who I really am freely." Isabel feels that this discomfort is propelling her somewhere, though she's not sure exactly where. "It's nebulous now. You'll have to interview me six months from now, and I'll tell you." She is only clear now that "It makes me really mad." When asked why she seems so pleased about her fall from happiness, she speaks appreciatively of a greater sense of awareness and purpose. "I used to think about [homophobia], but I didn't give it time. It was just yeah, too bad. This stinks. Next! Whereas now, it's really with me, the discomfort." She says that now she wants to write letters to government officials and read texts produced by the gay press which had "annoyed [her] at one point in time" because she had assumed that they represented a univocal, angry perspective that she could not share. She says that the class changed her in the sense that "I probably think about being gay every day now. . . . It made me think a lot about politics, about our government, about the way it's run. It made me question it a lot. It made me think about other groups, the way our system is, our society in general, our values. So many things came into the picture here."

Reiterating once more that the class has galvanized her desire, in her everyday life, to "set the record straight," Isabel clarifies that choosing appropriate contexts for corrective remarks is important to her. "I don't think I'll ever be a person that says, 'Hi, my name is Isabel. I'm a lesbian.' Just like I wouldn't say, 'Hi, my name is Isabel. I'm Puerto Rican.' It's just not my style."

Isabel says that as a consequence of our class's theme-based structure, her writing there was "much more focused" than her writing had been in other classes. "There's no hesitancy. I say what comes to me. A lot of times a lot came to me instantly that remained to be explored, so there was a lot of thinking in this class—but not a lot of editing, initially." By "editing," she says, she means "censoring," or what she calls "forethought." "I'm more impromptu now. My writing has improved as a result, because I zoom in on what I *want* to say." She explains that the kind of "forethought" that occurs for her in other writing situations often leads to aborted texts. "A very specific essay like 'Autohomophobia' I probably would never have written in another class, because I don't feel that another class would identify with the struggles of the community. I would find it a real difficult task to get that across, and I wouldn't have empathy from the audience." She explains that by inventing the word "autohomophobia" she was suggesting not "internalized homophobia," but "fear of someone in our community that appears different"—the "auto" drawing attention to the sense of identification that comes from the feared object's being a part of one's own community, the "homophobia" referring to the fact that the aversion is specifically to another gay person. She says that she would also be very hesitant to write "A Lesbian's Ongoing Endeavor" in another class because "It's very personal. It's very revealing. I think with these subjects I want immediate understanding."

Isabel feels that it would be a good idea to have more classes like this "because there *haven't* been any classes like this. And it helps in writing because you're discussing something that you really feel strongly about, and you really want to find out more about it because you're in that class, and it's—put this in quotes—a 'safe' environment. I think from the writing comes more writing, and probably better." She feels that mainstream writing classes should include an assignment on lesbian and gay life because it may afford "that opportunity for someone to come out and feel at ease to be out. And to contribute to the class."

Constructing Community

The texts that Isabel produced in the course seemed fairly consistently geared toward correcting what she perceived as errors in others' perceptions. Her primary objective in writing does appear to be precisely that which she articulates repeatedly in her commentary: a need to "set the record straight." Her writing style could probably best be described as journalistic and inductive: she draws predominantly on countless examples of injustice and distorted logic, competently arranging them so that they provide a panoramic view of what is "wrong with the picture" of dominant heterosexist ideology. Her mode of challenging ideology is to juxtapose it against "truths" accessed from the public domain of gay culture which highlight mass culture's distortions. By inserting herself into popular gay discourses as they appear in the gay press, at rallies and demonstrations, and at community events, Isabel makes these "truths" her own. She is adept at appropriating them and organizing pieces of them into texts of her own whose purpose generally seems to be to expose and to persuade—by unraveling falsehoods and emphasizing alternative viewpoints, constructions, and interpretations. She is rarely exploratory herself. "Setting the record straight" seems to have less to do with using her own experience to deconstruct the maxims of mass culture than with aligning herself with a counterculture that has already spoken powerfully to her, that she has already recognized as a significant counterdiscourse in the world, and that she wants to promote and be a part of so as to add to its force.

For example, in an informal draft called "Observations on Social Construction," she comments:

> I think social construction for women in general still dictates that they should be married at least by 30 years old. If they are not, it is for a reason other than free will; i.e., "She is a career woman, who puts her job before personal life" or "She's a bitch, no man will ever go near her." The thought of a woman willingly choosing not to marry or being a lesbian rarely enters the picture. Today, many people still think women become lesbians because they were abused as children, abused by men, or never had "the right guy." Moreover, our society has not accepted the notion of a significant other. With the exception of a handful of corporations, most organizations do not have a category for a relative or a gay lover to be listed as a beneficiary for insurance or medical benefits.
>
> The mass media, in particular, perpetuates the notion that everyone is straight. Books, publications, music, cinema, theatre, television, advertising all cater to a straight crowd. When the subject of homosexuality is introduced, it is almost always negative. The gay person is usually depicted as a fucked-up individual who has a difficult time living a "normal" life.
>
> If one adds more modifiers to a woman in our society it gets worse, i.e., Latina Lesbian Woman. A Latina lesbian woman has a much harder time living down stereotypes. As a Latina, she is expected to be "warm, loving, wild, sexy, and lovable and self-sacrificing to her man." If she happens to be gay, she is accused (a lot of the times by her own relatives and the Latino community) of trying to be "macho" like men.

Like many students trying to grasp what "social construction" actually means, Isabel envisions it from a rather liberal viewpoint: negative or restrictive dogma has enshrouded a particular identity, limiting the freedom of those bearing that identity. If we can just invoke basic logic to persuade employers, media, and the average person in the street to open their minds and see that that identity has been cast in an unfairly and irrationally pejorative light, a new valuation will supplant the old and liberation will occur. Of course, what

is obscured in such a view is the complexity that is involved in prejudice making to begin with: values and beliefs are predated by other
values and beliefs, and are entrenched in political structures that are
not only produced *by* discourse, but also must also produce it themselves if they are to continue to exist. The indignation in Isabel's text
takes as its object symptoms, not the underlying structures that have
manifested them. There is no indication here that there is any method
in the madness of homophobia, racism, or sexism, any system larger
than themselves that they seek to uphold. In its appeal to rationality
and democratic apportionment of individual liberties, Isabel's argument overlooks what *is* rational in the uneven delegation of rights in
a society desperate to preserve its hierarchies. As Shane Phelan writes
in her book *Identity Politics: Lesbian Feminism and the Limits of Community:*

> The acknowledgment that we are constituted, which is the first step
> away from an atomistic liberalism, must be followed by the question:
> By what or whom are we so built? The answer "language," or "cul-
> ture," or "tradition," is hardly an answer unless it is followed by more
> questions: Who controls the language, culture, and tradition? What
> interests and purposes are served by the present constitution of the
> self? (1989, 145)

Isabel's focus on unfairness, stereotyping, and false representation
is endemic in the mass lesbian and gay movement's struggle for civil
rights, where a widespread goal is social assimilation and equality for
people who are not heterosexual. The fact that the branches of the
mass media "all cater to a straight crowd" has been widely pointed out
and fought by popular organizations such as the Gay and Lesbian
Alliance Against Defamation (GLAAD), articles in gay publications,
empassioned letters to the editors of the mainstream press, and groups
of friends who gather in skeptical hope, chronic frustration, and wry
humor in front of made-for-TV movies and television shows "experimenting" with gay characters. That women become lesbians by default
rather than "free will" and choice is also a popular maxim that has
received popular debunking in the lesbian and gay community.[1] In fact,
Isabel doesn't seem to feel that her use of quotations around statements
representing homophobic social mythology require citations or docu-
mentation; they enclose remarks that are generally recognizable—both
because of their prevalence in social discourse and, I would argue,
because of the extent to which they have been highlighted and charged
with absurdity in queer counterdiscourse. In this light, her argument
can be seen not only as an enunciation of resistance to received
wisdom, but simultaneously as a manifestation of received counterwis-
dom. "Setting the record straight" is not a burden she sees herself
having to shoulder alone. A movement has already produced useful

countercultural critiques and objections to heterosexist commonplaces. Her task, it seems, is to be a responsible member of that movement, deploying these critiques wherever she collides with the falsified "record."

This is what I wonder over and over again as I read Isabel's work: She is writing about relatively "new" ideas, but are they *her* new ideas? They don't strike me that way, yet it seems to me that they may *feel to her* like "her" new ideas because she has only recently encountered them. If I buy a house, the house may not be new, but it is *my* "new house." Isabel's work, then, highlights for me the flimsiness of the line between what I would call "received wisdom" and what I would call "original thinking." If we reject romantic notions of a unique "self" capable of producing thought that is not derivative, that is not itself written by prior discourses, then what wisdom counts as "received," and what contrastingly counts as "original"? Is the dichotomy even a valid one? Rereading Isabel makes me think that it's not.

Take, for example, her essay called "Autohomophobia." She explains at the outset, "For the purpose of this essay, I am taking the liberty of inventing a new word, autohomophobia. Autohomophobia refers to homosexuals involved in their own existence who fear and neglect the virtue of the differences between themselves and their homosexual brothers and sisters." The subject of the essay (though not the word that supplies its title) is one that has been at the center of raging discussion in the lesbian and gay community for some time now, and the notion of "difference" or "diversity" within identity-based communities has been debated as well in other political movements and presses and throughout academia. Yet Isabel enters the discussion assuming that these social divisions need to be described before they can be redressed:

> . . . More often than not, we segregate ourselves. In more subtle ways or perhaps not so subtle, we socialize with those who look and think like us. Gays with gays, lesbians with lesbians, white middle-class gays socialize with the same, minorities with minorities from their respective backgrounds, etc.

> Limiting ourselves to those like us not only results in derision but in the long wrong-run, jeopardizes our common goal of being integrated into one society. All of us want to be accepted for who we are and desire the same rights and benefits extended to heterosexuals. How can we, then, aspire to be accepted as part of the general public when we ourselves do not make an effort to know each other? Are we perhaps as guilty as the feminists in Adrienne Rich's essay "Compulsory Heterosexuality" (who failed to take into account Lesbianism as an innate propensity in women) of disregarding a segment of our community just because their experience is not ours?

Converging once a year for Gay Pride Day is not enough to effectu-
alize our mutual aim of being taken seriously in our quest for equality.
In reality, this is an excellent example of what could really happen if
we all met regularly and showed by our presence and mutual interaction that despite our different backgrounds and belief systems, we
are able to coexist as a united group of people.

Having described the problem, Isabel alternately pushes toward utopian solutions and pulls back from the overoptimism they require:

Admittedly, this is easier said than done. While it is, no doubt, much
more comfortable to be in our own element with people of similar
backgrounds, we can overcome our autohomophobia if we make a
concerted effort to know about the respective struggles of different
groups in our community. But, how does one begin to identify and
fight for the struggles of another group when, in reality, all of us in
the gay community (black, white, women, men, young, old, parents,
etc.) have an ax to grind of our own?

As part of a minority group, we carry the great weight of living in a
biased society. However, this weight is a common ground for all of us
to get together and share with each other the experiences of our
respective backgrounds and hence build a strong support system for
the future. The question, however, remains. How can we do this and
when do we start?

. . . We could form a version of the United Nations where all special-
interest groups within the gay community meet regularly to voice
their needs and struggles through their elected representatives. ACT
UP, the Korean Lesbian and Gay Organization, Latino Gay Men of NY,
GLAAD, SAGE, et al. could all convene at a forum and discuss how
best to meet their individual needs with the cooperation of others.
Doing so will create greater harmony in the community which will
invariably allow us to be more effective in meeting our goals as a gay
nation.

Before forming a United Gay Nation, we must overcome the fear that
stems from believing that our individual problems will never be resolved if we take that of others. If we look at the big picture, we will
be able to determine that we have enough in common (i.e., we have
all been targets of homophobia) to build a strong support system that
can help us cope with our personal strife. . . .

On an earlier draft—which was not substantially different from this
draft—I had written to Isabel:

Your essay is about, I think, one of the most urgent issues in the
lesbian and gay community—the divisiveness that continually undermines and threatens the power we have when we are united in
action. In this draft, I think you do a really good job of setting the

reader up to regard this divisiveness as ludicrous and counterproductive. At the same time, I think dire problems exist for deeply rooted
reasons. Prejudices and angers and fears are usually not simple. You
ask many of your questions rhetorically—["Rather than condemning
members of our community who engage in S&M, why don't we just
accept it as a different expression of intimacy . . .?" "Instead of accusing lesbians of acting and dressing like men and accusing men of
emasculating women, why don't we praise them for not falling prey
to the dictates of convention?" "If we don't happen to be politically
active, why make fun of those in our community who lobby for our
rights . . . and stigmatize them as obsessive?"]—and maybe in your
next draft you could try to dig for some of the answers. What always
seems frustrating to me is that *most* of us (I think) ask these questions—just like I think most people pose questions like "Why can't
there be world peace?" and "Why can't everyone love and respect
one another?" with real wistfulness and sincerity, yet support wars
and feuds and all forms of oppression—because particular circumstances seem to them to necessitate it, to be unfortunate obstacles to
the harmony they crave. So I think you would be doing important
work if you really tried to explore just why we *do* pick on each other
so much, and resist the real unity that we all crave on some level and
that could propel us collectively into the position in the world so
many of us seem to be perpetually seeking.

What I was unsuccessfully suggesting was that Isabel backtrack from
her incredulity and her plan for action to consider the real difficulties
and tensions that divide the community. She is not atypical of student
writers in her desire to invoke the closure of the happy family, the
cohesive community, even if doing so requires creating a fairy tale in
which the deeper grittiness of our prejudices and alienation from
one another must be elided. Invisible here are the meanings of our
memberships in other communities, the competing allegiances which
produce different concepts of "identity"—and consequently, divergent
notions of "community." Isabel is confident that the "big picture"
reveals that "we have enough in common"—homophobia—to fuel the
construction of a "United Gay Nation." She seems unaware, however,
that this "Nation" is itself a heavily contested enterprise, and that some
of its sharpest critics are those who resent having to subsume their
ethnic, gender, or other identities to their sexual identity as the price
of sustaining the harmony of the queer collective. Prejudices related to
these identities are centuries-old; what magic tonic does the gay community possess that would so easily eradicate them at the moment of
sexual liberation?

It is important to bear in mind that Isabel wrote this essay near the
beginning of the course—a moment perhaps still within the era she
was describing when she said, "I used to think about homophobia, but

I didn't give it time. It was just yeah, too bad. This stinks. Next! Whereas now, it's really with me, the discomfort." It is the absence of this "discomfort," and of recognition of its sources, that seems to me to make this essay weak. As a reader who is both part of the lesbian and gay community and a consumer/observer of mass culture, I can't buy Isabel's defused, unproblematized renditions of S&M, gender bending, and political positioning.

Yet, looked at another way, the essay virtually rises out of other sorts of discomfort: discomfort with splittings, with the slow speed of social change, with internecine dislike and distrust. If I, as a reader, know that Isabel's utopia has already failed, that doesn't necessarily mean that she should know it, or that her writing should reflect it. She is writing from her point of entry into one conversation, before yet reaching the threshold of a more interior one. Poised at that point, she adds her voice to the others lamenting that the "common goal of being integrated into one society" is threatened by "limiting ourselves to those like us." The ideal of a "common goal" or "common ground"—or, as Adrienne Rich put it, the "dream of a common language"—is something that one must perhaps actively yearn for and even strive for in order to fully appreciate its impossibility. It is legitimate, maybe even necessary, to reinvent the wheel.

Several of Isabel's other early texts, both formal and informal, have these qualities of apparent overreliance on "received wisdom" and coasting perhaps a bit too smoothly along a road ostensibly bound for heaven. But by the time she writes an informal draft called "Reflections on Outing" in the beginning of the second half of the term, she seems to be moving someplace new. In this case, she takes a side in a well-publicized, highly polarized debate, but also, for the first time, she is able to use material that might seem contradictory or nonaligned with the main thrust of her argument, rather than simply avoiding it as a potentially problematic disruption. For instance, she writes:

> The mass publicity outing has received is reason alone to celebrate its birth. Articles on the subject have appeared throughout the nation and in all major papers and periodicals. Whether favorable or unfavorable articles, they have all contributed to gay and lesbian visibility.

In another section, she writes:

> In her article [in the *Village Voice*] opposing outing, C. Carr writes, "I am still waiting for the news of Malcolm Forbes to improve my life." Yet because of the outing of this public figure she has had an opportunity to write a lengthy article about a gay and lesbian issue in a mainstream paper and talk about the existing homophobia. Hopefully, this article will be read by someone whose lightbulb went off

and came to terms with another existence, that of the gay and lesbian community.

A formal essay later still, called "Being 'Out': A Lesbian's Ongoing Endeavor," reads initially like a feature article chronicling the difficulties of living as a lesbian. Many of the difficulties she cites are fairly predictable in that they have been widely discussed, though she elaborates them quite competently: no domestic partnership benefits, negative images (and nullifying absences) in the mass media, fear of disclosure in the workplace, harassment in the streets, strictures within the family. At the end, though, she adds something surprising:

> Since our culture assumes heterosexuality to be a given, a lesbian is always faced with setting the record straight and consequently coming out over and over again. When a gynecologist inquires "what method of birth control do you use," we explain none and why; when someone we barely know assumes the significant other is a man, we correct them; when we are asked out on a date by men who don't take no for an answer, we educate them with another fact in life—lesbianism. The coming out process—no matter how accustomed we are to doing it—is never stress-free, for we are always confronted with the possibility of rejection and condemnation. Very often fear returns and we experience the same symptoms we did when we first came out. Our throat goes dry, our voice becomes low and we stumble for words to disclose our sexual identity.
>
> Having to do something over and over can also create a sense of powerlessness. This sense of lack of control is a constant within our lives which we struggle to overcome every day in one form or another and that's the "catch": the perpetual coming out which interrupts the quest to live in peace with oneself and society.

The reason this section of her essay feels surprising to me is that it is not simply about an unfair material or social reality which can be changed by legal or educational reform. It is about a fundamental paradox of being out—that coming out is an act doomed to only briefly satisfy the need that provoked it. Being out is a "perpetual" and redundant process, requiring one to enter a stressful experience over and over again. One is only as out as one's last act of coming out; the refusal to do it on any given occasion throws into question one's entire status as an out lesbian or gay man. If one constantly has to redefine one's existence to the world, how out is s/he? And yet, if one doesn't do it, s/he's not out, either. Isabel calls attention to the feelings of "powerlessness" attached to maintaining a social identity which requires continually doing something threatening and risky that is nonetheless destined, each time, to undo itself. In this instance her willingness to engage with the contradictions inherent in the process of "setting the

record straight" propels her beyond the closure either of utopian resolution or of abandonment of the corrective project to a "catch" which,
while frustrating, may function as a gateway to deeper theoretical
exploration. No particular institution is responsible for this "catch";
therefore none can be enjoined to rectify it. There is no particular
record to be set straight here, but rather a reckoning to be had with
the immense complexity of identity. Judith Butler (1991) has written
that "being 'out' must produce the closet again and again in order to
maintain itself as 'out'" (16) because identity *is* nothing more than a
string of linked performances: "[H]ow and where I play at being [a
lesbian] is the way in which that 'being' gets established, instituted,
circulated, and confirmed" (18). Heterosexuality itself, she says, "only
constitutes itself as the original [sexual identity] through a convincing
act of repetition" (23); and "if heterosexuality is compelled to *repeat
itself* in order to establish the illusion of its own uniformity and identity,
then this is an identity permanently at risk, for what if it fails to repeat,
or if the very exercise of repetition is redeployed for a very different
performative purpose?" (24; emphasis Butler's). One difference between Isabel and Butler—other huge differences notwithstanding—is
that Isabel perceives only lesbian and gay identity (as opposed to
heterosexuality) to be at "risk," presumably because the dominant
society doesn't recognize it except for those moments when it is in-
jected into existence through speech, whereas for Butler, the "risk" is
inherent in the notion of identity to begin with. In any case, I read the
end of "Being 'Out': A Lesbian's Ongoing Endeavor" as a new kind of
theoretical moment for Isabel, her first excursion outside the administrative offices where "the record" is malproduced and straightened.

By the time she writes her final project called, "Is 'Outing' Ethical?"—an extended discussion of the subject she had touched on briefly
in an earlier informal draft—Isabel has consolidated all the techniques
that have worked for her over the course of the term. Once again, she
proves herself extremely capable of amassing numerous facts, quotations, and arguments culled from a wide range of media and pitting
them against one another, this time ultimately batting down the anti-
outing side with the weight of her pro-outing logic which "sets the
record straight." For example:

> [T]he logical . . . question is "Privacy (i.e., sexual orientation), accord-
> ing to whom?" Why is it, for example, that we know all about Liz
> Taylor's past and present husbands but nothing is ever printed on
> openly gay Congressman Barney Frank's domestic partner, Herb Moses,
> who accompanies him to the White House and numerous work-re-
> lated functions. Yet the mainstream press wasted no time in printing
> details of the Congressman's personal life when it was discovered that
> he had slept with a male prostitute years before. In their March issue

of 1992, *New York Queer* notes, "Ten times as many articles about Frank's involvement with Gobie (the male prostitute) appeared in 1989 and 1990 than articles about Frank's work in other years."

Likewise, she rests her argument largely on her faith in the media's power to overhaul deep-seated social beliefs, should it ever be so benignly inclined:

> The claim "blondes have more fun" is a myth created by the same society that insists heterosexuality is the only natural way to be. If, on the other hand, the mainstream press accepts and begins to depict homosexuality in the same matter-of-fact manner it treats heterosexuality, they will help remove the stigma they themselves perpetuate—that being gay is bad and should be kept private.

She also pursues her insight from "Reflections on Outing" that, in this controversy, the medium is the message:

> By debating the very issue of "outing" everyone—whether they know it or not—is contributing to gay and lesbian visibility. When the media or the public argue that Pete Williams should not have been outed, they are in essence confirming that he is gay and hence, restating the position of outers.

Disappointingly to me, Isabel did very little in the end of what I interpret as "taking risks" or venturing out on a theoretical or even speculative limb. She rarely seemed to find ambiguity useful or compelling, and except occasionally, it was hard for me to get much of a sense that she was writing to learn. Her writing was proficient, yet seemed to me to lack the excitement of student texts that are themselves scenes of encounter with new ideas, texts that read as if they are in motion, taking their writers as well as their readers someplace new. Isabel almost always seemed to be writing about what she *already* knew, and her project seemed to be to brandish that information in as persuasive a manner as possible in order to "set the record straight." She consistently challenged homophobic discourse by wielding popular counterhomophobic discourse that was itself packaged as if beyond the question of resistance. Even when addressing issues on which the gay community has been divided—such as dealing with diversity or outing—she refrained from resisting or playing with the borders of the side she had chosen.

Nevertheless, it seems to me that something important did happen for Isabel in this class: she discovered discomfort and anger, and at the same time she found her place in a community challenging the hegemonic discourses that provoked these responses. Her writing, though from one perspective geared solely toward puncturing and refuting those discourses, is from another perspective an act of solidarity with a group that she perceives as championing her interests, challenging the narratives that have undermined her. "Our class just made me think more of myself as a lesbian," she says. "I'm really *thinking* about gay now, where before I was just *being* gay." The time she spent there was a time of entering and solidifying the categories "lesbian" and "gay"; it was not a time to dismantle them. Across a wide range of academic and political circles, as I have discussed in Chapter 1, scholar/ activists are debating the very question of how to reconcile postmodern disassemblies of identity categories with the need to strengthen those categories in order to fight for social change. Questioning the meaning of those categories can be distressing for any activist, even one intellectually challenged and inspired to take up the enterprise; it can certainly seem altogether beside the point for someone just beginning to feel empowered by these categories, someone who is just starting to experience the comfort of membership in a "united" community battling the discomfort of oppression.

When Isabel self-mockingly says, "I just went in on a soapbox"— referring to her attempt to explain her identities as woman, Puerto Rican, and lesbian to another class—she seems to be implying that, on some level, she is using the familiar rhetoric of right and wrong that she grew up with in the Jehovah's Witnesses. She *is* perhaps a bit absolutist, perhaps a bit like the Bible in her deliverance of "truth" to the pagans of the world of identity politics; yet I also see extraordinary courage in her acts of giving language to her unfolding sense of self. From early childhood and, in relation to her family, into the present, she has lived with the knowledge that the "truth" about her sexuality, put into language, would sever her connections to people literally through excommunication. In Isabel's essays, her use of counterfacts and ideology from the lesbian and gay community to refute conservative social forces is fascinatingly reminiscent of her early challenges to her father in which she pointed out divergent meanings in Bible passages and his interpretation of Witness doctrine as it affected the environment of their household. As the recipient of absolutist thinking, she was imparted information that her own experience implicitly refuted, and yet the use of her experience as a counternarrative was forbidden. Instead, it seems that from a young age she used the approach of "setting the record straight" via the experience of others in order to crack the power of forces that controlled her agency. Later, she again put to use the strategy of rational correction she had tried on her father—this time the subject being sexual identity, and her audience, people to whom she had no close relationship, such as students in her other classes. In those situations she was finally able to more fully voice the "truth" of her own experience without huge personal penalty. In our class, in which there seemed to be the greatest opportunity to use her own experience in original and exploratory ways, she didn't. Was it perhaps because, once again, she feared excommunication from a new ideological and affectional family? Interpreted within that context, Isabel's work and her intentions for the future—to "set the record straight" in the public sphere through writing—seem quite understandable. Her writing seems to be concerned not so much with deconstructing the lesbian and gay community as, literally, constructing it for herself—and constructing a place for herself within it.

Note

1. Of course, the reverse is also true: The religious view of homosexuality as sin *does* posit it as a choice, and a segment of the lesbian and gay community debunks *this* by reclaiming the essentializing notion of inherent "orientation."

Chapter Ten

John Lee

Writing Fractured Identity

John is a twenty-five-year-old African American psychology major who has just completed his sophomore year at Municipal College. He originally attended college for two semesters immediately after high school; in his second semester, due to the tumult of coming out, two of his five classes remained unfinished and he left school for several years.

John grew up first-generation Northern-born in Brooklyn, New York. His mother has a bachelor's degree and a teaching certificate, and works as a pre-kindergarten teacher. His father—who is really his stepfather, but has filled the role of John's father his entire life and to whom John refers as "my father"—is a building contractor with a high school diploma. John describes his family as working-class, though he feels that he himself has become more middle-class—"in attitudes, not yet in economics." His father is "not religious at all," while his mother is a "badly practicing Jehovah's Witness" who became a Witness when she had children in order "to be a good mother." Raised Baptist, she was the last of many in her large family to convert. Although the Witnesses played a big part in John's upbringing, he says that his mother would nevertheless always prioritize open school night over a Witness meeting if there were a conflict between the two. He also feels that, as his stepfather was rather remote, his mother used the Witnesses as a way for John to have more male influences in his life. He loved the attention he got from the many men there and still has warm memories of the meetings, although he says that religion had no spiritual significance for him even as a child. As an adult, John never goes to church. "Religion in general doesn't interest me. I find other things to attach religious significance to—like knowledge, sexuality, and psychology, which borders on religion anyway."

He describes his father as "open and open-minded about sexuality." John feels "one hundred percent certain" that his father had homosexual relationships before he married John's mother, when John was four. He explains that his mother married him when he came up from North Carolina with a friend with whom he had been in the Peace Corps and with whom he had subsequently lived for several years. There have never been indications of women in either of the men's lives, and the details of that period have never been discussed in the family. John's mother, whom he describes as "heterosexual" and "very feminine in identity," spent most of her time during several years between high school and college with a gay male cousin who was a designer and made all her clothes. "She was constantly with gay Black men—that was the crowd she hung out with when she was young." She nonetheless held on to traditional ideas about family—"the whole Donna Reed thing"—a desire that John attributes to her not being from a traditional family herself, as her mother never married and raised many children alone. John is the oldest of five children.

Back in school for a full academic year now, John also holds down jobs in an independent art movie theatre and a public relations firm. He will give them up if likely prospects of two different research assistantships with psychology professors materialize next year.

John tells a story about a time when he became aware of difference in sexual identity: "I was in the seventh grade, and I realized that my best friend did not feel the same way as I. I had tried to get him undressed—and it didn't work out, it was completely botched—but I realized that he felt differently. We wound up going to different high schools, and I remember sitting with him on the train one day, and he was telling me about his girlfriend, or about this girl that was interested in him. And I suddenly realized that my identity had developed in a completely different way, and that I didn't think of those things at all. And it wasn't just that he had a girlfriend, but that I really felt very different. And it was kind of at that point that I recognized that yes, there were different sexual identities, and that it meant more than who you slept with. I knew that because I hadn't slept with anyone! And I don't think he had, either. I had no desire to sleep with him at that point, or to have sex with him, but I definitely felt something very different that I wasn't feeling was being radiated back toward me."

Earlier than that, when he was about ten or younger, John had heard his father speak disparagingly of homosexuals. "If there can be levels of disparaging comments, then I mean they weren't completely malicious—they were actually playful in some way. But they were definitely not affirming. And that's when I became aware that 'faggot' and 'gay,' 'queer' and a couple of other terms that I knew all meant pretty much the same thing. I really wasn't sure exactly what they were, but I knew there were negative connotations to them. They were kind of trivializing. I guess at that point I was becoming aware of what sexuality was, and more aware of how I was sexually different than my parents or my friends or anyone else that I knew. And it's funny, I wasn't sure if I *was,* but I had a feeling that when he called someone a faggot—I kind of felt that oh, well, you know, that term kind of applies to me, too."

What John does not notice—or at least, does not mention—is that in each of the two situations that he says were instrumental in promoting his consciousness of sexual identity, the other person in the conversation—his former friend, his father—had a vested interest in separating himself from the notion of homosexuality. In the first case, the friend was someone John had tried to seduce at a young age; in the second case, there was circumstantial evidence to suggest that his father might have had a homosexual relationship himself. In both cases, John felt inducted into a discourse in which he could only read himself as "different." Yet it is possible that both were specifically invoked *as* discourses of difference which sought his participation as Other, the audience whose homosexuality ratified the identity of the speaker as not-homosexual. His willing belief, in both cases, in the speaker's ingenuous disentanglement from homosexual identification— manifested in his conclusion both times that *he* was somehow "different"—seems to possibly involve him as an unwitting collaborator in a false dichotomy manufactured at his own expense.

John eventually came out when he was eighteen, a freshman in college, and working in the accounting department of a large, popular sportswear store. "The accounting department was run by this really nice lesbian, Nancy, whose lover was a daughter of the person that did all the contracting for the store. There were at least three other lesbians in the department. The entire buying department was gay. The personnel director was a lesbian into body building. And there I was. All of these people were very new to me because the only other gay people that I'd known existed were in dirty movie theatres. I really didn't have any other contact outside of that. I wanted to be more open because all of these other people were so open."

This new context for thinking about himself and about gay relationships helped to ready him for a first relationship of his own. "I didn't have the typical dating or intimate relationships, or semi-intimate relationships that most people who are somewhere between sixteen and twenty usually have. I was pursuing sexual identity at night and living a kind of asexual existence during the daytime." He became involved with a man named Vince, but kept it a secret. "There

I was, infatuated but not out, around people who *were* out—and it was so confusing, because I wanted to tell someone, 'Wow, I met this wonderful guy and I'm really happy, and I really want something to develop here, but I'm not sure what to do.' And so one afternoon I decided that I was just going to come out. Throughout that week, I had worked up my courage—he'd invited me to spend the weekend with him—and so the next weekend I did. I just didn't tell anyone where I was going. I just kind of went to work, met him at a bar over on the East Side, and we went back to his apartment. I hadn't told my mother where I was going. I was still living at home. So I just effectively disappeared for three days. I had left some of my things at home in my room, and my mother came across this number. She knew that someone had been calling for me at the house recently, so she assumed that, well, that's where I must be. So she called on Sunday night, and—I hadn't been expecting her to call. She said, 'Where are you?' and I told her I was at Vince's house, and she said, 'Well, is he gay? Is he white?' And I think it was, 'Are you in bed?' I answered yes to all of the above. I don't know why I answered yes to everything. Actually, it was probably kind of foolish to be that direct, without any real buildup to this happening. But I was.

"Well, I was out to family at that point. After I talked to my mother on the telephone, eventually I figured I had to go home, so that night I went back home. My Dad was sitting outside in the car—he had just driven up and he was parking the car—so I went over and I sat in the car with him, and I told him I thought I was gay, and that I needed to tell someone, and I wasn't sure how to go about telling my mother, other than the brief conversation we'd had earlier in the day. And, you know, he didn't really say much. Just a lot of nodding, actually, and then he'd cough. And it's funny, he didn't really give me any advice on telling her. He just said, 'Well, you know, you have to tell her about it.' It was helpful actually talking to him, and I was actually surprised because I had expected that he would have been the last person that I would have talked to, because we'd never actually had this great, intimate, father-son relationship. We were always actually pretty distant. So his response was kind of the last thing I'd ever anticipated happening. I mean, in his own way, he was kind of supportive. And that's something that's kind of continued on, ever since I've been out. He's always been more supportive than my mother has, though we never really *talk* about things much." John suspects that the "weird" feeling of bonding that resulted from his coming out to his father had something to do with his father's memories of his own earlier life, though he's not sure: "We never really had an in-depth conversation about *his* sexuality." Now, seven years later, John lives with a lover and though his family has met him, "there's just really no connection." The other people he came out to were his friends from high school, and he "lost all of them."

John says that he has always done a lot of writing privately about sexuality and relationships, but that piles of unfinished work have accumulated because "I lose either the inspiration or the motivation to actually do it. The only completed things I've ever done have actually been for classes in school." He has found that he has had a better track record completing work where there is "very little personal connection with the writing."

He does not recall ever having heard gay existence come up as a topic in any of his classes unless he himself brought it up—something he has done frequently. "The absence of it makes me angry. And so what I do is, I stick it into my writing. The absence has made me pursue it, and go, well, why isn't this here?" John has raised that question— "Why isn't this here?"—in class discussions as well as in writing that would only be read by the teacher. "I was always nervous doing it, but I always came across as being more confident than I actually was. I always figured that I had nothing to lose." Other male students in those classes avoided talking to him, he says, and teachers would simply "sidestep the issues that I raised." "It's kind of yes, that's nice, but let's go on. It's almost relegated to irrelevance in group discussions." He cites as an example a class that read *The Importance of Being Earnest* in which Oscar Wilde's homosexuality was omitted from the account of biographical data.

He feels that there is a very strong relationship between his gay identity and his writing. "I've become very comfortable with my gay identity, and I find it really has focused the things that I write about. I haven't written a thing that hasn't been in some way shaped by, or related back to, my gay identity. From the nature of the relationship between Hamlet and Ophelia to Lincoln's emancipating enslaved peoples and the relationship to queer rights—I always manage to get something tied in. It just seems to come naturally at this point." He feels that this is so because "those subjects are part of me. I can write about nice, abstract things, but I see them through the lens of my sexuality. I think that's a good thing. I think it actually opens up new perspectives for me."

His first experience writing about sexuality for school was in his freshman composition class, when the teacher assigned an open topic for the final research paper. John decided to write about Black gay men. "It was 1989. I wasn't sure if I was writing about myself yet. It was all still pretty much abstract, because I hadn't experienced a lot of the things that I was reading about." Yet he found, after reading several anthologies and articles in a gay political weekly, that his personal experience was "kind of leaking out into the paper." That paper took a long time for him to write because "it was a more personal thing that I was writing about, even if I wasn't completely aware of it at the time." Yet "the professor didn't say much about it. I remember him writing that it was a very interesting topic to cover, that he hadn't had anyone actually write about this before—but that was really about it. And I guess I was really looking for feedback. Whether it had been positive or negative, I was really open to provoke a reaction. And so I was kind of disappointed that I didn't get one. And I guess that's how I would actually describe any of the writing that I've done that in any way involved my sexuality—the reactions that I've gotten have been rather mild. And when I specifically include things like that, and then I don't get a reaction—then I understand, well, I'm ignored. I've never in my academic career actually come up against anyone who's had a strongly negative reaction to my being open about my sexuality. Most people just prefer not to deal with it, not to touch that issue." None of the writers that the class read in their freshman anthology had been openly gay. "The things that they wrote about were often rather limited to me. I had a difficult time accessing their experiences, because they were so removed. Most of the writers that you read in [freshman composition] are basically nice, white people. So while their experience was already somewhat removed from mine, it was removed that second step by the nature of their sexual identity." John feels that reading about experience that is unilaterally white or unilaterally heterosexual is of "limited" use for him. "I get to feeling lost if I don't find an anchor. And often with white writers, with straight writers, I can't find an anchor there to hold on to. And that makes accessing those stories more difficult for me."

John feels that when he "brings up" otherwise unexplored gay dimensions of subjects being discussed in his classes he is expressing an intellectual need that isn't being met. "In most classes, if I don't bring it up, it won't get brought up at all. No one's going to. And this has been the case in my psychology classes, and it's been the case in my English classes, and it's been the case in my history classes." In his American History class that covered the latter part of the nineteenth century to the present, he was surprised to find no mention of either gays or AIDS. "I don't think you can go through American history in the seventies without discussing gay liberation. But people manage to somehow or other. And AIDS was completely written out of history. Or in my Twentieth-Century History of Culture and Ideas class, we got up to the present day without ever discussing philosophy of lesbian and gay theory, what it's meant, how sexuality has affected the way people perceive the world." In that class, he says, "I was the only person of color in the room. All the people who were actually taking the class for credit were white philosophy majors. We all had to do oral reports, so I chose to do a report on James Baldwin—if only because he's the only gay person of color they were ever going to come across." He says that after he concluded his report, the class was completely silent, and then asked questions "all of which started with, 'You know, I didn't know that,' and 'You know, that's interesting,' or all the other usual responses." The teacher, too, said it was "interesting" and "a good report," and asked him "about other notoriously gay people of the time," all of which left John feeling once again that the subject of Black gay identity was getting a polite nod but had no great prospects of commanding deeper exploration or inclusion in the larger sphere of academic inquiry.

John rates himself a "9.5" or a "10" on an "outness" scale of one to ten because he feels he is now out virtually everywhere, the only exception being "people and places that I don't have much contact with at all." When asked to describe what it means to be "gay," he says, "It means, for me, a way of looking at the world that is very, very different from the way other people look at it. That incorporates a greater degree of understanding, an integration, of things that I guess are typically considered masculine and feminine. And being comfortable with that integration." He catches himself in surprise at his own definition: "It's actually the first time I've gotten beyond using sex as the first few words of the definition of what it means to be gay." He says that he's moved beyond a sex-bound definition because of "more contact with gay people, and more discussion of how other people perceive their sexuality, or what their sexuality has meant to them." He says of the words he uses to describe himself, "I've never been fond of 'fag' or 'faggot.' I guess I use 'gay' more than anything else, but I find myself slipping toward 'queer' when I write—and when I really am writing in a more political vein, and speaking in a more political vein, then I'll use 'queer.' I tend to use 'homosexual' when I'm being very technical, because I think it only has validity as a very technical term."

Matters of Access

John says of his work in our class, "I've put more effort and more thought into all of the things I wrote this term than anything I have ever written. Because they accessed something that was very intimate to me, and in some respects that made this class the most difficult that I've ever taken. It was accessing one of my identities that's extraordinarily strong—a very primary identity for me, but that I hadn't really actually sat down to focus on and go, OK, what is the nature of this identity? So when I did most of my writing, on being Black and gay, and on the effect of AIDS, and on coming out—they were things that really have been some of the most important factors in shaping my life overall, but that I'd never actually sat down and put down on paper, and worked out and saw exactly how they did what they did. In other classes there really hasn't been an opportunity to make an exploration in that way."

John feels that many of the readings in our course enabled his writing. He mentions John Boswell's essay on the problem of creating categories for historical analysis, and comments, "I think it's really relevant to sit down and discuss—is gay and lesbian identity essence? Or is it existence? Does it come afterward—is it something added—or is it something that's there from the very start, and how shall we go about naming all these things?" He also liked Adrienne Rich's "Compulsory Heterosexuality" very much, and says he wasn't bothered by it as many of the other men were because he concurs with Rich that misogyny among gay men is "far more rampant than anyone is willing to express. I've never been one to really think that gay men should be excluded in some way from the way that people basically think of men." He thinks that his attitude "probably goes back to my first formative gay relationships being with lesbians as opposed to being with gay men."

John also cites John D'Emilio's "Capitalism and Gay Identity" as a text that "confirmed" and "crystalized" things he had been trying to think through on his own: "That the nature of what we call 'gay identity' in this latter part of the twentieth century is something that is not eternal. Or it hasn't always existed. I remember when I read that, I had been arguing the week before with Sean [his lover] about how much of what we call 'gay history' is made up by us. So we've kind of gone back and invented a history. Because you can't really apply the term 'gay' or 'lesbian' to someone who lived in ancient Rome. You can't apply it to Plato, or Socrates, because the concept as it exists for us now just wasn't there. The way we think of society and what things mean in society are so different. And so that essay was really very helpful for me, and actually, I remember taking it the other way and saying, well, now I understand more why gay white men are at the level they are in terms of gay identity, and why people of color develop gay identity along different lines. Because they haven't had the material advantages that white communities have had. In some ways, they're just getting there. So their perceptions of what gay and lesbian people are are different. I think it's the old, 'if you have enough money to get away from your family and establish a life of your own, then you're more likely to be able to access and nurture your lesbian or gay identity.' If you don't have the economic resources to do that, and your existence is very much tied to the welfare of the family unit—whether that be immediate family or the community you're in—then it's really unlikely that you're going to do something that goes so strongly against family or community thought, like establish a positive gay or lesbian identity."

John feels that the lesbian and gay history he has read tends to leave out African Americans and other people of color, even when it purports to include them. He seems to be sensing both the limits and the possibilities of social history when he says, "[The lesbian and gay history I've read] gets restricted to the Harlem Renaissance and entertainers and the popular poets, but that's really about it. And I don't think that's completely it. You don't get much exploration into the day-to-day lives of actual Black gay people. I don't think it's an appropriate representation, or an accurate representation, of everyone's experience."

He was disappointed that there weren't more people of color in the class. (We discovered at the time of the interview that he had categorized several members of the class as "white" based on appearance though they did not define themselves that way.) Gratified by the sense of community in one sense, frustrated in another, he remarks that his concept of "diversity" underwent some revision: "One of the most interesting things about the class was the great amount of diversity outside of racial and ethnic diversity, although there were a moderate number of people of color in the class. What was more striking is that there were people of all age ranges, and all different types of experience there. And so one of the things that I realized is that there really is, and can be, no one definition of gay or lesbian." The composition of the class helped him to realize, too, that even within a group that seems homogeneous in certain ways, diverse experience ends up emerging and informing the collective conversation. "I think [diversity] becomes more prominent as familiarity grows," he says, remarking too that people often choose to keep matters of difference to themselves. "Diversity can be a matter of your perception." He points as an example to "the straight people not coming out. I didn't know that they were straight until the middle of the term." And: "I didn't *know* that some of the people in our class were people of color. Or that they weren't white Anglo—for lack of a better term. But then I also wonder—were they just comfortable in other people not knowing?" He conceives an important connection between representation—which involves self-identification—and the discourse of a classroom. "If there isn't diverse representation in a class, then you're not going to get as much diversity discussed in the class. In a class like this people want information about, basically, themselves, and the more diversity you have, the more likely you are to get a greater diversity of information."

The competing demands for representations of various strands of experience become more urgent in a class packed with people who already feel deprived of information about themselves; yet the cross-experiential forms of knowledge that get produced in such a situation yield surprising benefits. "I still think one of the most amazing things is how much I learned about lesbians this term," John says. One thing that had been enlightening was a debate that had occurred over whether the terms "lesbian" and "feminist" necessarily coincided. "I found myself saying last night in conversation with someone, 'Well, da da da da da, and lesbians—whatever that means.' Just, you know, realizing the question of what these terms—gay and lesbian—actually mean. And it comes more from lesbians than from gay men, who somehow seem to be quite secure in exactly what that means."

John also feels that the subject matter of the course, but lesbian theory in particular, helped him find an entry point into the wider realm of theory, which "tends to evade" him generally. "I've become the academic person that I always thought I was, but never was encouraged to be," he says. Queer theory "really helped me to actually utilize [my gay identity], as opposed to just, you know, going along with it." He felt that the lesbian theorists were "a much more inclusive lot than any of the men were," as well as more accessible.

John points out that important meanings don't only reside in diverse groups. "I think it's important, if it's a class that's a homogenously white group, to go, 'OK, this is what we are. What does this mean?' I also think it would be very worthwhile for straight people to do that. To sit down and go, 'OK, we're a group of straight people. What does this mean? How does it come about, and why isn't there anyone else here?'"

In the class, John became more aware of a tendency in himself to deliberately write in opposition, as Other, as "a subset, or a member of a subgroup of a minority," with the immediate context of his writing presenting a necessary friction that frames the way he will present himself as a subject. This tendency exists in curious counterpoint to a simultaneous need for the comfort of sameness, for an audience composed of like-minded others "where you can feel acceptance." It also paradoxically coexists with his anger at *having* to take recourse in "combative definition[s]" that are predicated on "what I am versus what they are." Because the notion of "difference" so much defines his writing, he says, within the gay community he writes differently than he does elsewhere, "not so much against a background of a majority of people being straight and everything that goes along with that, but as a Black gay man immersed in a white gay world." He feels he wrote more about being Black in our class "because it was a thing that set me apart from everyone else," whereas in classes that are more racially mixed but silent about sexual identity he writes about being gay. "I guess I really do look for that point at which there is difference, and write from that standpoint," he says, asserting emphatically that a class of gay Black men "wouldn't be any better than a class full of gay white men all together. I'm not a person for homogenous groups."

John thinks it would be a good idea to have more classes like ours, especially for "people who are young and just coming out, and who think that academic settings are not an appropriate setting to express their sexual identity in." He thinks all classes should include more lesbian and gay reading because "it is identity-affirming for students. And one of the things you get from being in school is identity-affirmation. For people who are in school, it's a major part of their life. If you don't do it, you definitely shortchange them, you're doing them a terrible disservice. Because they're not going to find this anyplace else. There are few other forums for positive affirmation of sexual identity outside of big cities." He thinks that the benefits for heterosexual students engaging with lesbian and gay material are that "you get to undo a lot of the damage that's probably been done to them over the past eighteen or nineteen years of their lives—in the way of perceiving gay or lesbian people as being bad, wrong, deviant, or anything like that. And I think a class like this is much better than a class where you just sit down and discuss the problems of being gay or lesbian, because you have people—that are in the life. You get real people, not abstractions or images in books."

The Crossover Kid

Issues relating to race in the gay community are at the center of the work John produced throughout the term. His first paper—initially entitled "Helpful Hints for People of Color on Being a Gay White Male—The Tale of the Crossover Kid" but called simply "State of the Queer Nation" in his final draft—addresses both ironically and analytically the tendency within the gay community to subsume all differences other than those based on sexual preference in order to preserve a sense of "community," a notion which, in its most frequent constructions, depends on the identification of masses of individuals with one another based on one overarching common characteristic. He opens:

> I have some experience with being gay white and male. Not hands-on, personal experience: it's closer to vicarious experience. I am a gay black male. But many of my friends are gay white males. And I've been told that we all, all of us who are gay men, go through about the same series of stages on our way to attaining our gay identities.

His text is not simply an invective against cultural colonization and racism. Knowing that this argument has been articulated before and continues to expand in the gay press and cultural milieu, he is sophisticated enough to insert himself into that larger conversation by deconstructing its context, searching for clues to the genesis of the problem. Several pages later, he writes,

> The first question that begs an answer is why be a part of a gay community, especially a predominantly white gay community, at all? I think the answer to that question will be different for each individual. Some may be geographically restricted. The only gay community in their area may be a gay white community. For many gay people of color the choices are few: acceptance by ethnic/people of color communities, acceptance by a gay community (most commonly a gay white community), acceptance by both, or isolation from both.

> To gain access to gay white communities, one had to subvert any other identity. What this usually meant to people of color who wanted access to these communities was jettisoning a host of cultural traits and attributes to gain acceptance. (They were not alone in this; gay ethnic whites had to do the same thing with no less difficulty than did people of color. Perhaps, less noticeably because they could superficially blend in with the community as a whole.) Further, once these other difference markers had been divested and a conditional access had been granted there was the demand to fit into the stereotypical mold that the community had cast for people of color.

John goes on to explain that a dawning consciousness of multiculturalism altered the community's perceptions.

> . . . [M]ulticulturalism means opening up to the different and diverse experiences of these outsider communities, it means breaking down the myth of the single monolithic gay experience. It means recognizing that gay identity is only one of many identities for many people. That other identities can be just as important as sexual identity.

Yet,

> Multiculturalism in white gay communities is still not so much a synthesis of ideas and ways of being gay as it is a mosaic, a collection of ideas on being gay that have agreed upon certain commonalities of purpose. Those people of color who had not assimilated into white gay communities continually found that they were trapped between an ethnic community that did not want them because they were gay and a gay community that rejected them for being too ethnic. . . .

> . . . Recognition of these growing people of color communities by the white gay communities was slow. It was easier to acknowledge groups like Men-Of-All-Colors Together that promoted a form of interracial experience as a basis for erotic relations. But, it was harder for the mainstream community to understand all-Black, all-Asian, or all-Hispanic groups. . . .

> . . . Although comparisons about the ubiquitousness of racism versus the pervasiveness of homophobia and heterosexism can be made it is

still less likely that a person of color will be discriminated against for being queer than for being black or Hispanic. The latter simply tends to be much more obvious than the former.

Gay white men often have only one focus for experiencing discrimination, their sexuality. Consequently they are free to devote more time fighting this discrimination. For people of color discrimination on the basis of sexuality is probably encountered more among other persons of color, while discrimination on the basis of race or ethnicity can be encountered almost anywhere.

Why then don't people of color concentrate on the homophobia of other people of color? First, that would not solve the problem of racism in white gay communities. Second I suspect that targeting racism among white gays is easier; it has fewer emotional attachments. Attacking homophobia and heterosexism among minority communities means attacking home and family—an anathema to any minority group, as community is often perceived as extended family.

John D'Emilio in his essay *Capitalism and Gay Identity* makes the case that only when the notion of the primacy of the extended family is diminished can gays and lesbians actually work toward forming separate communities. While the influence of the family has waned for most white gays allowing communities to form, this has not been the case for many gay persons of color. Family for gay people of color continues to be a potent source of economic and emotional sustenance and support, even for those gay persons of color who have formed alternative gay communities and families. Unwilling to attack their first communities, the battle for acceptance has shifted overwhelmingly to the white gay community front.

He goes on to say that "gay people of color limit the effectiveness of discussions on racism in the gay community by not addressing the right audiences. Too often the issue of race is discussed only in a group of people of color or with whites who are sympathetic to racial issues." Part of the problem is that

ignorance and prejudice is even more insidious in white gay communities because we (men at least) have a tendency to act with our genitals first and think later, though what happens most often is that we forget about the latter. Gay men are all linked by their sexual attraction to other men. Until the gay activist movement this was almost always the primary reason for the community's existence. Gay white men, like anyone else, tend not to realize that their worldview is not everyone else's worldview unless they are told of other viewpoints.

For academics, John's ruminations on identity are likely to evoke the familiar postmodern theme of the fractured self in which multiple perspectives simultaneously demand recognition. Yet John is writing not from entrenchment in academic discourse, but from his position within social and political self-defined "communities" whose overlapping and contradictory discourses fashion him, in his own words, as "the crossover kid." Self-consciously inhabiting several discourse communities at once produces ideological and rhetorical confusion. In our interview, John says that what he sees as a quasi-"separatist" tone in his paper—or, in his words, a stance of "Hey, we don't need you to define us, and we don't need to be part of this community"—surprises him, and doesn't precisely represent his view. "It was really kind of weird, because I'm not terribly involved with people of color communities," he says, a bit perplexed, adding that "this was the most difficult paper I had to go through. And I didn't really rewrite it until the end of the term. But what came out of it was the last paper [his final project], and just writing about Black gay men. Writing about the uniqueness of that experience, compared to gay experience and Black experience and why gay men are neither one nor the other, but that being both is something completely different. Both of those identities— Black identity and gay identity—work equally to shape the person. I realize that that's what I was trying to write all along, and wasn't getting it." He says that "in the end, all the work that I did was a product of this class," in that the readings, the discussions, the workshops, and the intertextuality of student work continually reshaped his thinking. Within that context, he also began to chart events from the past that had epistemologically located him, as evidenced in these excerpts from several journal entries:

> Coming of age in the time of gay rights activism was a weird thing. I remember walking into my first ACT UP meeting at the [Lesbian and Gay Community Services] Center and attending GLYNY [Gay and Lesbian Youth of New York] meetings with some acquaintances. I have never not known activism. Consequently I have always felt that I must be involved. I must present my experience. I must demonstrate my difference. Out. Loud. Proud.

> People—teachers and elders—have always tried to instill black pride in me through a sense of historical relevance. They never backed up their h.r. with any real facts. This makes me angry, that I am denied my history but it incenses me further that people try to string together a group of events into a true fluid history. Anyway I take pride in being part of a new historical group.

> I guess that coming from a created culture—Black American culture, with its synthesis of old African ideas lost in postslavery institutions and values—I always felt lacking in a sense of history.

> I moved out of my community, a predominantly black family neighborhood, quite by accident into a white and gay (kind of). . . . [sic]

> This is important because I became separated from aspects of my black identity and restricted in my understanding of gay identity. I think this happens fairly often with people with dual identities; one identity gets shunted or underdeveloped at first. Unfortunately I think that when people come out often other identities are cast off for the moment. . . . I remember when after a year of living among gay whites, a new and strange experience for me, I started to need my blackness, my repressed identity.

> The first gay-oriented newspapers and magazines that I found had no photos of people of color. I didn't notice this at the time.

Operating largely within an epistemic of resistance, John uses different parts of his "identity" to test the other parts and puncture the illusion of their coherence. "Out. Loud. Proud."—the credo of the "Queer Nation" whose "nationhood" he wryly questions in his paper—rings a bit monotonic in the wake of the dictums John has received from that community and what he has found when he has duly acted upon them—"I must present my experience. I must demonstrate my difference." He resents the convenient fiction of a "true fluid history," all the more so because its creation obfuscates a more available and, for him, perfectly legitimate source of "pride"—the experience of "being part of a new historical group." He yearns for the repressed in himself, is interested in his capacity to overlook his own nonrepresentation. Over and over, he finds meanings in gaps and absences, particularly insofar as they prohibit false totalizing of that which appears as present. "The crossover kid" is the dismantler of reified homogenous realities; his place, to borrow Audre Lorde's much-quoted phrase, is "the very house of difference rather than the security of any one particular difference" (1982, 226), and he recognizes the efficacy of this place as a site of social critique.

Certainly one of the most apparent "absences" for gay men in the 1990s is the tangible human absence of those who have died of AIDS. John writes about the loss of his best friend in "Jorge's Socially Constructed Epidemic," which begins,

> Before Magic Johnson made AIDS safe for anybody to get, back when AIDS was something that only happened to queers and IV-drug users, a librarian-in-training by the name of Jorge Morales fell into a coma and died from an AIDS-related brain infection.

In mock-fairy-tale tones, John situates his friend's death in an unspecified chronological time that is metonymically linked to social epistemic time. It is clear from the start, then, as well as from his title, that John's subject is not simply illness and loss, but the constructedness of those events by public discourse. Jorge is seen not as an unfortunate Other befallen by sad circumstances, but as one who, along with John, has been written into an impossibly constraining cultural narrative.

> [Jorge's] death reminds me of the price that AIDS has exacted from gay men, from me. While there have been many factors that have gone into the construction of my sexual identity—my gay identity— the most important of these has been acquiring this identity in the era of AIDS. I am just one of many people who has watched their friends, lovers and family members die of this plague. And, like many people my age, I cannot remember a time when AIDS did not exist. The experience of this plague has done more to shape the ways that I perceive gay identity and sexuality than any other personal circum- stance or sociocultural movement.
>
> . . . AIDS made sex "dangerous," "risky," and "unsafe." It was desig- nated as a disease of "perverts"—gay men and IV-drug users. . . . When I first heard of AIDS I was terrified. I was a teenager just realizing that I was gay and recognizing the implications of accepting gay as an identity. I did not know it then but I was being abused by a psychology created by the government, the medical-industrial com- plex, and assorted homophobes that equated being gay with having AIDS. This for me and others like me was probably the start of having an identity that seemed intimately linked with a virus.

John's exposition relies on the writer's and reader's shared subtextual knowledge that his "I" actually represents a "we"; that it is his mem- bership in a community of similarly positioned people that gives his story epistemic significance and cultural meaning. As he goes on to narrate the scene of bereavement, he enlists the reader's sympathy by challenging popular social discourses about "family"—discourses in which "family" is biologically or matrimonially constituted, in which habits of care and solidarity among people related in that way are assumed, and in which ties of affinity based on choice and circumstan- tial factors like being "intimately linked with a virus" are considered subordinate. At the same time, his challenges are mounted with the help of popular counterdiscourses in which relatives' pledges of endur- ing connection are often hypocritical—a view most potently demon- strated by the fact that a member's homosexuality effectively waives the right to unconditional familial love and support:

> When [Jorge] died I had known him for four years. He was the second gay person that I had met after I came out. At 30 years old he retained the innocent character of a person far younger. We three—my lover, Sean, Jorge, and I—lived together, more family to each other than any of our birth families were. As he slipped closer into death, Jorge's family returned to make provisions to return his remains to his hometown. Tuesday, August 2nd, at 9:48 P.M., Jorge's body gave out and finally died after outliving his brain by about 48 hours. His family

had come from Trenton [New Jersey] to see him in the hospital; many of them had never been to New York, though Jorge had lived in the city for more than a decade. They did not stay long. Sean and I were entrusted with any further decisions regarding Jorge's care and with the solemn task of sending his remains home once he had expired. We were glad, as we had looked after him for so long; we felt that this final act of care was our right.

Jorge was buried in Trenton. He was eulogized by a family-chosen priest in Spanish (Jorge spoke almost no Spanish) that he had probably never met. His family asked that no mention be made of the cause of his illness and death. No one in the family mentioned that he was gay. The funeral was held at 9 A.M. in Trenton. Few of Jorge's adult friends—his gay friends, boyfriends and lovers—were able to make it to the ceremonies. Sadly, bitterly, we could do little but watch as Jorge's life was placed into a coffin of familial denial and buried away.

Implicit in John's narrative is the notion that he, like a prosecuting attorney, carries the burden to establish "proof" that Jorge's biological relations' claim to the title of "family" is impeachable, and that he and Sean are the ones who, instead, deserve that designation. His assertion that the three friends were "more family to each other than any of our birth families were" is substantiated by the comment, thrown in with casual deliberateness, that many members of Jorge's family "had never been to New York, though Jorge had lived in the city for more than a decade" and that they "did not stay long." This information frames Jorge's burial in Trenton (in "a coffin of familial denial") as a meaningless ritual, the purpose of which is to sanctimoniously preserve the form of Jorge as "son" while emptying the appellation of its content. The location of the grave, like the presence of the relatives, the language of the service, and the absence of Jorge's chosen "family," are all details that enable John to substantiate his case.

The audience of this text—our class—is a crucial component of its production in that it could be relied upon to catch and appreciate the bitter ironies the story offers in a way that Jorge's biological family—most infuriatingly to the author—did not. John describes the act of writing this piece as "cathartic," and something that was largely possible because of the class environment. In fact, in his interview he cites this essay as an illustration of the way that Dennis's text, "The Audience I Have Waited My Entire Life For," was an appropriate summation of his experience of the class.

He mentions several other texts he wrote that he doesn't believe he would have written in another class. One of them is what he calls his "definition-of-gay piece." He explains, "I'd have difficulty actually making a definition of what it means to be gay and presenting it to a

bunch of people who are not. I'd probably create a much more combative definition. Or one that defined what I was versus what they
were. I'd have started to explore a definition of life-style, orientation,
and of the opposite of being straight. And I probably would have been
stuck at just the opposite of being straight." Instead, his text begins,

> Gay is a life. It is not a life-style. It is not an orientation or a fixation.
> It is not the opposite of straight.

He goes on to examine and refute each of the popular conceptions,
moving toward his own definition yet inevitably foundering even
there.

> Gay is a life-style. I used to think that this definition was more in line
> with what I felt. Life-style though comes with baggage of freedom of
> choice. Life-style says that like fashion, gayness can be changed as
> easily as a hemline or a pair of shoes. It insults me because it presumes
> that all gay people are the same. That we have whimsically chosen to
> be gay. Life-style is invariably used by straight people who haven't an
> inkling of what the term actually means. (These same people would
> never consider being straight a life-style.)
>
> Orientation. . . . (I've never figured out how to use the term in polite
> conversation. Do you say, "I'm gay-oriented" or "my orientation is
> gay"? I either sound like a marketing executive or a navigator.) . . .
> Orientation, like life-style, has an air of the artificial. Both terms make
> what is an integral part of my self-concept seem like a veneer or a
> coating to be stripped off or discarded. Neither accounts for the in-
> definiteness of gayness. . . .
>
> Identity. I am most comfortable with the term identity. . . . I'm told
> that an identity is an amalgam of different ideas and perceptions of
> one's self. Identity combines aspects of various roles (ideas of what a
> person who is involved in a specific set of actions does and is);
> experience and learning; self-esteem; what I (we) perceive that others
> think of me (us)—positively and negatively. An identity is both innate
> and learned so it encompasses the feeling of difference (gayness) that
> I have always had and incorporates those things about being gay that
> I have learned through social interaction.
>
> What is gay then? What does it mean?. . . .
>
> Gay represents a primary identity. . . . Gay identity cannot be changed
> or discarded, it can only be acknowledged or ignored, encouraged or
> repressed. Expression can vary but existence cannot. . . .
>
> I don't think that you can truly say that you are gay until you've been
> called a faggot or a cocksucker by a straight. . . .
>
> Coming out defines gay and gayness for me. Not the singular act of
> coming out but the ceaseless process of coming out. . . .

Being gay means that one seeks out the company of other gay people, for purposes other than sex. . . .

How then is gay a life? . . . I think the expression "In the life" describes it best. A life is not a thing or an event but the totality of the person and his experiences. My experiences always seem to come back to the extent to which homosexuality has shaped my interaction with my environment. . . . If I am vague it is because the definition of gay is so palpable but so elusive. I know it when I see it. . . .

In his discovery that the category "gay" is slippery, John engages with the mercurial nature of definition itself. His struggle to locate and pin a solid meaning on a term he so deeply identifies with and so frequently uses sends him lurching between the opposite poles of meanings that are "so palpable" and those that are "so elusive." The "palpable" side might be described as the drive toward essence and absolutism—"I know it when I see it"—supported by strong assertions that in their glib totalization impose firm boundaries of the sort he elsewhere vehemently objects to: "I don't think that you can truly say that you are gay until you've been called a faggot or a cocksucker by a straight." In this view, society can only mold the outer manifestations of an inner core reality that is immutable: "Expression can vary but existence cannot." The "elusive" side, on the other hand, is supported by various statements indicating that identity is a matter of performance, and is thus by nature indeterminate, since roles are assumed, tried out, and rejected based on what one has "learned through social interaction." The endless string of actions that one must perform in the "ceaseless process of coming out," "seek[ing] out the company of other gay people for purposes other than sex," and one's "interactions with [one's] environment" all posit gay identity as something one makes and maintains, rather than simply has. Yet that definition can hardly satisfy John, either, since it reverts to dumping upon him the "baggage of freedom of choice."

Ultimately, what is frustrating for John about the creation of this text is the key to its heuristic value: definition is impossible, since meaning appears to be indeterminate. Yet living in a world of socially inscribed meanings deployed as capsules with definite parameters, John will be vulnerable if he does not find some provisional meaning of "gay" with which to rebut homophobic definitions. He has in effect hiked to what must feel like land's end of both epistemological theory and social exigency. The resulting impasse is a painful one; yet out of it rise some of the most critical questions of gay life in the postmodern era. Standing there, John is in a position to confront these questions. He has written himself, however uncomfortably, out of the naïve belief that agency is simple and toward a deeper understanding of language's refusal to cooperate with the drive toward stability and coherence. From this understanding a new kind of agency becomes possible—a kind that is more aware of its own discursive nature, and that can thus self-consciously use discourse to manipulate cultural capital.

The relevance of John's suggestion that people who belong to domi-nant groups stand to benefit from reflection about the meanings they create through those identities is borne out when I cross-reference his writing in response to one particular assignment with that of several white students. The assignment was to pick one piece of AIDS activist art reproduced in the book *AIDS Demo Graphics* and analyze it, explain-ing whether or not it is effective in ACT UP's attempt to "confer a new kind of power." (The quotation is taken from a longer one by art historian John Berger which was used to frame the assignment.) John was one of several students among my two classes who chose a poster with a headline in large bold letters at the top that said "AIDS: 1 in 61" (see Appendix). In the space immediately below the headline on the right half of the page is a picture of a doll, its arms and legs helplessly splayed and partly ensconsed in its own shadow. On the left side, across from the doll, is written:

> One in every sixty-one babies
> in New York City is born with AIDS
> or born HIV antibody positive.
>
> So why is the media telling us
> that heterosexuals aren't at risk?
>
> Because these babies are black.
> These babies are Hispanic.
>
> **Ignoring color ignores the facts of AIDS.**
> **STOP RACISM: FIGHT AIDS.**

Below this text is the same text translated into Spanish.

Although several white students wrote enthusiastically about this poster and its power to educate, John, in his paper called "ACT UP: Do the White Thing," is the only one who sees racist biases embedded in the poster itself. The following are selected passages from his text:

> The poster raises the issue that almost anyone can be infected with HIV while focusing on Blacks, Hispanics, women, children, and ra-cism. Conspicuously absent in the poster's message are heterosexual whites. Although the message is the equation of AIDS with racism, the subtext is that white heterosexuals need not worry about AIDS or passing it on to their children.
>
> *1 in 61* amplifies the indisputable fact that the AIDS crisis is laden with racism. The correlation is crystalline in the poster: "Ignoring color ignores the facts of AIDS. STOP RACISM: FIGHT AIDS." The first

sentence makes a salient point: that AIDS is inexorably linked to race. But, the second sentence makes an offensive generalization that could only be made by someone with little experience of racism. AIDS is important, but to say that stopping AIDS will stop racism is to belittle what racism is and how it affects people of color. **AIDS may be racism but racism is not AIDS.** I wonder how a group of gay white men can in good conscience call on others to stop racism when racism goes unchecked within the gay community. "STOP RACISM: FIGHT AIDS" illustrates the depths of gay white male insensitivity toward people of color, women, and children on AIDS issues. The word racism is used here without any concept of what it means or implies. The poster's creators further demonstrate their ignorance and insensitivity toward people of color by using an Anglo doll as a symbol for Black and Hispanic children lost to AIDS. Apparently, it did not occur to the designers that a white doll might be out of place in a message about Black and Hispanic people. The same ignorance seems to have led the poster's creators to believe that printing a message in Spanish is enough to demonstrate an interest in the Hispanic community. Inclusion, involvement, and an understanding and appreciation of unfamiliar cultures: none of these elements seemed to enter the minds of ACT UP/Gran Fury, or to have gone into the *1 in 61* poster.

It is no surprise then that this poster is not really directed at the communities it invokes. . . . This poster is a response in a discussion exclusively between white people about racism and AIDS: no people of color are involved, invited or included. . . . [T]he poster is simply another tool employed by whites to provoke other whites to guilt. Just think about it. How many ACT-UPers (gay middle-class white men) actually interact regularly with "young minority-group women"? Where would these women come across these posters? Were contingents of wheatpasters sent out to Williamsburg? Bushwick? Brownsville? or Castle Hill? Would these posters really be effective in inspiring people of color to think about AIDS?

Hearing John's text for the first time in a small peer-group workshop, I was jolted into realizing my own misreading of the poster. Each of the many times I had seen it, I had unconsciously edited the line "STOP RACISM: FIGHT AIDS" to read "STOP RACISM! FIGHT AIDS!" Switching the colon between the exhortations to an exclamation point, I had managed to avoid negotiating with the simplistic causal relationship set up there: that fighting AIDS will stop racism. None of the white students who analyzed the poster had noticed anything wrong with the logic suggested there, nor had they noticed the incongruity of the blond baby doll. Perhaps because the creators of the poster unwittingly fashioned the wrong audience for it, that "wrong audience" constituted the group who accepted the message it purveyed, while John, a member of a group discussed in the poster (a group for whom he sees its message ostensibly intended), automatically used his vantage point from within that community to deconstruct the poster. "I really kept getting back to how people are defined" he says of his work on that paper. "And how when other people define you, you're living by their definition, which can be totally ridiculous."

He feels that this matter of definition has grown, for him, from being a purely textual matter to one that translates into action outside the classroom. "I've noticed that I've started to be really adamant about not being defined by other people, and about setting my own definition for myself, and letting other people's definitions work for themselves, and not ascribing to someone else's definition. Lately I've been prone to say, when someone says, 'They say this, they say that'—'Who's they? Tell me, who specifically are you speaking about?' Which is something I didn't do before I started to write in here. And I think this has given me, actually, a better means of being an activist than I had before. Because I'm probably a better writer/activist than actually going out and organizing a demonstration."

Chapter Eleven

Mary Donoghue
"Let's Assume These Things Are True"

Mary Donoghue is a drama major at Cosmopolitan University who has just completed her freshman year. An eighteen-year-old of Catholic, predominantly Irish American background, she grew up in a Virginia suburb of Washington, D.C., where most people's livelihoods were tied to the government, primarily through the military. Her father, a C.P.A. who has been self-employed for the past six years, has a client roster primarily of businesses with government contracts; her mother, who has a high school diploma with some secretarial school and college, works for a computer firm that also does government contracting. Mary describes her family as upper-middle-class now, after having navigated the pathways of upward mobility through her childhood, and "more on the liberal Catholic side." Her father has grown increasingly religious with age, and she says that his two basic tenets are "Don't mess with family" and "Don't mess with religion." Her brother, who is three years older, has declared himself an atheist, and Mary, bisexual and not yet out to her family, observes that "he's messed with religion, I've messed with family." The family is pro-choice—the mother more vociferously so than the father—and Mary sees most of her other relatives split on the abortion question along gender lines. Mary at this point considers herself "just not Catholic," explaining that she is "more spiritual than religious" and that "Catholicism is like a cultural thing." Though her parents both consider themselves heterosexual, she can imagine her mother "maybe having been a dyke if she'd grown up in a different time and not in a military family."

Mary describes her experiences with writing throughout elementary and junior high school as "bad" and "boring": "You put a thesis sentence, and then after that you put the three ways in which you're going to try to prove it. It was just like, why am I writing this, when everyone is turning in the exact same thing?" She says that writing "has kind of been like a recovery since then." In high school she was introduced to freewriting and forms of composing that felt like "less of a nightmare." In her first-term college freshman writing workshop, the class was allowed to write essays that "could be more personal. . . . I started paying more attention to the language, and it was kind of like the difference between writing a play and writing a medical journal. You can say the same thing, but with a play, it's how you say it, while with a medical journal it's just that you *do* say it."

Mary remembers only one or two vague academic references to homosexuality in all her years of school before college—a brief mention that Oscar Wilde was gay and that a writer might be talking about a gay experience in a literary passage. "It wasn't like people would even make negative comments, most of the time—because no one would say anything. So anything you thought of was something you thought of on your own, and it was something that you had to pick up from pieces of things and put together." She heard occasional references to "fags" and "fairies," but she had the impression that they were fairly benign, and her understanding of them was fragmentary at best. "I thought 'fairy' was just an effeminate man. I had *no* idea that it was a *gay* man—a man who loved other men." She recalls other students misreading poems in order to de-gay them—for example, assuming that a male writer was making a literary choice to take on the persona of a woman rather than that he was a man writing love-texts to another man. She herself never wrote anything about being gay "because it just wasn't something you wrote about" and because she vaguely sensed that the teacher might feel put on the spot, as if required to "do" something.

Midway through high school, Mary found out that her best friend was exploring coming out. She, that friend, and another female friend decided to go to the senior prom together—"We went as dates, but we weren't lovers." Nevertheless, they enjoyed spooking the rest of the crowd of graduating seniors with a bit of lesbian performance: "We were being cute with each other, and we were goofing around, and we'd give each other little kisses and stuff." She feels that they were given some license for such behavior because they were by then known around school as "art people" whose eccentricity was explainable and tolerated. They relied on that explanation to a large extent themselves, the women speaking with studied sophistication about gay men but never about lesbians "because that was kind of maybe hinting that you *were* a lesbian." Among the art crowd it was also popular to hypothesize that everyone might be capable of having sex with different genders, though they were always quick to add, "But I've never done it!" "Everybody was sort of feeling out the territory," which involved experimenting with ambiguous self-descriptive language as well as sexual practice. By the end of her senior year there was a chain reaction of people in her crowd saying to each other, "I think I'm bi," although that referred more to "experiences" than "relationships." Almost no one was out to their parents; the one friend who did come out to his family had an initially easy time of it, though his parents began trying to constrict his activities as time went by, and his grandfather "tried to rent him a hooker."

In her first-term college freshman writing workshop, the instructor did mention homosexuality, but, Mary felt, rather awkwardly—"I think a lot of it was, he didn't want to seem too queer-positive because then people might think he was gay"—and it seemed to her that he and the other students quickly retreated to casually mentioning their girlfriends or boyfriends when the subject came up. She is quick, though, to point out that it isn't only heterosexuals who struggle with discussing gay topics in public forums: "Even with gay people, when they say, 'Oh, I'm gay,' the word kind of gets swallowed, like sucked back into you." Mary didn't consider the students in the class to be "violently" homophobic, but felt that they did see gays as negatively marked figures. "There was nothing blatant like 'Let's go kill all those faggots' kind of remarks, but just remarks like, 'Well, I don't think gay people should get to have equal status. I don't think they should get to be married and stuff. It's not that I feel it's wrong, it's just not kind of totally normal.' You know, there was just a sense of 'other.' Like, this person is not-me, and even if I know gay people, I'm knowing these people *as* gay people—like, 'my gay friend.' It's not just 'my friend.'"

Because of all these factors, despite some class discussion of homosexuality, she never used it as a topic in her essays, even peripherally, though she notes that she did feel free to write about a male ex-lover. The erasure of that part of her experience disabled her as a writer of other texts, she says, as the course was largely structured around the theme of identity. "I dealt with a lot of other pieces of identity, but when all of that other identity is so influenced by being gay, to not talk about being gay, which is such a huge, huge thing, is just like to ignore the right half of my body." Ultimately, the situation felt paradoxical: the class's homophobic comments silenced her, and in her view that silence allowed them to remain entrenched in their homophobic positions. Looking back, the stasis of their views seems inevitable to her: "How can you expect anyone to ever be comfortable about gay issues and about gay people when the gay person isn't comfortable herself?"

Mary describes herself as "bisexual," her conversation is peppered with the word "gay" in reference to herself and the groups with whom she identifies, yet when asked directly what words best describe her she says she prefers "queer" and "dyke" because they are strong and positive and have political implications. "There's no word for a bisexual woman," she points out. "I've started saying the word 'byke'—like, 'I'm a byke, and this is my friend who's a bag.'" She feels that a tough word like that would be useful because "bisexual women are kind of viewed in the heterosexual community as a neat kind of erotic thing, making them so much more exciting for het men—which totally isn't what it's about." When asked how out she thinks she is on a scale of one to ten, she gives herself a "five or six" in Virginia, because even though she thinks people there "have a good idea," she hasn't "directly said it," and "when you think people have a good idea, it might mean that they have no clue at all." Her New York rating is higher, an eight or a nine, based on a greater number of people to whom she has come out "officially" and others who were more obliquely informed. "I was talking to my roommate about it and I put it in this context—'And since I'm a lesbian, blah blah blah'—and I think it just went totally over her head."

To Mary, anyone's decision not to come out contributes to the promotion of homophobia; yet at the same time she perceives that a lesbian speaker is often unwittingly transformed in her audience's eyes into something that feels untrue and uncomfortable to her. She recalls her own tendency—in the days when she thought of herself as "liberal" rather than "bisexual"—to think when people told her they were gay, "Oh, that's so neat! This is a gay person! How exciting!" Now, that memory helps her to intuit the ways her own discourse may be mentally annotated by outsiders to gay culture. "When you come out, you're taking on all this stuff. You have to deal with the fact that when you say 'I'm gay,' to you it's really a casual thing and it's part of what you are, but for everyone around you, chances are it's going to be some big, huge deal. And when you're talking about your lover, people are not going to be going along with what you're thinking, like—'Oh, my lover and I went and got coffee yesterday and we were talking about the weather.' They're going to be thinking stuff like 'Lover—lover—lover' and 'Gay—gay—gay.'" Likewise, she perceives the defensiveness behind enthusiastic fetishizing. "Even if it's like, 'Wow, that's so exciting for you to be gay!' it's still a distancing thing, like—'It's so great that *you* can be gay.'"

During the same period that Mary felt silenced in her first writing workshop, she found the courage to experiment with gay themes when she directed scenes in her theatre studio workshop. "I was the first one in my group to do a gay scene. I got these really homophobic men to do it because I wanted to make them do it. And they did. And they dealt with it—better than I expected them to. But at the same time there was that whole, like, after the scene is done you have to readjust and talk about your girlfriend. That happened after every single gay scene I think the entire year that it was done, there was that readjustment." She found that when she herself projected a sense of being at ease with the material, the actors followed suit. When they protested, she would tell them, "Just pretend it's your girlfriend" or "This is acting. Don't worry, no one's going to actually think you're gay," and she discovered that such assurances and suggestions for translation were effective: "When they did it, there was definitely some nice hot action. It wasn't like this really ginger, afraid thing. It was kind of like an out. Once they knew [that nobody would think they were gay], they could go all out. They could do whatever they wanted." When I ask her how she felt about giving them this kind of direction, she says, "Well, this is the easy way out. But I'm going to give it to them. Because I feel like, when people are first coming out, or even when they're first discovering things about themselves, their tendency is to make excuses—like, 'Oh, but I'm not a gay person. I just had this one experience.' And I kind of felt like, OK, if I give them this excuse that they can use, then maybe that's freeing them up a little more to really explore how they feel." She notes that a virtual avalanche of gay scenes followed in the wake of her own. "At least once a week there was a gay scene. The most homophobic people in the class were directing gay scenes." She feels that part of the reason people felt comfortable doing these scenes was because she, the initiator, was perceived by them at the time to be straight. "It was kind of like, 'Oh, a straight girl's directing these scenes, and no one's assuming *she's* gay, so I guess we can do one, too.' I think it may have thrown them a curveball when I came out, which I did later." She speculates that some of them were interested in experimenting with gay scenes to be liberal, others because they were not out and wanted to be, and others because they were "kind of questioning." Yet everyone ultimately got to play with gay themes and personas under the rubric of the governing tenet "It doesn't mean we're gay."

Mary also noticed in studio that her queer sensibility informed her readings of scenes when she was the audience. She cites as an example an instance in which two women on stage related intimately to each other. The director had, in fact, intended it to be assumed that they were mother and daughter, not considering that this automatic inference required the audience to bracket out the possibility, raised afterward by Mary in a studio workshop discussion, that they could be lovers.

Mary says she realizes that the confidence she feels about her sexual identity in New York, in theatre and art milieus, and in a place like our class where queerness has become incorporated into the sphere of learning can easily fizzle when the context in which she is operating changes. She plans to come out to her parents when she is home in Virginia for the summer, and is sure that "things are going to change drastically. That's the scary part about coming out. I don't know how they're going to react. They're both pretty homophobic, and I know it's not going to be like, 'Oh, yay! Our daughter's gay!'" Her fear is that they will tell her, "You're doing this to get attention. You're just trying to be different. You're just trying to be artsy. You went to New York, and now you're gay." She anticipates this response because "whenever I do anything that they don't like, they assume I've done it to piss them off." She's also sure that they'll believe she's going through a "stage." When they visited her at school several months ago, she kept her pink triangle pinned to her bag and she is "pretty sure" they know what it means.[1] However, when they all attended St. Patrick's Cathedral for Easter services with relatives, she made the decision to take it off. "It felt kind of weird. It was just really uncomfortable. I really didn't want to be taking it off. It was kind of like, 'Why am I doing this?' And I didn't know. But when I had church, my parents, *and* my relatives, then it was kind of like—'OK, I'm going to take this triangle off.'" She feels her parents "sense these things, like where my lines are, and they know which questions not to ask me because they have a pretty good idea of what the answer would be."

Nevertheless, she and her family do engage in abstract ideological arguments about homosexuality which function as rehearsals for the personal confrontation they all sense is coming. Mary tells the story of a discussion they had about a "Family Life" class her brother took at college. According to her brother, several lesbians "disrupted" the class by interrogating the definition of the category "family" and asking the professor where he saw gay people fitting in. Mary's parents concurred with her brother's assessment that the lesbians had been inappropriate and "annoying"; furthermore, her mother surprised her by bringing the subject up again while visiting Mary at school. Mary objected to the portrayal of the lesbians as disruptive on the grounds that "their point of view was not being presented." Her mother countered by saying that "they knew the class was about family life, and they should have known what [the professor] would be talking about."

Such interchanges signal to Mary that planning the coming-out scene will require her appraisal of multiple rhetorical strategies. On the one hand, she envisions simply saying, "It's family talk time, let's all go sit down in the living room and let me come out to you." On the other hand, she imagines spontaneously responding to a homophobic remark by saying, "Oh, really? Because I'm gay." "In a lot of ways, I don't want it to be in that kind of situation," she says, "because if that was the context, it would be like them saying something negative, and me responding. And that will just lead into, 'Oh, you're being a rebel. You're trying to get attention.'" She has similar quandaries about telling them she's bisexual. "I know they'll take that as a way to dismiss the gay side. But at the same time, if I say I'm gay, and then I do later have a relationship with a man, and if I never add the addendum that I'm bi, then they'll think, 'Whew, that was a stage. Thank God she was just being a rebel.' And if I go back to a woman, there'll just be, you know, a total conniption explosion."

Despite the no-win situation she anticipates, she feels better equipped to enter the scene because she is armed with information about others' experiences from a series of coming-out narratives we read in class. "There were all kinds of particular little quotes that I think will come in handy when I'm talking to my parents."

Vaulting Off the Springboard

Mary feels that the sharp focus on language in her first college writing workshop carried over into our class the following term, and partly manifested itself in our looking at the different connotations and uses of words such as "queer," "gay," and "homosexual." The "personal" aspect of writing that she experienced in the first writing workshop also felt amplified here: "These were essays that we could put some of ourselves into, instead of like where, before, it was you never speak in first person, you never mention yourself, you don't ever say what you think, because teachers would say, 'I don't want to know what you think. I want to know how the book works.' Which is—especially with the stuff we talked about in writing workshop this time—you can't. I mean, there's no such thing as writing without yourself. Because you're always—even if it's like a medical journal—in the most clinical writing, you're always there, because everything you've ever done affects your writing and how you look at things."

Many of Mary's observations of her own and others' discourse reflect an awareness of how positioning, timing, subtext, and context function rhetorically. Looking back at the time she was in Writing Workshop I, she sees herself having responded to homophobic remarks only abstractly. "I would say stuff, but always in the third person—'Well, you know a gay person would—' or 'Well, gay people might not feel that way,' 'Gay people have legitimate relationships'—all this stuff. But it was always very removed from me. Like I would never have said, 'Well, listen, I'm queer, and you're homophobic.'" During the second term, though, she feels that her mode of self-presentation changed. For one thing, she carefully recalculated the insertion point of her coming-out statement in conversations with new people. "I used to think that, OK, when I first meet someone I'm not going to tell them I'm gay. I'll get to know them and then I'll tell them I'm gay later, so that way they'll be like, 'Oh, OK, so this person who is my friend is a gay person. I guess that means all gay people are just like normal people.' I mean, part of that was just total internalized homophobia—like, 'I'm not going to tell this person I'm gay until I get to know them because that way it will be easier for them to accept that I'm gay,' when a lot of it was really, 'I don't know this person well enough. I don't want to risk losing their friendship because I'm gay and they're freaked out.'" Or, as she wrote at the end of the term:

> Before I used to say "I don't have to tell this person I'm queer because it shouldn't even be an issue" while I was thinking somewhere in my mind "If I tell this person I am queer s/he may hate me before even getting to know me."

Over the course of the second term Mary became increasingly conscious of the ways she could choose to authorize her own statements, and how the presence or absence of an "I" could alter the way statements were heard and felt. She explains that she used to fear that revealing the gay part of her identity would lead to her being pigeonholed, filed under one heading—"Oh, this is a gay person telling me this. Of course they're going to feel that way." Yet she came to realize that if she omitted the "I," she ceased to command the credibility of a speaking subject. "If I say to someone, 'I'm gay, and this is what I think and feel,' then they can't say, 'Well, I don't think gay people agree with you.' It's like, 'Well, I *am* a gay person and I *do* agree with me.'"

Mary feels that our class offered a different context, conceptually and discursively, than anything she had experienced before for considering the meanings of gayness. "In this class we could explore things—with the readings and with what we wrote—beyond just 'I am gay.' It's like a base that you can shoot off from into other questions, while before it was like trying to put together some kind of a base to even think about these issues. It was like there was nothing to shoot off from." That's why, she explains, "the sense of community I think is a big thing." Had there not been a substantial and visible gay presence in the class, "we would have been just trying to prove that there's such a thing as a gay person. . . . And we could get into politics, and into AIDS activism, but since you don't have any basis for thinking about them, you end up thinking more about the fact that they exist instead of thinking, 'OK, let's say for now, for the context of this conversation, these things are true. Assuming these things are true, what does that mean for everything else we've been talking about?' Like—let's assume that people are somewhat socially constructed. Assuming that, then what does that mean in how the world interprets gay people? Like, if we're socially constructed, then is being gay a choice? And if it's a choice, then is it a political act naturally?"

Much of what Mary says reveals an underlying conviction that possibilities for social and political change are intimately bound up with the rhetorical calculus of audience appraisal, rhetor positioning, and highly context-sensitive textual logic. She imagines, for instance, futile conversations with right-wing homophobes. "If you say a person was born gay, then in their eyes it would be like being born handicapped, because it's something you can't do anything about, and it deserves pity. While if you choose to be gay, or if you're socially constructed to be gay, then it can be like, 'Oh, you social rebels, radical people, choosing to just be difficult.'"

The sense of audience she had in our class, then, was crucial. "A lot of anger and frustration I would be hesitant to express in another class, simply because a lot of people—I don't think they would understand. Or maybe it's not that they wouldn't understand, it's just that it would take so long to explain to them what it's about, and why I'm angry. If I was writing a paper about why gay people should be accepted and why there shouldn't be antisodomy laws, I would cut back on the anger a lot, for fear of alienating people who were reading my paper." Although direct-action groups such as ACT UP and Queer Nation are premised on the open expression of anger and the use of "in-your-face" tactics and *do* alienate many people, she thinks that's OK because their relationship to their audience is significantly different. "With ACT UP and being angry, it's kind of like getting in the faces of people who are not going to otherwise pay any attention to you at all. But I feel like if you've got a paper, or you're talking to someone, this is your opportunity to really convince them, where they're kind of a captive audience—like if they're your teacher, or they're someone you're reading this paper to. With ACT UP, you have to be louder than that, because they're not going to listen to you otherwise. If I read my paper, a calm paper, to twelve million people on the street, they're just going to totally dismiss it, and they can walk by."

Mary feels that having a gay academic community was a unique and critical experience for her. "The fact that we were reading and writing about gay topics legitimized them. When you write about something, and you can read about it in a book, in school, then it makes it more real in a way." Subjecting gay themes to critical academic inquiry in that context gave her writing "a really solid springboard from which I could explore all kinds of other things that I never would have thought about writing about before. Like if I'd written a paper in my other Writing Workshop class, it would have been about *being gay*. I see myself making a lot more statements where I *assume* things like I'm gay and that people tend to be homophobic, but before it would have been like I don't know *why*. A lot of it was the *why*. And [in this class] I kind of started to understand why I was thinking what I was thinking more. And then I could write about it more, and it was more in-depth, instead of just kind of generally what it's like to be gay. It's kind of like my emphasis now is on 'I'm coming out because . . .' instead of 'If I come out . . .'"

The class community was also unique for her in that it allowed for a good deal of gay intertextuality. "It made a big, big difference, the fact that there was this group of people that were bouncing ideas off each other." Mary had believed before in an abstract way that it was useful for both gay and heterosexual people to come in contact with gay-themed work, "but it never totally occurred to me the amount of impact that it would have on other people, seeing my work." In our class, someone might read aloud a text she had written and "it would be something that was either on the border of your mind that hadn't quite solidified yet, or just an idea you hadn't thought of. And someone would say something, and you'd be like, 'Oh, yeah! OK, *that's* what I've been thinking about!' And then in turn, since someone said that, then all of the thoughts that had been surrounding this kind of unsolid thing, you could say to them, and then *they* would be like, 'Oh, yeah! I hadn't thought about that!' And it was just this feeding process. It was really cyclical." Because of the sorts of conversations between texts that occurred in class, as well as impromptu class discussions and assigned readings, she feels that she now writes about gay issues with greater authority. "I had a lot more background, a lot more backup, a lot more support for the things I was saying. It wasn't as vague, and I had a way to say them now that made sense. And I could make sense to these other people."

Looking through her portfolio of work for the whole term, she observes, invoking a theme she seems to keep coming back to, "The overall feeling I have about these papers is that I would never have gotten into this much depth if I was in another class, because I would have been just defending the fact that gay people existed." She also says that in this class "I haven't been running away from topics that I would have avoided in other classes. And now I feel I can go and write in other classes."

Mary repeatedly cites social construction theory as one of the critical factors that shaped the new perspectives, analyses, and modes of reading and writing that she developed in our course. Yet at a certain point in our conversation I begin to sense that her enthusiasm for social construction theory and for lesbian and gay history may in fact be at odds with one another. She speaks of the excitement she felt reading about lesbians in Native American populations and in World War II— "suddenly the world where you just assumed everyone was straight, and you're this weird little pocket, this rare community that happened to be gay" is altered and a different demography becomes conceivable. Yet though the social constructionist historians we read explicitly tried to *dismantle* the popular slogan born out of the euphoria of the early gay liberation movement, "We are everywhere," by showing that the dual concepts of homosexuality and heterosexuality were Western productions of the late nineteenth century, Mary nonetheless exults, "Suddenly when I think about the Puritans, they have this entirely new dimension—like some of these Puritans were gay. Oh my God, how strange. What was it like to be gay when you were a Puritan?"

I confess to her that I'm puzzled about how she reconciles her belief in social construction with her belief in gay Puritans. I tell her, "Most of the historical readings we did claimed that gay identity *didn't* exist in every historical period—for example, the Puritans. That there *weren't* gay Puritans. There might have been people who had feelings towards the same sex, or attractions, or experiences, but they didn't think of calling them 'gay people.'"

She agrees, in part. "I don't think that there were gay people as we know them now in past societies, because there wasn't a community and there wasn't an identity. But at the same time, I kind of feel like some of the things that gay people were feeling then are things that gay people feel now. Just about feeling—I like women. Everyone else around who's a woman likes men. What's that all about?" At the same time, she acknowledges, "I think if I had grown up in the fifties, I wouldn't have been as openly queer as I am now. There's no way. And I think there's a chance that if I was raised in another society, maybe I never would have come out."

I am beginning to understand that she is thinking of behaviorial choices—being "openly" queer, coming out—as the material that society constructs. The meanings of feelings, on the other hand, still seem to be innate and transhistorical in her view. So I press on. "Let's say for Puritans, maybe nobody would have ever said you should marry somebody that you're attracted to. Because you weren't *supposed* to be sexual. You got married because you were an economic unit. Sexuality wouldn't even interfere with that at all. So in a way, I wonder how could the Puritans have had this feeling like, 'Oh, I'm different,' when nobody was supposed to be sexually attracted to anybody anyway."

Mary persists: "Even back then, when there was no one saying, 'You should be sexually attracted to the opposite sex,' I feel like there would still be some kind of feeling like, 'You *should* be'—not really sexually attracted, but—I mean, there were all these love poems and stuff—you should feel some kind of love/lust thing, even if it wasn't in those terms."

I'm still concerned about the role of the observer in all this, and I ask, "But how do we know how much we're projecting from our current perspective? Because when you're in a society where lust is not allowed, and not talked about, you probably don't feel like you're deficient for not lusting after your marital partner."

Mary thinks that this is a good point, but takes it further: "Especially with women. Women weren't supposed to enjoy sex. It was just like a duty for a lot of women. And women who *did* enjoy sex too much a lot of times were thought of as hussies. I guess women would feel different not even because they were attracted to the same sex, but because they were attracted to anyone."

It strikes me that in our conversation Mary is thinking like a social constructionist, in that she searches for evidence of how Puritan women's sense of sexual identity was produced discursively and ultimately revises her hypothesis about what those women "would feel" based on her reassessment of available data about that discourse. At the same time she is, perhaps, *feeling* like a romantic, newly out queer, assigning universal meanings to some of her own subjective experience as a way of legitimizing her own identity. From early gay liberation until now, conceiving affinities of identification across historical and geographic boundaries has provided a reassuring sense of enduring and global gay community, and has been used to refute what "they" have "always" said: that "we" don't exist. Although social constructionists and essentialists have been fashioned as two opposed camps within lesbian and gay studies, I suspect that many of us in fact scramble those perspectives as Mary does, the impetus to dismantle inaccurate categorizations crashing against the yearning to connect and belong. Beyond that, Mary's re-envisioning of history makes me wonder in what ways our students interpret and apply social construction theory that we don't imagine.

Mary has several observations about the heterosexual women in the class and the roles they took. "With Lorna and Pamela—just the fact that both of them used the word 'homosexual' I thought was really interesting. That kind of related back to how there's still that distance between straight people and what they think of gay people. Just the word 'homosexual'—it's really clinical, and the fact that both of them used that, and almost everyone else used 'gay' or 'lesbian' or 'queer'— kind of really stuck out in my mind. It kind of emphasized the fact that I still feel like we're kind of a 'neat thing' to them. And how Pamela was talking about how she 'got to know some gay people.' And I kind of felt like when she was saying that, she was kind of thinking, 'These are my gay friends, these are my straight friends.'"

Yet she says of Lorna, "The fact that she was bulimic—I think that helped her make a lot of connections, too. It was something she understood—what it was like to come out. And although it was a different thing, I think she understood the feeling more about having to tell someone something that they're not going to like, and that to some extent you're a little uncomfortable about telling them, because you don't know how they're going to react, or if they're going to support you."

Mary's observations about Jennifer, the heterosexual student she believes went through the greatest amount of change, are also based on her perception of Jennifer's use of language and her capacity for genuine reflection about issues pertaining to sexual identity. "Jennifer I feel was the most comfortable. Just terminology-wise, I feel like she got more comfortable more quickly. And even the fact that she was saying, you know, 'I started honestly thinking about if I could be attracted to a woman, and I decided that I couldn't'—I feel she was more relaxed about it." Mary had also been impressed by Jennifer's sensitivity to the dynamics between queer and straight people. Mary had described in class an awkwardness she believed existed between straight and lesbian women due to straight women's fear, "Is this woman in love with me?" Mary recalls, "Jennifer said something like, 'Do you think it's less likely for you to make friends with straight women now, because of this tension?' And I was like, 'Wow, that's a really good point!' Because I think to some extent, that's totally right. Just dealing with that is like another thing to have to worry about."

Mary is one of several students who describe the class not simply as a way to learn about their lives, but also as a factor that shaped their lives. One way it did this had to do with the placement of course artifacts in their dormitory rooms—as Jennifer experienced when her friend "read" her room as an indication that she was a lesbian. Mary similarly writes in her "Final Reflections":

> Now being gay is a political issue and a personal identity instead of a personal issue. In other words I am finally comfortable with being gay and when I come out I am not asking for anyone's approval. How has this class helped that? Well even silly things like having gay books around and writing gay papers with my roommate and her friends in the room. I don't carefully put away my books anymore; I leave them on the bed as I do my other books. I wear my T-shirts and my buttons where people can see them. We fags and dykes are real; we have a history and we can be studied in a class at Cosmopolitan.

Mary thinks that in an ideal writing curriculum, "there wouldn't be a gay unit," but instead, "multiculturalism would include queerness." In such courses heterosexuals would learn something new and gays would discover role models. In addition, "students who were gay would become more involved in what they were studying—it would be related to them, not abstracted—just as Black students and students from other groups can relate when their group is included, when what they're learning is not removed from them, but related to their life and how they live, and is something they can take with them when they leave the classroom."

Just as many of the students I interviewed said that this course felt more "personal" to them than their other courses even when they had written about personal experience in those courses, Mary feels that she has "a very personal stake" in queer activism that supercedes her investment in, for example, her work for ecological groups or Amnesty International. "It occasionally hits me that I could be put in jail when I go home to Virginia, for being *me*," she says, referring to the fact that Virginia is one of many states in the U. S. with antisodomy laws. "John D'Emilio says in *Sexual Politics, Sexual Communities* that once you come out, you cross that line, and you're in a place where now you can't really go back. You're in a place where now you've got a commitment to it, because you *have* to fight, because now you're in that kind of danger, that situation where you can't say, 'Oh well, I'm not going to think about it anymore.' Because it's your life."

Queer Positionality and Everyday Speech Acts

When she first came into our class, Mary didn't think her bisexual identity affected her writing. The first week, writing informally and exploratively in response to the question, "How does sexual identity affect us as readers and writers?" she—like many others in the class—focused on "labels" and their consequences. Her text begins with a parody of the standard censuslike autobiographical confession that prefaces many feminist texts.

> As a gay bisexual heterosexual Asian White Black woman man it is easy to become obsessed with labeling instead of finding the meaning behind the labels. Are labels merely convenient ways of giving others a description of personal history in general terms or are they ways to ignore the varied experiences of individuals by clumping them together? If it is assumed that labels or identities were meant only to give a preliminary view of one person to another person, then they are taken as a starting point into another person's history. Often though, they become trapping when mental and emotional characteristics are assigned to each person of a group even if his or her history may have been extremely different. . . .
>
> Also these labels set apart groups from each other often based on physical characteristics while disregarding the hundreds of other bonds

which might make people relate across differences. While labels may give a needed sense of security to some by assigning them to groups with histories and group identities, it also may prove limiting with never allowing or inviting people to explore other sides of themselves. It also may force people into groups which do not fit them as well as other groups of people might. Even when a person voluntarily joins a group she may be pigeonholed into a stereotype. . . .

Later, she illustrates some of the perils of "labeling" in regard to the category "gay":

When writing does this labeling serve to limit the exploration or does it give a basis to question further? . . . Unfortunately because of what society has become the caution often overtakes the curiosity so people never discover the basic similarities which almost all people have. In relation to queerness there is the fear both of the unknown—just of being "gay," the fear of gayness by association, the fear of finding something socially unacceptable within yourself, and also the fear of being hit on. In some heterosexual contexts being hit on is a compliment which may include having to tell someone you are not interested which is not a fun thing to do, but when a heterosexual interprets the actions of a homosexual, whether the heterosexual is just being paranoid or not, as being hit on, the compliment is seen as a threat.

Shortly after, she concludes, "As a writer I have to try to write from more perspectives."

There was a tendency among many of the students at the outset of the course at Cosmopolitan to blame "labels" for prejudice, with the implication that if people could "just stop labeling other people and recognize that people are just people," prejudice would dissolve. "Labeling" was regarded suspiciously as an unwelcome stamp of identity imposed from outside, like a yellow star or a pink triangle in Nazi Germany—something designed to brand a person, evacuate her complexity, and draw a strict circle around her locus of movement in the world. It suggested predetermination, denial of three-dimensionality, and a fencing off of other parts of one's personhood. The source of the danger seemed primarily to be mainstream society, but many also perceived it to be identity-based groups themselves who sometimes deployed homogenizing discourses to ensure the solidarity of their members. There was a sense, then, that liberating people from their "labels" would make them full-fledged, holistically actualized and respected beings. People would enjoy greater mobility, fulfillment, and agency as unmarked wholes, unfettered by pesky parts which would always be vulnerable to forces of bigotry, repression, manipulation, and false representation. Mary was unusual in her willingness to consider that "labeling" might actually serve some provisional heuristic purpose by providing "a basis to question further." That is, it could serve in a "preliminary" and "convenient" way to delineate a "starting point" from which one could identify categories of experience that might more easily submit to examination and generate different forms of knowledge. Yet the ending of this text suggests that she, too, feels that any particular viewpoint will dead-end in limited insight, as if the democracy of "more perspectives" is not only readily available, but constitutes an authentically objective view and an antidote to writing from within the myopic and totalitarian confines of one's own positionality.

Often students in mainstream classes who write about the need to embrace "more perspectives" approach the project from pluralist or relativist impulses. They are willing to grant the abstract fairness of "one opinion, one vote" in electing what will count as truth (generally when the subject is one that has no life-or-death significance for them), or else they graciously experiment with decentering their own "viewpoint" as the "open" or "interesting" thing to do. But there remains a big difference between the adventure of peering through perspectives that one would barely have imagined existed because one's own perspective is so ubiquitously reflected that it appears universal, and the sometimes desperate maneuver of those perennially "pigeonholed into a stereotype" to demonstrate that they are whole enough to transcend their particularity. The latter is frequently the social requirement and thus the breathless enterprise of the doubly conscious (those in our society who, ironically, have *most* transcended particularity). A project of our class, then—and one that is suggested by Mary's text—was to figure out what might be intellectually valuable and socially important about queer subjectivity. This involved conceiving of it not only as something affixed *upon* oneself, delimiting one's agency—the "label" model—but as something constructed *by* oneself that buttressed one's agency by generating new forms of knowledge. As the term went on and queerness began to seem (in the words of many of them) like a "legitimate" player in the sphere of academic inquiry because of the many published books, articles, and essays that they read (as well as because of their own writing and discussions in the class), Mary did drop her use of the word "label" and began to employ concepts like "identity" to discuss marginally situated subjectivities. This switch in fact gave her the tools to more effectively pursue her legitimate concern with issues of difference and conformity among oppressed groups.

Mary feels that she made choices to write essays on particular topics in our class because they were "really relevant" to things she was experiencing and thinking about. She mentions an essay that she wrote toward the end of the course that was an analysis of a piece of AIDS activist graphic art entitled "RIOT" (see Appendix). Though she wasn't particularly enthused about the poster "graphic-wise," she selected it from among many others because she felt it offered rich possibilities for answering the assignment—which involved interrogating the forms and notions of power that the poster attempted to address and represent. In the poster, which is deliberately derivative of Robert Indiana's 1966 pop art sculpture "LOVE," the letters of the word "RIOT" are robustly drawn, the first two perched atop the latter two; above them is written "STONEWALL '69," below them, "AIDS CRISIS '89."

"Stonewall was born out of the frustrations of a small band of drag queens prompted to action by the police," Mary writes in her paper. The situation involved some "ironic humor because of the fact that drag queens were winning in a battle to evade trained police." This irony, she writes, is "the precedent of the gay rights movement." Intrigued by the notion of a riot partly because she had never seen one, she decided to make her final research paper a comparison of the Stonewall Rebellion and queer and AIDS activism as she knows them today. In her text, called "Queer Activism: In the Tradition of Stonewall," she argues that "although the Gay Liberation Front no longer exists, the impact that Stonewall and the organization of the newborn movement had can still be seen in the tactics of queer street activism today in an evolved form."

"Evolved" is the key word here, since her text also employs a crucial distinction: "Stonewall was a spontaneous explosion of rage and frustration, while groups like ACT UP and Queer Nation are organized expressions of rage and frustration." She catalogues some of the attributes of that "organization": legal demonstrations, training in safe civil-disobedience techniques in which the likely consequences of such tactics are clearly explained to participants, regular meetings in well-publicized locations, graphic arts teams whose job it is to produce information in a compelling and persuasive way for nonmembers, committees to work on specific focus areas, public education, and direct confrontation of appropriate parties in the government and business sectors. Yet, she recognizes, such a planned and reasoned response was not possible at Stonewall: "Activism fits the circumstances in which a group exists and then when the group sees that traditional methods of protest do not work for it, then it must find an alternate method by which to be heard."

She draws on the printed account of Bob Moss, an eyewitness to Stonewall who lived just across Christopher Street and was sitting on his roof having drinks with friends when the disturbance started. As bottles started to be thrown at the police, they mistook Moss's party for the perpetrators and began to bang on the door of his building. "In the eyes of many people," Mary writes,

> whether or not Mr. Moss and his friends had thrown the bottle was irrelevant, since many people believe that if someone is gay, that is enough of a reason to beat them up. Circumstances such as these, which commonly explain the situation in which gay people lived and to a large extent still live, in which you are assumed to be guilty because you are gay, call for nonconventional action in order to combat the situation gay people are placed in by society.

Later on she writes:

> In the words of Mr. Moss, "They were just queens. They weren't political." However, any group becomes political when it reaches a line of human pride over which it refuses to be pushed. When the people at Stonewall Inn were assaulted by the police, it happened to be at a moment when people were tense enough because of constant injustice that any incident would have set them off. Quite often the incident which sets off a riot is not at all the reason for the riot, but is instead an example of what happens all of the time to an oppressed group of people. Even if the police had not invaded Stonewall Inn on June 27, 1969, an incident like Stonewall would have happened eventually simply because no group will stand oppression forever.

In our interview, Mary pointed out that immediately after she had struggled, through the course of writing two drafts of this paper, to understand the social and psychological forces that had produced a riot some years before she was born, the riots in Los Angeles in the wake of the first Rodney King verdict occurred. "All the stuff I'd been writing about became really real," she said. "[Stonewall was] about people reaching a frustration level, and having to do stuff that they wouldn't have otherwise done. And then, the Rodney King riots happened, where people were just pushed too far. Of course, there are going to be people who take advantage of the fact that there's a riot going on and go like, oh, isn't this a great place to steal stuff. You know, there's some of that thrown into any riot. But people don't have any faith in what the government's doing anymore—and it's just so ironic that President Bush is sitting on his little TV, talking about, you know, 'Let's go back to the due process of law.' While—why did this riot happen? Why did this whole thing start?" Amazed by the government's conundrum-like rhetorical strategy in addressing the L.A. crisis—i.e., urging faith in a justice system whose very failure fueled the despair that unleashed the riots—Mary perceived a relationship to the official rhetoric of the AIDS crisis, where prolonged government indifference and inaction have provoked the fury of people with AIDS: "—and then these token gestures that politicians make, like, 'Oh, we're doing something, we care, really.'"

Mary says, "To have [the L.A. riots] happen right after [my paper], it was easier to understand why things happened at Stonewall, and what it was actually like to be at Stonewall. It made more sense. If I went back and rewrote that paper, I would emphasize the parallels a lot more between the levels of frustration that are here now and the level of frustration that was at Stonewall. Because it makes sense to me now, these people have been putting up with all of these police raids and people getting these bashings and everything, and no one could do anything about it—you know, you can't go to the police with it back in 1969, because they're going to be, like, 'You deserved it.'"

As I read over Mary's texts and the transcript of her interview, it seems to me that she is preoccupied above all else with the ways that manifestations of justice and human dignity are essentially speech acts, created and impeded by rhetoric and the interpretive frameworks which contain them. In 1969, there was no accessible response to gay bashing except "You deserved it"; in 1992, though gay bashing continues to exist, there are gay citizens' patrols, antiviolence organizations, and hate crimes bills that recast it (or "relabel" it) as "homophobic" and a "bias crime." The president says about AIDS, "We're doing something," or about Rodney King, "Let's go back to the due process of law," and an "official" policy has been enacted, contrary actions notwithstanding. The strength and "precedent" of the gay rights movement is that it is built on a critical "irony"—that of seemingly powerless drag queens "winning in a battle to evade trained police." For Mary, the language of the political moment—the enunciation of who has power and who doesn't, of who acts and who does not act—*is* the political moment; there is no stepping outside it. Political change means linguistic change and the concomitant production of new knowledge; empowerment entails creating a new discourse within which to fashion and position yourself.

It seems to me that way before social construction theory came along and "explained" to Mary how knowledge is made, she was interested in playing with social signifiers and choreographing provocative rhetorical moments. I think of her adventure at the high school prom, disrupting the eternal Noah's ark-like symmetry of conventionally gendered pairs; or her deft direction of homosexually panicked men in gay theatre scenes; or her invention of new hybrid words like "byke" and "bag" to provide hip, affirming slang for semantically neglected bisexuals. I think, too, of her astuteness in detecting the play of meanings in everyday speech acts: her sense of the power of speaking in the first person rather than in the third; her observation that students in mainstream classes found it easier to mentally put literary

narrators through sex-change operations than to entertain the notion
of a gay poem; her perception that students in her first writing workshop manifested their low-level homophobia through a conceptualization of gays as "not-me" or Other; her awareness that in the simple
utterance, "My lover and I went and got coffee yesterday," the word
"lover" will be disproportionately foregrounded in a homophobic context, in effect abducting the meaning from the purpose the lesbian
speaker had intended.

I remember that in the early days of the semester, someone commented that all the men in the class were gay and all the women were
straight—as no woman, besides me, had come out, and I as the teacher
apparently didn't count. Mary looked at the speaker evenly and said,
"What makes you assume that all the women here are straight?"
Afterward, she identified herself as bisexual, but the effect of responding in the form of a question, rather than with an immediate correction, was to highlight for the rest of the class that their perceptual
apparatus was programmed to a default setting, assuming heterosexuality unless specifically told otherwise. It was a tactic she employed on
other occasions, too—not to be coy or didactic, I felt, but to make public
utterances of questions provoked for her by the ordinary interactions
of everyday life. In other words, it seemed to me that Mary recognized
the ways she herself functioned as a social signifier, and rather than
simply avoiding or bluntly refuting these encounters with alien productions of her "self," she chose to exploit them for the rhetorical
insights they offered. One day she described for the class how she
perceived men with whom she interacted changing in response to the
information that she was bisexual; another time she observed that
many people are afraid to entirely purge their discourse of homophobic
assumptions out of fear that they will be perceived as gay; and on
another occasion she hypothesized that women often speak from their
throats—when in fact their voices are "naturally" fuller and from a
lower register—in unconscious acquiescence to social mandates for
acceptable feminine behavior. In all these cases, she was revealing an
awareness of how we position ourselves through our habitual and
occasional speech acts, and the ways we are constantly reading and
writing ourselves in a variety of social scripts.

Mary greatly contributed, then, to what I have described as the
"inside/outside the classroom" dialogic which was a highly significant
part of the process of both classes. She brought her rhetorical readings
of interpersonal dynamics into the classroom; and there was also much
that she clearly needed to take out. Like many of the younger students,
she was especially on the alert for those "particular little quotes that
. . . will come in handy" at the emotionally laden moment of coming

out to her parents. Her portrayal of her family's dispute over her brother's college course on "Family Life" suggests many of the difficulties she will have to rhetorically navigate when that moment comes. Although ostensibly arguing the distanced and "academic" question of exactly what is contained within the definition of "family life," the challenge to the notion of "family" is, of course, particularly potent for this family, which is using theoretical discussion and representative others to camouflage its desperate sparring over its own self-definition. Mary, unready at this point to come out to them and tangibly symbolize a new dimension of "family," knows—and is frustrated—that she lacks the agency to rupture the seamlessness of their definition, whose hegemonic power lies in its very claim to self-evidence—in her mother's words, "They [the 'disruptive' lesbians] knew the class was about family life." Similarly, the nuclear family—*the* nuclear family and Mary's particular nuclear family—will not register Mary's language and relegates it to a place beyond the perimeters of discourse. In the terms that Mary has established in reference to her classroom utterances, to speak with an "I"—"I *am* a gay person"—would recast her own biological nuclear family as a site of contestation by problematizing its borders and dismantling its premises: "If I am a gay person and this is a family, then gay people *do* exist within 'family life' and should be considered legitimate parts of its discourse." Of course, the act of reifying "the family" generally entails refuting one of the premises upon which that syllogism is built—either "You're not really gay" or "Then you're not part of this family"—possibilities which have foreclosed upon many a coming-out statement. The power of the family is maintained through the forms of representation it chooses; if Mary is sufficiently intimidated by the cultural power her family enjoys from its representation of itself, her own critical task of self-representation may be subverted and her gay identity will carry no symbolic value in that domain.

This, I think, was a major project for Mary in our class: to register her symbolic value in public and private domains by learning to use language and knowledge in new ways. Just as Adrian longed to get beyond the need to "justify" his life to those who would contest its legitimacy, Mary too has emotional, intellectual, and political yearnings to move beyond "just trying to prove that there's such a thing as a gay person" and establish "a base that you can shoot off from into other questions." Speaking of the conceptual and historical artifacts of queer existence that are usually invisible to the naked eye of mainstream society, Mary said in our interview, "OK, let's say for now, for the context of this conversation, these things are true. Assuming these things are true, what does that mean for everything else we're talking about?" Cutting her way through the rhetorical jungle of the homophobic

Part Five

Conclusion

Chapter Twelve

Queering the Brew

Much of this book has been about the experience of students' textual reorientation from mainstream contexts of learning to the highly unusual milieu of a lesbian- and gay-themed writing class. I realize that such a scenario may seem rarefied and off the beaten track for many teachers of writing who may have simply wondered how to be more lesbian- and gay-inclusive in their mainstream classes. Yet I hope what has been portrayed here does serve to address that need by illustrating the limited usefulness of "inclusion" as generic, if well-intentioned, practice. That is, I hope I have shown that mere "inclusion," which is widely practiced as the incorporation of material about one more social group into a smorgasbord of diversity to be "celebrated," renders impossibly simple the experience of the margin, which is a site both of annihilation and actualization, of disempowerment and electrifying resistance.

What I am suggesting in place of "inclusion" is a pedagogy that takes into account the often very *un*celebratory conditions which underwrite the exclusion one is trying to cancel. Whether or not one will actively participate in changing those conditions will depend on the interest, energy, and commitment of whoever is doing the investigating; but at the very least, such inquiry may produce an appreciation of how complex, risky, difficult, and often even outright paradoxical or counterproductive it is for someone on a social margin to take up residence at the center of a structure where her subjectivity is unrecognized and, as a result, her capacity to exercise her talents is diminished. The sort of pedagogy I am proposing would entail thinking about the ways margins produce not only abject outsiderhood but also profoundly unique ways of self-defining, knowing, and acting; and about how, though people usually want to leave the margins, they *do* want to be able to bring with them the sharp vision that comes from living with friction and contradiction. Writers who are marginally situated need to know that readers located within dominant discourses have some apparatus for recognizing them, for hearing and *utilizing* the note of dissonance that they may introduce into commonsensical language.

Chuck Schuster, a composition colleague who lives in Milwaukee, has told me of an "old Milwaukee expression" he once heard from a beermaker. When a brewer says that something "queers the brew" he means that for some reason the brewing process goes awry, and he has to throw out the beer. There is no doubt that whatever "queers the brew" is not regarded very affectionately by the brewer—and the etymology of the expression is probably just as homophobic as one would imagine it to be. Yet there is something I like about this expression. If "queering" means having the power to disrupt by the sheer force of weirdness, if it means that one anomalous ingredient can completely alter the quality of an old, standard recipe, then I suspect that it has a usefulness which the brewer—who is concerned with making and selling beer, not with analyzing its capacity to be alchemized into some other, perhaps even more valuable, substance—has overlooked.

Lesbian and gay writers—like other marginalized peoples—have the capacity to "queer" the master narratives of our culture simply by throwing their unexpected presences loudly into the brew. By claiming public discursive space in which to compose representations of themselves, they change the nature of that space for everyone who inhabits it. As William Cook (1993) has put it, when marginalized subjects attempt to "read, write, and speak the texts of our culture" they need not "approach them as closed systems, that is, as spaces already covered with the inscriptions of others" (24). Unlike "Ralph Ellison's nameless protagonist in *Invisible Man* . . . [who] is nameless because he refuses to wrest the act of naming away from others"—who "writes and speaks on the line, on the white line, and seems to have no conception in his early life that there are spaces left above and below that line, spaces which are available for his own appropriation" (18–19)—those who willfully queer the brew know their power to mutate public spaces. As teachers, we will inevitably react to this potency; we may embrace new ways of intoxicating the imagination, or, like the brewer, we may throw the whole brew out and try once more to replicate old, distilled formulas. We must remember that "inclusion" itself doesn't indicate that the brew is queered; queering comes from the possibility that alien discourses will not only, like silent partners, *be* in the brew, but will *reconstitute* it as an altogether new concoction. As I suggested in Chapter 4, it is possible to "include" new discourses and yet simultaneously deny the tensions that exist around their proximity and their competing claims for territorial definition. Naming and engaging with these tensions is what sparks the chemical reaction that ineluctably queers the brew.

The classes I have described in this book were structured to facilitate that sort of queering. These classes didn't meet, in John Mayher's (1990) terms, the "common sense" objectives of current-traditional composition practice, which is about the teaching of forms abstracted from the charged personal and political content of students' daily lives. Neither did they quite resemble many alternative models of writing pedagogy with which I am familiar: they didn't consciously foreground the process of "teaching students how to write" by supplying them with strategies such as freewriting, peer review, and revision, but rather made these strategies implicit, employing them in the service of a particular "content" that made them indispensable. They didn't invite students to simply "express" their feelings and opinions in an uninhibited "natural flow" of ideas; on the contrary, anything that felt "natural" was systematically subjected to scrutiny, probed to unearth its roots in culture and discourse and tested against experience. The classes even broke with conventional liberatory pedagogy, which is usually concerned with empowering students to recognize and challenge economic inequality and the systems that perpetuate it. The closest models I can think of for these classes are feminist classrooms and that small but growing number of composition classes informed by cultural studies.[1] Lesbian and gay studies classrooms themselves are ambiguous models, since most of those I have known of have been more traditionally concerned with the acquisition of knowledge, rather than the production of knowledge, and have not foregrounded the relationship between class product and process.[2]

It certainly made "uncommon sense" to me to use sexual identity as the thematic basis of a writing class. It has abstractly become "common sense" wisdom to try to get students to write about things they "care about." Yet, as my student Adrian put it, this often means writing about "a childhood experience on your bicycle or something like that." It is without doubt more "uncommon" to ask students to write about the dangerous, forbidden, yet consuming things they care about, like sexuality—and even more "uncommon" to have students write about "uncommon" forms of sexuality. "Classes that were saying, on the surface, go in and look at yourself, really didn't reflect that," said Adrian. "The one place where you could really explore continued to be a place that was just—not there."

Rhetorical Knowledge

After I taught the classes and interviewed the students in my study, I realized that there was a particular rhetorical significance to these students' experience of living as lesbians and gay men in homophobic culture. Dealing in myriad situations with issues of secrecy, conceal- ment, and disclosure, as well as anticipating the consequences of dis- closure, strategizing how to time and pitch utterances that might reveal something about themselves to various others, trying to figure out appropriate circumstances for revealing or concealing different sorts of information—all of these things have produced a form of rhetorical self-consciousness that is a very frequently utilized instrument in these students' lives. Obviously, everyone is involved in some way with fashioning their self-presentation to the world, and anyone who lives with any sort of social stigma or occupies a socially subjugated space is going to inevitably become more involved than people in socially dominant positions will with decisions about how to present herself, because her stigmatization or subjugation has raised the stakes of what she says and how she behaves. For lesbians and gay men, the issue of self-presentation is heightened because the dual options of coming out or not present themselves numerous times every day; each time the benefits of coming out have to be weighed against the benefits of concealment, and an array of factors have to be quickly assessed in order for that decision to be made. These factors include sizing up one's audience, appraising the various ideologies at play in a situation, con- sidering alternatives, deciding what kind and what degree of danger or reward is involved, and taking measure of one's own capacities at the moment. The notion of choice is key here, and can mainly be compared to the experience of ethnic minorities or certain gender transgressors involved in the phenomenon of "passing." Lesbians and gay men repeatedly find themselves in the position of taking this inventory and making the subsequent choice to come out or not, with all that either choice entails. Further, they not only decide how to present informa- tion *about* themselves, but *to* themselves, since internalized homopho- bia usually plays a significant role even in the private thought of lesbians and gay men.

For example, in my interview with my student Tina I asked her how "out" she would rate herself on a scale of one to ten. She gave herself a very high rating—9.8. She noted with some amusement that her *intentional* acts of being out often spilled over into realms and situations where she had not consciously prepared to come out. She pointed, for example, to the T-shirt she was wearing at the time of the interview, which said, "BLACK LESBIAN AND GAY PRIDE DAY. PRIDE=POWER. WASHINGTON, D.C." and which bore silhouettes of, as she said, "supposedly identifiable African American people."

"I'm wearing this T-shirt," Tina explained, "and I live in a very Black, working-class neighborhood right now, and I was walking along the street where there were these young men hanging out, and I was going into the cleaners on my way over here and—and I totally forgot I had it on." To walk around with print emblazoned on one's clothing and to lapse into forgetfulness about its presence is to enter potentially dangerous rhetorical (and thus, physical) territory. Tina was aware that her T-shirt would command sharply different responses in the various social spaces she inhabited, as shifting and unpredictable audiences encountered it. Political messages on clothing—principally in the form of T-shirts and buttons—often function as compasses pointing to kindred folk in an otherwise murky, unmarked world. For instance, another lesbian on the street spotting Tina's T-shirt might point and give her the thumbs-up sign or a raised fist, or comment suggestively, "I like your T-shirt," or engage in sexually provocative eye contact. Such T-shirt messages are intended, in other contexts, to be transgressive, literally "telling" people outside the community something they may not know or even wish to hear. Bearing the message in such a context is often said to serve a "political purpose"—which may involve education, confrontation, or militant assertion.

The concept of "gay pride" assertively inverts the prevailing pre-Stonewall assumption of "gay shame"; likewise, "power" preempts the "powerlessness" that served as the fulcrum of repressive practices in preliberation homophobic culture. While we are tacitly to understand that "SHAME=POWERLESSNESS" was the formula that guaranteed queer submissiveness in such a culture—and the absence of any T-shirt bearing such a statement ratified the message (as Foucault says, silence *is* a discourse)—"PRIDE=POWER" is in-your-face metacommentary: "By being proud enough to tell you, a stranger, that I'm gay, I have power." Yet Tina, forgetting that her sheer physical/textual presence "spoke" to all passersby, was startled by her sudden consciousness that she had borne her message out of the zone of her assumed audience—where her intentionality gave her some control over resulting interactions—and into one in which she might be frighteningly *out* of control. "Very Black, working-class neighborhood" was her shorthand for a world at counterpart with the "queer" world where she purchased the T-shirt—where, although many people might also be Black and working-class, words like "lesbian" and "gay" had a radically different valence. Yet because she belonged to both these communities, she was continually crossing borders, negotiating perilous shifts in social meanings.

"It goes back and forth," Tina said. "I mean, there were times when I'd sit on the train and read newspapers and magazines that have 'gay, lesbian, dyke, faggot' written all over them, and be OK, but you know, other times when I'm aware of the violent potential—I'll continue reading it, but I'm very self-conscious about it." Tina's awareness of the way her own intended meanings reshaped themselves vis-à-vis different audiences was responsible for the ".2" that she felt she was *not* out. "I think there are just times when I'm more and more picking and choosing my battles. Depending on my mood, if somebody says something I may or may not respond to it." Deciding *not* to always come out to everyone, everywhere, may be a choice that one is more apt to make later in the coming-out process—a process that Tina described as "a constant evolution."

The rhetorical complexities of everyday life extend well beyond political choices for lesbians and gay men. For example, psychotherapist Lee Zevy (Zevy and Cavallero 1987) has written about the complicated tangle of cues a lesbian must manipulate when she is not out and desires simultaneously to "pass" in the straight world and to connect with other lesbians who are, unfortunately, similarly disguised:

> Rules [of sexual interplay] are based on a communication complex of linguistic, paralinguistic, and nonverbal behavior. When people want to be heard and seen as clearly as possible, they send messages over a tightly braided cable of their own and their partner's communicative intentions and modalities: What is said must be supported by gaze pattern, voice features, body posture and movement, facial expression, turn-taking behavior, and a synchronization of all of these with the partner's behavior. When partners are to be deceived or hidden from, one or several channels are used in contradiction. For example, a lie can be delivered successfully behind the screen of a warm, open face. Or a lesbian's sexual preference can be made ambiguous by a clutter of feminine dress and body gestures. (85–86)

Zevy describes what it was like realizing in her late teens in the 1950s, after growing up as a tomboy/butch, that she was a lesbian:

> Now the deceptive communication that I had practiced since childhood took on a frightening new twist. I could either avoid women entirely or assume very sophisticated communication strategies. Such strategies involved my providing cues and signals that would achieve three ends simultaneously: First, I wanted the occasional woman who would be a possible sexual liaison to know I was interested. But second, my communications would have to be ambiguous enough to provide an out in case the woman was not interested. And third, I had to play the heterosexual game with no intention of winning; that is, I had to play the game without really playing, to appear genuine and interested in men for whom they appeared to be—perhaps colleagues and friends, but also potential mates—while still seeming unavailable for sexual liaison with the man who asked. And I needed to look disinterested in women for whom they appeared to be—colleagues and friends, but not potential mates—even though I would have been available to them had they asked. Successful job interviews as well as other public presentations depended on my ability to balance appropriate sex-role behavior against no-nonsense competence. This is a very difficult game for the heterosexual woman to play, but

it is even more difficult for lesbians, who must play the game well enough so that everyone remains comfortable, but not *so* well that princess charming, should she happen by, would not recognize a potential love through the heterosexual disguise. (87)

Lesbians and gay men in homophobic culture, even when out, are constantly confronted, as my student Isabel Serrano pointed out, with having to repeat the act of coming out. Because for many intents and purposes, as Mary Donoghue illustrated, the culture is programmed to read everyone at the default setting of "heterosexual" until an act of coming out alters their reading, even lesbians and gay men who are not caught in the particular web of deception that Zevy illustrates are working some of the same channels, endlessly interfacing with the assumptions, prejudices, and threats of heterosexist society. Thus, lesbians and gay men do come to the writing class seasoned with a kind of rhetorical self-consciousness which, if creatively utilized, could be a huge asset in their attempts to position themselves within the locus of audience and meaning that is at the center of the writing act.

Unfortunately, though, although these students may be highly skilled rhetoricians, they are not necessarily skilled writers, often because their rhetorical prowess has actually been put to the purpose of *sabotaging* their writing. My students (though many of them are very skilled writers) have described and illustrated some of the ways that they have sabotaged their own writing in mainstream writing classes: Adrian succumbed, when he wrote about being gay at all, to the need to "justify" and "explain" his existence, which kept him tied to fairly basic forms of discourse and curtailed deeper exploration; Isabel would "get on a soapbox" in order to "set the record straight" for ignorant homophobes; John took several plunges and wrote about Black gay men, but always for a teacher-audience who did not give him a seriously critical response and thus cut off the possibility of serious revision; and Mary avoided writing about queer material altogether, which in the context of her first freshman writing workshop felt like "ignor[ing] the right half of my body." Other students, too, reported avoidance of the topic altogether as a common tactic—which could often mean becoming embroiled on a textual level in the complications that Zevy described, since "personal experience" essays are common assignments and the material that comprises the rest of a person's life must be shuffled around to successfully enact the gay discursive deception.

Whether or not such acts of sabotage occur can depend very much on the environment of a writing class. Thus one of the pedagogical implications of my study has to do with the construction and presentation of such an environment. A writing class which is overtly gay-positive

and antihomophobic, in which outness is supported (though not required) and in which lesbian and gay existence can be creatively
explored, provides a place in which lesbian and gay students' rhetorical
knowledge can be utilized, drawn on, and used as a foundation for
their development as writers. On the other hand, a writing class that
merely replicates the homophobic conditions of mainstream life is
likely to incur the same acts of sabotage of the students' self-expression
as those which occur in their daily lives: students will perceive risks
which might inadvertently "out" them as foolhardy, and see the benefits
of experimenting with writing as secondary to the need to maintain
safety for themselves. The occasions when these sorts of decisions arise
extend far beyond the obvious times when they may have the option
of writing about sexuality or relationships, since their lesbian or gay
identity touches virtually all parts of their lives—as Mary asserted.
Thus, a question that we can put to any writing class might be: Are
the conditions that produced lesbian and gay students' rhetorical self-
consciousness reproduced, or altered in the class? And as a result, is
their language subverted, or supported?

Subverting Homophobia in the Classroom

Of course, no teacher can completely control such conditions; but a
teacher can promote and encourage a classroom environment which,
beyond being "affirmative," is structured to creatively tap the involvement of queer subjectivities in the class's epistemological brew. Since
many readers of this book are doubtlessly waiting for the moment
when I answer the inevitable question—"What can I do?"—I will offer
some suggestions, though with the caveat that none of them are simple
directives for classroom implementation. On the contrary, the suggestions I offer here involve teacher self-education and only signal points
of contact with the manifold dimensions of lesbian and gay experience.
In other words, I am suggesting building a base of knowledge from
which to construct pedagogical praxis around lesbian and gay realities
in writing classes. For me to do anything more than that would be to
enter the reductive domain of recipe mongering. My umbrella suggestion is: Learn about lesbian and gay people. (This can be useful even
if you are one.) Here are some ways to go about it:

- If you live in or near a city that has one, go to a lesbian and gay
  (or feminist) bookstore and browse for a couple of hours. An
  increasing number of nonspecialized bookstores—ranging from independent sellers whose stock principally consists of critical theory
  to the B. Daltons at the mall—now have "gay" sections. Look

through the periodicals and anthologies. Think about which essays might be useful to include on your syllabus.

- Go to lesbian and gay cultural events on your campus, if there are any—lectures, forums, literary readings, plays, films.

- If your campus has a Lesbian, Gay, and Bisexual Alliance, contact them and ask for suggested readings and other leads. Women's studies programs can also be helpful sources.

- Check out sessions on lesbian and gay issues at professional conferences and contact the lesbian and gay caucuses of the MLA, CCCC, the National Women's Studies Association, etc.

- Get your campus library to stock titles in lesbian and gay studies and subscribe to national lesbian and gay publications such as the biweekly *Advocate,* the scholarly journal *GLQ, Lambda Book Report,* and the *Washington Blade,* which has national weekly news coverage.

- Get a copy of the annual *New York City Pride Guide,* published in May of each year for Gay and Lesbian Pride and History Month, which provides comprehensive listings of regional and national resources (Pride Publishing, Inc., 80 Eighth Avenue, Suite 902, New York, NY 10011).

- Investigate lesbian and gay studies. Contact the Center for Lesbian and Gay Studies (CLAGS), affiliated with the Graduate School of the City University of New York, 33 West 42nd Street, New York, NY 10036 (212 642–2924) for information. CLAGS describes itself as "a fully accredited research center" whose mission is "to gather, disseminate and encourage research on the lives of gay men and lesbians from a multicultural perspective." CLAGS publishes a newsletter and a nationwide directory of scholars working in lesbian and gay studies, and has plans to disseminate in print and on video some of the material of its symposia and conferences. An extensive collection of course syllabi is also on file there. On the West Coast, The Institute of Gay and Lesbian Education (626 North Robertson Boulevard, West Hollywood, CA 90069; 310 652–1786) is, according to its brochure, "a nonprofit educational institution, dedicated to furthering the intellectual development, self-awareness, and pride of the gay and lesbian communities in Southern California." The Institute offers a Certificate in Gay and Lesbian Culture and a range of courses such as "The Psychology of Gay Culture" and "Queer Screenwriting."

- Obtain newsletters from prominent lesbian and gay organizations such as the Gay and Lesbian Alliance Against Defamation (80 Varick Street #3E, New York, NY 10013), the Lambda Legal Defense and Education Fund (666 Broadway, New York, NY 10012), the Human Rights Campaign Fund (1012 14th Street, NW, Suite 607, Washington, D. C. 20005), and the National Lesbian and Gay Task Force Policy Institute (2320 17th Street, NW, Washington, D.C. 20009). They will keep you up-to-date about issues in media, the law, lobbying, government, and other areas in which the movement is active.

- Find out about resistant readings of lesbian and gay experience in religious discourse. National organizations you can contact include Metropolitan Community Church, with hundreds of congregations in North America (International Offices, 5300 Santa Monica Blvd., Los Angeles, CA 90029; 213 464–5100); Integrity, Inc.: Gay and Lesbian Episcopalians (P.O. Box 19561, Washington, D. C. 20036; 404 892–3143); Presbyterian Church, USA/Presbyterians for Lesbian/Gay Concerns (c/o James D. Anderson, Box 38, New Brunswick, NJ 08903; 201 846–1510); Dignity, Inc./Roman Catholic Church (1500 Massachusetts Ave., NW, Washington, D. C. 20005; 202 861–0017); and World Congress of Gay and Lesbian Jewish Groups (Box 18961, Washington, D. C. 20036).

- Experiment with using lesbian and gay topics in your classes. Encourage your colleagues to do the same, and exchange narratives about what happened. Bring lesbian and gay existence up in department and committee meetings as a matter of curricular importance.

I would like to console those who still rue the absence of more "practical" suggestions among my concluding remarks by pointing out that such suggestions wouldn't work, anyway. I have been asked things like, "How can we best handle the issues of coming out, of acceptance and understanding in freshman classes made up predominantly of straight students?" "Can/should straight people offer classes such as yours—or would gay students be outraged?" "How can straight teachers more successfully address these issues in their classrooms?" These sorts of issues have been, and still are, heavily contested in a variety of situations involving the admittedly problematic relationship between *discourses* and *experiences* of identity. But the very disparate answers only begin to unravel with immersion in those discourses—whether or not one has been immersed in those experiences. Short of that, the questions are patently unanswerable because, in deferring to the authority of an "expert," they implicitly divest the asker of the authority to make the very judgments that are requisite to dealing responsibly with the subject in the first place. Furthermore, these questions suggest that "gay students," "straight students," and "straight teachers" can be formulated as generically constituted and manageable sets emptied of all the complexity, heterogeneity, and particularity that

I have tried to depict throughout this book. Lastly, I would invoke a truism from the vintage days of identity politics that still strikes me as highly relevant: those occupying socially dominant identity positions place an undue burden on those in subordinate positions when they expect them to do all the work of deconstructing and rectifying systems of oppression. One tends to be aware of prejudice when one is the recipient of it; but we are all embroiled in the symbolic order that regulates prejudice, and therefore anyone who is really interested can become aware of it if he makes the effort to find out about it. Or, as radical subalterns used to say: *Educate yourself.* Progressive educators will surely agree that such an approach promises greater pedagogical returns than arranging to have deposits of curricular advice "banked" in one's intellectual account. For those who teach language, the logical way to begin such a project is to think about what you know—and what you need to know—about the ways that identity manifests itself in discourse.

Identity and Composition

If identity is shaped by language, then how are questions of identity being played out in composition? Usually, progressive writing classes favor the "inclusion" of various identities, just as contemporary anthologies published for use in freshman writing courses are increasingly presenting themselves as "multicultural" in order to "represent" a diverse spectrum of identities. Whether the identities represented are meant to correspond to the identities of various student readers, who will then be able to "identify" with issues raised in the texts they read, or whether they are meant to raise the consciousness of readers by virtue of encounters with identities of multiple others, is not always clear. In either case, the courses that result represent significant departures from those modeled on the white, male, and ostensibly heterosexual canon of essays used until very recently. As I have shown, though, it is important that we question what the limits of academic discourse are—even in environments promoting such a sense of diversity—for students actually located along the axes of some of those more socially marginalized identities. Furthermore, it is important to distinguish (though such distinctions are not always clean and simple) between issues that arise for students with identities that are "marginalized" and those that may be blatantly "vilified" in class, as well as those that are rendered obvious by appearance and those which involve options of "passing" or "coming out," and those which have a place (even a begrudged one) in public discourse and those which "dare not speak their names."

Of the students I interviewed, several had had positive experiences in earlier writing courses with teachers who genuinely supported them in their attempts to write about whatever they wanted to—though many had not. Several students, whether or not they felt supported by the teacher or classmates, had chosen to write gay-themed texts in earlier writing classes—though many had not. Yet of those who did choose to produce such work, none felt that the context of those texts' production enabled them to explore lesbian and gay experience in writing in the depth and complexity that our class did. Others said that they simply had not felt comfortable writing about sexual identity at all because of the usual constraints that homophobia places upon such expression.

I *do* think that finding ways to make use of knowledge generated by lesbian and gay subjectivities—as well as the knowledge of heterosexual students about sexual identity—is a good idea in mainstream writing classes. Furthermore, in my interviews students overwhelmingly and unhesitatingly suggested—not very surprisingly—when asked what recommendations they would have for teachers in mainstream writing classes if they were to consult with them about future curriculum design that teachers include lesbian and gay readings and assignments. Yet it is clear to me from the stories they tell me of their experiences and from my own experiences of including lesbian and gay issues in mainstream contexts that, although this inclusion can have very important results, it falls radically short of what can happen in a class which is structured to utilize the knowledge generated within a lesbian and gay discourse community.

What I am suggesting is that others also experiment with fashioning composition classes as discourse communities predicated on features of identity. Such an idea is more novel than the more frequently seen practice of establishing "themes" for writing courses which may be about a particular subject—writing about utopias and dystopias, the environment, science fiction, the West, spirituality, or the media, to use the examples of several other honors sections that were taught simultaneously with mine at Cosmopolitan. There is no doubt that these subjects may be engrossing and inspire writing; but I think it is safe to say that they do not draw students who are moved by the same sense of urgency as does a subject that is about a part of themselves which is daily immersed in conflict, subjected to joys and humiliations, drenched in contested meanings, and which plays a key role in the orchestration of their social existence.

Lesbian or gay identity, insofar as it fulfills all of those criteria, has much to offer composition—not only as a subject in itself, but insofar as it prompts us to think of how composition classes might be conceived as identity-based communities concerned with the production of knowledge through discourse. Even when such classes are not homogeneously populated by the bearers of such an identity—and I think that my experience has illustrated that the notion of a "homogeneous" identity collective is necessarily an illusion, anyway—it is pedagogically important that the members of the group be self-selected, deliberately convening to explore the meaning of a particular identity that has *some* relevance for them, as opposed to the relatively random manner in which the constitutencies of most writing classes are formed. Even "outsiders" to the identity under discussion, when making the conscious decision to relate to the theme of the course, can become in certain vital senses "insiders" in the discourse community because they are there intentionally, propelled by some concept of personal relationship to the material—even if the nature of that relationship is ignorance. The recognition of ignorance not just as a gap, but rather as a presence, a meaningful discursive field which one can prod, interrogate, and alter, marks one as eligible for at least provisional membership in the discourse community.

For example, during the academic year 1979–1980, while I was a graduate student in an M.F.A. program in creative writing in western Massachusetts, I sat in on a two-semester course taught by Gloria Joseph at nearby Hampshire College called "The Significant Role of Black Women in Women's Studies." Faculty, administrators, graduate students, and undergraduates who were involved with women's studies in any of five local colleges were invited to attend. In the previous year I had become very involved with women's studies, but I knew very little about Black women's lives and had thought very little about racism. However, within women's studies—a community in which I had become extremely invested—there had started to be a great deal of discussion about racism and the lack of recognition of Black women's experience in the curriculum. The "gap" that had originally been an omission that had evaded my notice became problematized to the point where it occupied a central place in the work of the women's studies community. Others were constantly talking about this gap, so that soon I, because of my location in the community of women's studies, was drawn into talking about it, too. In addition to working on filling in the gap with texts and courses by and about Black women, we talked about why the gap was there, who had made it, how it had formed, and how we ourselves might have, even if unwittingly, contributed to its existence. We were also always asking one another how we were going to contribute to its eradication.

When Gloria Joseph's course was announced, I decided to take it because though I didn't know very much about racism, I knew by then that it didn't only affect other people (the "not-me"), but that it had something to do with myself. The course, filled with the tension of the "confrontational" politics that were popular at that time, was populated by Black women, white women, a few Latina women and one Asian woman; there were also many lesbians as well as heterosexual women. One's "identity" counted for a lot there; it was an era in which feminists had become hyperconscious of speaking "as" particular features of their identity—for example, "as" a "white, Jewish, middle-class lesbian." Revealing one's ignorance about women of color was generally regarded as exposing "the problem" as rooted in oneself, so that speaking "as a white, Jewish, middle-class lesbian" who hadn't had much prior experience of radical politics of any sort, and none of antiracism work, was terrifying. For myself at least, the weekly experience of the class was traumatic, and yet something kept me there not only all of the first semester, but all of the second. I think that what that "something" was, was hatred of my own ignorance. As the year went by, discourses of race and racism increasingly informed the way I thought about not only Black women, but about people. It wasn't that I was starting to believe that "people were people"; on the contrary, I had *begun* with that rosy premise, and was starting to understand the forces that marked people as distinctively *different* people. Most unsettling was what I was learning about my own role not just as recipient of those "forces" in society that did such things, but also about my role as producer of the kinds of knowledge that bolstered those forces even as they were produced *by* them. Expressions like "Deal with your own racism" and "If you're not part of the solution, you're part of the problem," which some dismissed as didactic and simplistic, in fact had complex and catalytic power for someone like me in that they served as linguistic and conceptual epicenters for entire new shock waves of thought. Locating myself at the center of such aphorisms, I experienced the sensation of being in an altogether new discursive space, and I found that in that space I had company; I was in a new discourse community.

That course, in conjunction with others—because it was, after all, others that had led me there, and that course that led me to others— permanently repositioned me, made me identify with discourses of race and insert myself into social and political spheres that were concerned with issues of race and that were themselves multiracial. It made white spheres, discourses, and thinking glaringly visible to me, whereas before they had seemed unmarked and unremarkable. It also made me speak and act; *seeing* and *knowing* about racism made *doing* imperative. Its imprint is on all of the intellectual and political work I have subsequently done: on decisions I made later to go to Central America, to take positions that left me vulnerable at work, to become involved with multicultural education and multicultural organizing, to demonstrate against the Howard Beach murder and the Rodney King verdict, and to teach in an urban, multiracial college; and it is certainly on my writing—including academic writing, journalism, grant writing, course syllabi, leaflets, and letters to newspapers and public officials.

My experience in Gloria Joseph's course and my experience in my own lesbian and gay writing classes both lead me to a question: What kind of space/place might the classroom be? On the one hand, I am wary of answers like "a socially transformative space" or "a personally tranformative space," just as I am wary of "a space in which students become writers"—only because each seems so partial, so much not the others. On the other hand, I am wary of answers that in their claims to include "all of the above" get lost in the blur of their own diffuse idealism. It is true that there were things that didn't happen in my classes that might have happened in a class more generically focused on "writing"—there might have been more discussion of the writing process itself, for instance, or more "playing" with language, or more conscious experimentation with different forms. This wasn't that kind of class—but neither was it a class in which lesbian and gay experience simply supplied the "content" material as serviceably as anything else could have.

It was a class predicated upon the existence of a particular discourse community where new rhetorical relationships among writers, readers, subjects, and contexts made the production of new forms of knowledge possible. It was an environment that I described in my introduction to this book as "queercentric," though it was not exclusively populated by queers—just as Gloria Joseph's course managed to be "Afrocentric" without rendering the presence and realities of others void or paradoxical. This course was just as concerned with problematizing identity and questioning the formation of the categories into which we insert ourselves as it was with affirming the needs of students to speak and write "as" queers or heterosexuals.

Yet writing "as" *was* also a big part of what happened, because most of the students came with pent-up frustrations about the limits they had previously felt in authorizing their academic reality in any way *as* queers. In addition, some of them weren't used to being in *any* social space in which being queer was generally regarded as a good thing. In our class, queerness was affirmed and enjoyed, so that whole new realms of material became available that could not be utilized in a homophobic context. But in addition, subjecting homophobia itself and our behavior in a homophobic world to critical inquiry added new dimensions of possible material.

Mary Donoghue wrote in her "Final Reflections": "We fags and dykes are real; we have a history and we can be studied in a class at Cosmopolitan." Many students expressed amazement during the term that lesbian and gay studies could be considered a "legitimate" subject for academic inquiry. Like Mary, they seemed far more convinced of their own "realness" once it was reflected back to them by the authority of a university curriculum. The power of school to confer existence was more than a match for the knowledge of experience; many reported that finding the queer part of themselves institutionally legitimized gave them an entryway into academic discourse that neither their *extra*curricular lives nor their other academic pursuits had opened up. While many teachers, particularly those involved with liberatory pedagogy, urge students to problematize the authority of social institutions such as the academy, there is no question that the point is undermined and etched in their disbelief when we—students and ourselves—are all clearly, by our presence there, committing huge amounts of our personal resources to it. More to the point, then, what does it mean to be delegitimized by the very institution to which you are entrusting your education and your future? What kind of message does your absence in the realm of valid knowledge give you about your own power to authorize knowledge and participate in public discourse?

On the other hand, what does it mean to have a space in which to come out to the institution that has heretofore negated your entitlement? Coming out is a speech act that, as the lesbian and gay movement grows and mass public discourse is increasingly infused with information about lesbian and gay existence, we can expect to see attempted more and more in our writing classes. The forms that that act takes will vary. In some instances it will emerge as an "expressionist" moment—a "voicing" of an "authentic" inner reality whose enactment involves transcending prohibitions and inhibitions to project a "truth" which may then take its place in the wider realm of discourse. For others, coming out may be conceived as a social-epistemic moment, one which not only heralds the entrance of the writer's message into the world of discourse but which in turn is examined for its roots and origins in discourse. What, we might ask such a writer, is s/he coming out *of?* Where is s/he going? What does it mean to publicly assert one's identity as that which, in the words of a number of queer theorists, is still constructed as "haunting abject" in our society? What are the forces that would motivate one to claim such an alignment? How does one have faith in the prospect of self-actualization even in a changing society that "accepts" one's homosexuality when, as Sedgwick (1991) points out, the *real* wish in our culture is "that gay people *not exist*" (23)? The first response of the liberal pluralist academy to a coming-out statement at the dawn of queer "inclusion" is likely to be applause and "affirmation"—the expressionist response. Yet although important on an immediate affective level, such a response avoids the complexity of the experience and represents a failure of the academy to deal with this information on its own "academic" terms. Ultimately it shortchanges the student by reinscribing this speech act as extracurricular event rather than as intellectually worthy subject whose repercussions might be felt across the curriculum.

Such shortchanging can be devastating because it strikes at both cognitive and affective faculties—the juncture of which is the site of learning. What comes to my mind here is the expression that one hears across the country in relation to the gay rights movement—"gay pride." "Pride" is a term I usually tend to shy away from in gay contexts because, unlike its use in certain other contexts—the birth of a child, the achievement of a societally valued goal—the notion of gay "pride" tends to suggest to me a bittersweet and always ambiguous triumph over shame. It is not that gay "pride" can't or doesn't exist; I simply believe that what is called "pride" is often in fact something else—perhaps a feeling of ecstasy or relief in discovering that the values attached to being gay comprise a contested realm, after all, and are not unremittingly negative. I find it difficult to see why the condition of being homosexual should be any more a source of "pride" than the condition of being heterosexual—and thus it seems to me that, paradoxically, the more one overcomes one's internalized homophobia, the more one's "pride" (and one's need for it) may wither away. On the other hand, I believe that the long intermediate moment—which may, certainly, last forever—of being involved in the *act* or *project* of overcoming is the real moment of pride. Certainly successfully maneuvering through that frictional space in which a new discourse displaces the dense weighty matter of seemingly ubiquitous homophobia is an occasion for pride.

It is this sort of "pride" that my classes seemed to me to be involved in: creating a new kind of discourse through community, and a new kind of community through discourse.

Notes

1. See, for example, Berlin 1991; Berlin and Vivion 1992; Spellmeyer 1991; Clifford 1991; Schilb 1991; Jarratt 1991; Bizzell 1991, 1992; Faigley 1992; Villanueva 1991.

2. In a 1991 graduate seminar in lesbian and gay studies taught by Martin Duberman at the CUNY Graduate School, I was surprised to see many of the younger graduate students fiercely resisting Professor Duberman's attempts to create democratic, participatory structures and to connect class process to the "content" of the course. Their longing, it seemed, was to "legitimize" lesbian and gay studies by having it replicate the conventions, or "common sense," of the traditional disciplines. The desires some of them indicated for a teacher-centered classroom in which the line between "knowledge" and "feelings" was responsibly drawn made me wonder whether the diverse ages of people in the room represented competing allegiances to "sixties" and "eighties" models of learning.

Appendix

OUR GOVERNMENT CONTINUES TO IGNORE THE LIVES, DEATHS AND SUFFERING OF PEOPLE WITH HIV INFECTION BECAUSE THEY ARE GAY, BLACK, HISPANIC OR POOR. BY JULY 4, 1989 OVER 55 THOUSAND WILL BE DEAD. TAKE DIRECT ACTION NOW. FIGHT BACK. FIGHT AIDS.

AIDS: 1 in 61

One in every sixty-one babies
in New York City is born with AIDS
or born HIV antibody positive.

So why is the media telling us
that heterosexuals aren't at risk?

Because these babies are black.
These babies are Hispanic.

**Ignoring color ignores the facts of AIDS.
STOP RACISM: FIGHT AIDS.**

Uno de cada sesenta y uno de los bebés nacidos
en la ciudad de New York nacen con SIDA,
o con el anticuerpo HIV positivo.

¿Pero, por qué es que los medios de comunicación
nos dicen que los heterosexuales no corren riesgos?

Será porque estos bebes son negros,
o porque estos bebes son hispanos.

**El SIDA no discrimina entre razas o nacionalidades.
¡PARE EL RACISMO! ¡LUCHE CONTRA EL SIDA!**

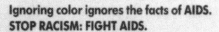

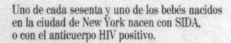

References

Acey, Katherine. 1993. "Lesbian Chic!" Fundraising letter for Astraea Foundation, New York, November.

Adair, Nancy, and Casey Adair. 1978. *Word Is Out*. New York and San Francisco: Delacorte Press and New Glide Publications.

Adam, Barry D. 1987. *The Rise of a Gay and Lesbian Movement*. Boston: Twayne.

Adams, Frank. 1972. "Highlander Folk School: Getting Information, Going Back and Teaching It." *Harvard Educational Review* 42(November).

Alarcón, Norma. 1990. "The Theoretical Subject(s) of *This Bridge Called My Back* and Anglo-American Feminism." In *Making Face, Making Soul: Creative and Critical Perspectives by Women of Color*, edited by Gloria Anzaldúa. San Francisco: Aunt Lute Books.

Allen, Paula Gunn. [1986] 1990. "Lesbians in American Indian Cultures." In *Hidden from History*, edited by Martin Duberman, Martha Vicinus, and George Chauncey, Jr. New York: Meridian/New American Library.

Anonymous Queers. 1990. "I Hate Straights." Broadside distributed in New York City, June.

Anzaldúa, Gloria. 1987. *Borderlands/La Frontera: The New Mestiza*. San Francisco: Aunt Lute Books.

———. 1990a. "Bridge, Drawbridge, Sandbar or Island: Lesbians of Color *Hacienda Alianzas*." In *Bridges of Power: Women's Multicultural Alliances*, edited by Lisa Albrecht and Rose M. Brewer. Philadelphia: New Society Publishers.

———, ed. 1990b. *Making Face, Making Soul: Creative and Critical Perspectives by Women of Color*. San Francisco: Aunt Lute Books.

Associated Press. 1992. "Levi Strauss OKs Benefits for Unmarried Partners." *Los Angeles Times*, 24 January.

Atkinson, Ti-Grace. 1973. "Lesbianism and Feminism." In *Amazon Expedition: A Lesbian Feminist Anthology*, edited by Phyllis Birkby, Bertha Harris, Jill Johnston, Esther Newton, and Jane O'Wyatt. Albion, CA: Times Change Press.

Avrich, Paul. 1980. *The Modern School Movement: Anarchism and Education in the United States*. Princeton, NJ: Princeton University Press.

Bakhtin, M. M. 1981. *The Dialogic Imagination*. Edited by Michael Holquist and translated by Caryl Emerson and Michael Holquist. Austin: University of Texas Press.

273

Bartholomae, David. 1985. "Inventing the University." In *When A Writer Can't Write,* edited by Mike Rose. New York: The Guilford Press.

Bartholomae, David, and Anthony Petrosky. 1986. *Facts, Artifacts and Counterfacts: Theory and Method for a Reading and Writing Course.* Portsmouth, NH: Boynton/Cook.

Bauer, Dale M., and Susan Jaret McKinstry, eds. 1991. *Feminism, Bakhtin, and the Dialogic.* Albany: State University of New York Press.

Beck, Evelyn Torton, ed. 1982. *Nice Jewish Girls: A Lesbian Anthology.* Watertown, Mass.: Persephone Press. Revised and updated, 1989, Boston: Beacon Press.

Belanoff, Pat, and Marcia Dickson, eds. 1991. *Portfolios: Process and Product.* Portsmouth, NH: Boynton/Cook.

Benjamin, Jessica. 1988. *The Bonds of Love.* New York: Pantheon.

Berger, John. 1972. *Ways of Seeing.* London: British Broadcasting Corporation and Penguin Books.

Berger, Peter, and Thomas Luckmann. 1967. *The Social Construction of Reality.* Garden City, NY: Anchor Books.

Berlin, James. 1988. "Rhetoric and Ideology in the Writing Class." *College English* 50(5): 477–94.

———. 1991. "Composition and Cultural Studies." In *Composition and Resistance,* edited by C. Mark Hurlbert and Michael Blitz. Portsmouth, NH: Boynton/Cook.

Berlin, James A., and Michael A. Vivion. 1992. *Cultural Studies in the English Classroom.* Portsmouth, NH: Boynton/Cook.

Berthoff, Ann E. 1981. *The Making of Meaning.* Portsmouth, NH: Boynton/Cook.

———. 1982. *Forming, Thinking, Writing.* 2d ed. Portsmouth, NH: Boynton/Cook.

Bérubé, Allan. 1991. *Coming Out Under Fire: The History of Gay Men and Women in World War II.* New York: Plume Books.

Bizzell, Patricia. 1982. "Cognition, Convention, and Certainty: What We Need to Know about Writing." *Pre/Text* 3.

———. 1991. "Marxist Ideas in Composition Studies." In *Contending with Words: Composition and Rhetoric in a Postmodern Age,* edited by Patricia Harkin and John Schilb. New York: Modern Language Association.

———. 1992. "What Is a Discourse Community?" In *Academic Discourse and Critical Consciousness.* Pittsburgh: University of Pittsburgh Press.

Bleich, David. 1989. "Homophobia and Sexism as Popular Values." *Feminist Teacher* 4(Fall).

Bordo, Susan. 1990. "Feminism, Postmodernism, and Gender-Scepticism." In *Feminism/Postmodernism,* edited by Linda J. Nicholson. New York: Routledge.

———. 1992. "Postmodern Subjects, Postmodern Bodies." *Feminist Studies* 18(1): 159–75.

Boswell, John. 1990. "Concepts, Experience, and Sexuality." *Differences: A Journal of Feminist Cultural Studies* 2(1): 67–86.

Bowen, Peter. 1993. "AIDS 101." In *Writing AIDS: Gay Literature, Language, and Analysis*, edited by Timothy M. Murphy and Suzanne Poirier. New York: Columbia University Press.

Bowles, Gloria, and Renate Duelli Klein, eds. 1983. *Theories of Women's Studies.* London: Routledge & Kegan Paul.

Brodkey, Linda. 1989. "On the Subjects of Class and Gender in 'The Literacy Letters.'" *College English* 51(2): 125–41.

Brown, Cynthia Stokes, ed. 1990. *Ready from Within: A First Person Narrative (Septima Clark and the Civil Rights Movement).* Trenton, NJ: Africa World Press.

Brown, Rita Mae. 1975a. "Living with Other Women." In *Lesbianism and the Women's Movement*, edited by Nancy Myron and Charlotte Bunch. Baltimore: Diana Press. First appeared in *Women: A Journal of Liberation* II(2).

———. 1975b. "The Shape of Things to Come." In *Lesbianism and the Women's Movement*, edited by Nancy Myron and Charlotte Bunch. Baltimore: Diana Press. Written on behalf of *The Furies;* first appeared in *Women: A Journal of Liberation* II(4).

Bruffee, Kenneth. 1980. *A Short Course in Writing.* 2d ed. Cambridge: Winthrop.

———. 1983. "Writing and Reading as Collaborative or Social Acts." In *The Writer's Mind: Writing as a Mode of Thinking*, edited by Janice M. Hays, Phyllis A. Roth, Jon R. Ramsey, and Robert D. Foulke. Urbana, IL: NCTE.

———. 1986. "Social Construction, Language, and the Authority of Knowledge: A Bibliographical Essay." *College English* 48(8): 773–90.

Bruner, Jerome. 1986. *Actual Minds, Possible Worlds.* Cambridge, MA: Harvard University Press.

Bunch, Charlotte. 1975. "Lesbians in Revolt." In *Lesbianism and the Women's Movement*, edited by Nancy Myron and Charlotte Bunch. Baltimore: Diana Press.

———. 1987. *Passionate Politics: Feminist Theory in Action.* New York: St. Martin's Press.

Bunch, Charlotte, and Sandra Pollack. 1983. *Learning Our Way: Essays in Feminist Education.* Trumansburg, NY: The Crossing Press.

Butler, Judith. 1990. *Gender Trouble: Feminism and the Subversion of Identity.* New York: Routledge.

———. 1991. "Imitation and Gender Insubordination." In *Inside/Out: Lesbian Theories, Gay Theories*, edited by Diana Fuss. New York: Routledge.

Christian, Barbara. 1990. "The Race for Theory." In *Making Face, Making Soul: Creative and Critical Perspectives by Women of Color*, edited by Gloria Anzaldúa. San Francisco: Aunt Lute Books.

Clifford, John. 1991. "The Subject in Discourse." In *Contending with Words:*

Composition and Rhetoric in a Postmodern Age, edited by Patricia Harkin and John Schilb. New York: Modern Language Association.

Cohen, Ed. 1991. "Who Are 'We'? Gay 'Identity' as Political (E)motion (A Theoretical Rumination)." In *Inside/Out: Lesbian Theories, Gay Theories,* edited by Diana Fuss. New York: Routledge.

Coleman, Eli. 1985. "Developmental Stages of the Coming Out Process." In *A Guide to Psychotherapy with Gay and Lesbian Clients,* edited by John C. Gonsiorek. New York: Harrington Park Press.

Colombo, Gary, Robert Cullen, and Bonnie Lisle, eds. 1989. *Rereading America: Cultural Contexts for Critical Thinking and Writing.* New York: St. Martin's Press.

Combahee River Collective. 1983. "The Combahee River Collective Statement." In *Home Girls: A Black Feminist Anthology,* edited by Barbara Smith. New York: Kitchen Table/Women of Color Press.

Common Threads: Stories from the Quilt. 1989. Produced by Bill Coutrie, Robert Epstein, and Jeffrey Friedman. Directed by Robert Epstein and Jeffrey Friedman. 79 minutes. A Telling Pictures/Coutrie Company co-production.

Comstock, Gary David. 1991. *Violence Against Lesbians and Gay Men.* New York: Columbia University Press.

Cook, William W. 1993. "Writing In the Spaces Left." *College Composition and Communication* 44(1): 9–25.

Cooper, Marilyn M., and Michael Holzman. 1989. *Writing as Social Action.* Portsmouth, NH: Boynton/Cook.

Crawford, Mary, and Roger Chaffin. 1986. "The Reader's Construction of Meaning: Cognitive Research on Gender and Comprehension." In *Gender and Reading: Essays on Readers, Texts, and Contexts,* edited by Elizabeth A. Flynn and Patrocinio P. Schweickart. Baltimore: Johns Hopkins University Press.

Crimp, Douglas, ed. 1989. *AIDS: Cultural Analysis/Cultural Activism.* Cambridge: MIT Press.

Crimp, Douglas, with Adam Rolston. 1990. *AIDS Demo Graphics.* Seattle: Bay Press.

Crowley, Sharon. 1991. "Reimagining the Writing Scene: Curmudgeonly Remarks About *Contending With Words.*" In *Contending with Words: Composition and Rhetoric in a Postmodern Age,* edited by Patricia Harkin and John Schilb. New York: Modern Language Association.

Culler, Jonathan. 1982. *On Deconstruction: Theory and Criticism After Structuralism.* Ithaca: Cornell University Press.

Culley, Margo, and Catherine Portuges, eds. 1985. *Gendered Subjects: The Dynamics of Feminist Teaching.* Boston: Routledge & Kegan Paul.

Daly, Mary. 1973. *Beyond God the Father.* Boston: Beacon Press.

———. 1978. *Gyn/Ecology: The Metaethics of Radical Feminism.* Boston: Beacon Press.

Danto, Arthur C. 1990. "Inventing Innocence." *The New York Times Book Review,* 24 June.

D'Emilio, John. 1983a. "Capitalism and Gay Identity." In *Powers of Desire: The Politics of Sexuality,* edited by Ann Snitow, Christine Stansell, and Sharon Thompson. New York: Monthly Review Press.

———. 1983b. *Sexual Politics, Sexual Communities: The Making of a Homosexual Minority in the United States, 1940–1970.* Chicago: University of Chicago Press.

Duberman, Martin. 1991. *Cures: A Gay Man's Odyssey.* New York: Dutton.

———. 1993. *Stonewall.* New York: Dutton.

Duberman, Martin, Martha Vicinus, and George Chauncey, eds. 1990. *Hidden from History: Reclaiming the Gay and Lesbian Past.* New York: Meridian/New American Library.

Du Bois, W. E. B. [1953] 1961. *The Souls of Black Folk.* Greenwich, CT: Fawcett Books.

Dunker, Buffy. 1987. "Aging Lesbians: Observations and Speculations." In *Lesbian Psychologies,* edited by the Boston Lesbian Psychologies Collective. Urbana and Chicago: University of Illinois Press.

Elbow, Peter. 1973. *Writing Without Teachers.* New York: Oxford University Press.

Ellsworth, Elizabeth. 1989. "Why Doesn't This Feel Empowering? Working Through the Repressive Myths of Critical Pedagogy." *Harvard Educational Review* 59(3): 297–323.

Escoffier, Jeffrey. 1990. "Inside the Ivory Closet." *Out/Look* 3, no. 2(Fall): 40–48.

Faderman, Lillian. 1981. *Surpassing the Love of Men: Romantic Friendship and Love Between Women from the Renaissance to the Present.* New York: Willliam Morrow.

———. 1991. *Odd Girls and Twilight Lovers: A History of Lesbian Life in Twentieth-Century America.* New York: Columbia University Press.

Faigley, Lester. 1989. "Judging Writing, Judging Selves." *College Composition and Communication* 40(4): 395–412.

———. 1992. *Fragments of Rationality: Postmodernity and the Subject of Composition.* Pittsburgh: University of Pittsburgh Press.

Fiore, Kyle, and Nan Elsasser. 1987. "'Strangers No More': A Liberatory Literacy Curriculum." In *Freire for the Classroom,* edited by Ira Shor. Portsmouth, NH: Boynton/Cook.

Fischer, Hal. 1977. *Gay Semiotics.* NFS Press. Excerpted in *Out/Look* 11(Winter 1991): 44.

Fish, Stanley. 1980. "Is There a Text in This Class?" In *Is There a Text in This Class? The Authority of Interpretive Communities.* Cambridge, MA: Harvard University Press.

Fishman, Stephen M., and Lucille Parkinson McCarthy. 1992. "Is Expressivism Dead? Reconsidering Its Romantic Roots and Its Relation to Social Constructionism." *College English* 54(6): 647–51.

Flexner, Eleanor. [1959] 1979. *Century of Struggle: The Woman's Rights Movement in the United States.* Revised ed. Cambridge, MA: The Belknap Press of Harvard University Press.

Flower, Linda, and John R. Hayes. 1988. "The Cognition of Discovery: Defining a Rhetorical Problem." In *The Writing Teacher's Sourcebook,* edited by Gary Tate and Edward P. J. Corbett. 2d ed. New York: Oxford University Press.

Foucault, Michel. [1978] 1990. *The History of Sexuality: An Introduction.* Vol. 1. New York: Vintage Books.

Fraser, Nancy, and Linda J. Nicholson. 1990. "Social Criticism without Philosophy: An Encounter Between Feminism and Postmodernism." In *Feminism/Postmodernism,* edited by Linda J. Nicholson. New York: Routledge.

Freire, Paulo. 1970. *Pedagogy of the Oppressed.* New York: The Seabury Press.

Freire, Paulo, and Donaldo Macedo. 1987. *Literacy: Reading the Word and the World.* South Hadley, MA: Bergin & Garvey.

Freire, Paulo, and Ira Shor. 1987. *A Pedagogy for Liberation: Dialogues on Transforming Education.* South Hadley, MA: Bergin & Garvey.

Fulwiler, Toby. 1987. *The Journal Book.* Portsmouth, NH: Boynton/Cook.

Fuss, Diana. 1989. *Essentially Speaking: Feminism, Nature, and Difference.* New York: Routledge.

———, ed. 1991. *Inside/Out: Lesbian Theories, Gay Theories.* New York: Routledge.

Giroux, Henry. 1983. *Theory and Resistance in Education.* South Hadley, MA: Bergin & Garvey.

———. 1992. "Liberal Arts Education and the Struggle for Public Life: Dreaming about Democracy." In *The Politics of Liberal Education,* edited by Darryl J. Gless and Barbara Herrnstein Smith. Durham, NC: Duke University Press.

Goldberg, Suzanne. 1993. "'A Sack of Stones for Throwing': Ballot Measures and the Right Wing Assault on Lesbian and Gay Civil Rights." *The Lambda Update: Newsletter of the Lambda Legal Defense and Education Fund* 10(3): 1, 21–22.

Goldstein, Richard. 1993. "Don't Ask, Don't Screw." *The Village Voice,* 27 July.

Goleman, Daniel. 1990. "Homophobia: Scientists Find Clues to Its Roots." *New York Times,* 10 July.

Gómez, Alma, Cherríe Moraga, and Mariana Romo-Carmona, eds. 1983. *Cuentos: Stories by Latinas.* New York: Kitchen Table Press.

Graves, Bingham. 1979. "What Is Liberating Education? A Conversation with Myles Horton." *Radical Teacher* (May): 3–5.

Hairston, Maxine. 1992. "Diversity, Ideology, and Teaching Writing." *College Composition and Communication* 43(2): 179–93.

Halliday, M. A. K. 1978. *Language as Social Semiotic.* London: Edward Arnold.

Haraway, Donna. 1990. "A Manifesto for Cyborgs: Science, Technology, and Socialist Feminism in the 1980s." In *Feminism/Postmodernism,* edited by Linda J. Nicholson. New York: Routledge.

Harkin, Patricia, and John Schilb, eds. 1991. *Contending With Words: Composition and Rhetoric in a Postmodern Age.* New York: Modern Language Association.

Harris, Joseph. 1989. "The Idea of Community in the Study of Writing." *College Composition and Communication* 40(1): 11–22.

Hart, Ellen Louise. 1988. "Literacy and the Lesbian/Gay Learner." In *The Lesbian in Front of the Classroom: Writings by Lesbian Teachers,* edited by Sarah-Hope Parmeter and Irene Reti. Santa Cruz: HerBooks.

Hart, Ellen Louise, and Sarah-Hope Parmeter. 1992. "'Writing in the Margins': A Lesbian- and Gay-Inclusive Course." In *Social Issues in the English Classroom,* edited by C. Mark Hurlbert and Samuel Totten. Urbana, IL: NCTE.

Heath, Shirley Brice. 1983. *Ways with Words.* Cambridge: Cambridge University Press.

Herzberg, Bruce. 1986. "The Politics of Discourse Communities." Paper prepared for Conference on College Composition and Communication, New Orleans, LA. Quoted in Patricia Bizzell, "What Is a Discourse Community?" In *Academic Discourse and Critical Consciousness.* Pittsburgh: University of Pittsburgh Press.

Highlander Research and Education Center. 1992. *Highlander Reports.* New Market, TN: (Fall).

Hollibaugh, Amber. 1990. "Writers as Activists." *Out/Look* 3, no. 2(Fall): 69–72.

Holmes, Steven A. 1994. "Gay Rights Advocates Brace for Ballot Fights." *New York Times,* 12 January.

hooks, bell. 1981. *Ain't I a Woman: Black Women and Feminism.* Boston: South End Press.

———. 1984. *Feminist Theory: From Margin to Center.* Boston: South End Press.

———. 1990. *Yearning: Race, Gender, and Cultural Politics.* Boston: South End Press.

Hubbard, Ruth. 1993. "False Genetic Markers." In op-ed "Dialogue": "The Search For Sexual Identity." *New York Times,* 2 August.

Hull, Gloria T., Patricia Bell Scott, and Barbara Smith, eds. 1982. *But Some of Us Are Brave: Black Women's Studies.* New York: The Feminist Press.

Jarratt, Susan C. 1991. "Feminism and Composition: The Case for Conflict." In *Contending with Words: Composition and Rhetoric in a Postmodern Age,* edited by Patricia Harkin and John Schilb. New York: Modern Language Association.

Jay, Karla, and Allen Young, eds. [1972, 1977] 1992. *Out of the Closets: Voices of Gay Liberation.* New York: NYU Press. First edition, 1972. New York: Douglas.

———. 1978. *Lavender Culture.* New York: Jove/Harcourt Brace Jovanovich.

———. 1979. *The Gay Report: Lesbians and Gay Men Speak Out About Sexual Experiences and Lifestyles.* New York: Simon & Schuster. Quoted in Eli Coleman, 1985, "Developmental Stages of the Coming Out Process." In *A*

Guide to Psychotherapy with Gay and Lesbian Clients, edited by John C. Gonsiorek. New York: Harrington Park Press.

Katz, Jonathan. 1976. *Gay American History.* New York: Avon Books.

Kennedy, Elizabeth Lapovsky, and Madeline D. Davis. 1994. *Boots of Leather, Slippers of Gold: The History of a Lesbian Community.* New York: Penguin.

Knoblauch, C. H., and Lil Brannon. 1984. *Rhetorical Traditions and the Teaching of Writing.* Portsmouth, NH: Boynton/Cook.

Kramer, Larry. 1985. *The Normal Heart.* New York: New American Library.

Kristeva, Julia. 1986. "Women's Time." In *The Kristeva Reader,* edited by Toril Moi. New York: Columbia University Press.

LeFevre, Karen Burke. 1987. *Invention as a Social Act.* Carbondale and Edwardsville: Southern Illinois University Press.

Lorde, Audre. 1982. *Zami: A New Spelling of My Name.* Trumansburg, NY: The Crossing Press.

———. 1984. *Sister Outsider.* Freedom, CA: The Crossing Press.

Lunsford, Andrea. 1991. "Intellectual Property, Concepts of Selfhood, and the Teaching of Writing." Keynote address at Fifteenth Annual Conference of CUNY Association of Writing Instructors (CAWS):"Is All Writing Autobiography?" New York, 25 October.

Marotta, Toby. 1981. *The Politics of Homosexuality* Part I. Boston: Houghton Mifflin.

Marriott, Michel. 1993. "Rap's Embrace of 'Nigger' Fires Bitter Debate." *New York Times,* 24 January.

Mass, Lawrence D. 1990. "Sexual Categories, Sexual Universals: A Conversation with John Boswell." In *Dialogues of the Sexual Revolution, Vol. II: Homosexuality as Behavior and Identity.* Binghamton, NY: Harrington Park Press.

Mayher, John. 1990. *Uncommon Sense: Theoretical Practice in Language Communication.* Portsmouth, NH: Boynton/Cook.

McQuade, Donald, and Robert Atwan, eds. 1991. *The Winchester Reader.* New York: Bedford Books/St. Martin's Press.

Miller, Nancy K. 1986. "Changing the Subject: Authorship, Writing, and the Reader." *Feminist Studies/Critical Studies,* edited by Teresa de Lauretis. Bloomington: Indiana University Press.

Mohr, Richard. 1988. *Gays/Justice: A Study of Ethics, Society, and Law.* New York: Columbia University Press.

Mooney, Carolyn J. 1992. "Homosexuals in Academe: Fear of Backlash Clouds Reaction to Increased Tolerance." *Chronicle of Higher Education,* 23 September: A17–A19.

Moraga, Cherríe. 1983. *Loving in the War Years.* Boston: South End Press.

Moraga, Cherríe, and Gloria Anzaldúa, eds. 1981. *This Bridge Called My Back: Writings by Radical Women of Color.* New York: Kitchen Table Press.

Morrison, Toni. 1992. *Playing in the Dark: Whiteness and the Literary Imagination.* Cambridge, MA: Harvard University Press.

"The Names Project: A National AIDS Memorial." 1987. Brochure distributed at National Lesbian and Gay March on Washington, 11 October.

Neel, Jasper. 1988. *Plato, Derrida, and Writing.* Carbondale: Southern Illinois University Press.

Park, Douglas. 1988. "The Meanings of 'Audience.'" In *The Writing Teacher's Sourcebook,* edited by Gary Tate and Edward P. J. Corbett. 2d ed. New York: Oxford University Press.

Parmeter, Sarah-Hope, and Irene Reti, eds. 1988. *The Lesbian in Front of the Classroom.* Santa Cruz: HerBooks.

Patton, Cindy. 1990. *Inventing AIDS.* New York: Routledge.

Penelope, Julia, and Susan J. Wolfe, eds. [1980] 1989. *The Coming Out Stories.* Expanded edition. Freedom, CA: The Crossing Press.

Phelan, Shane. 1989. *Identity Politics: Lesbian Feminism and the Limits of Community.* Philadelphia: Temple University Press.

Pomeroy, Sarah B. 1975. *Goddesses, Whores, Wives, and Slaves: Women in Classical Antiquity.* New York: Schocken Books.

Powers, Ann. 1993. "Class Conflicts: A Vindication of the Rights of Women's Studies." *Voice Literary Supplement* 119(October): 10–12.

Reagon, Bernice Johnson. 1983. "Coalition Politics: Turning the Century." In *Home Girls: A Black Feminist Anthology,* edited by Barbara Smith. New York: Kitchen Table Press.

Rich, Adrienne. 1978. *The Dream of a Common Language: Poems 1974–1977.* New York: W. W. Norton Company.

———. 1979a. *On Lies, Secrets, and Silence: Selected Prose 1966–1978.* New York: W. W. Norton & Company.

———. 1982. *Compulsory Heterosexuality and Lesbian Existence.* Denver, CO: Antelope Publications. First published in *Signs: Journal of Women in Culture and Society* (5): 4.

———. 1986. *Blood, Bread, and Poetry: Selected Prose 1979–1985.* New York: W. W. Norton & Company. Includes "Notes Toward a Politics of Location" (1984) and "What Does a Woman Need to Know?" (1979).

Rubin, Gayle. 1989. "Thinking Sex: Notes for a Radical Theory of the Politics of Sexuality." In *Pleasure and Danger: Exploring Female Sexuality,* edited by Carole S. Vance. London: Pandora Press. First edition, 1984. London: Routledge & Kegan Paul.

Rushin, Donna Kate. 1983. "The Bridge Poem." In *This Bridge Called My Back: Writings by Radical Women of Color,* edited by Cherríe Moraga and Gloria Anzaldúa. 2d ed. New York: Kitchen Table Press.

Schilb, John. 1991. "Cultural Studies, Postmodernism, and Composition." In *Contending with Words: Composition and Rhetoric in a Postmodern Age,* edited by Patricia Harkin and John Schilb. New York: Modern Language Association.

Schweickart, Patrocinio. 1986. "Reading Ourselves: Toward a Feminist Theory of Reading." In *Gender and Reading: Essays on Readers, Texts, and Contexts,* edited by Elizabeth A. Flynn and Patrocinio Schweickart. Baltimore: Johns Hopkins University Press.

Sedgwick, Eve Kosofsky. 1990. *Epistemology of the Closet.* Berkeley: University of California Press.

———. 1991. "How to Bring Your Kids Up Gay." *Social Text* 29(9): 4.

Shor, Ira. 1980. *Critical Teaching and Everyday Life.* Boston: South End Press.

———. 1987. *Freire for the Classroom: A Sourcebook for Liberatory Teaching.* Portsmouth, NH: Boynton/Cook.

Smith, Barbara. 1977. "Toward a Black Feminist Criticism." *Conditions* 2: 25–44.

Smith, Barbara, ed. 1983. *Home Girls: A Black Feminist Anthology.* New York: Kitchen Table Press.

Smith, Barbara, Gloria Hull, and Patricia Bell Scott, eds. 1981. *But Some of Us Are Brave.* Old Westbury, NY: The Feminist Press.

Snitow, Ann, Christine Stansell, and Sharon Thompson, eds. 1983. *Powers of Desire: The Politics of Sexuality.* New York: Monthly Review Press.

Solomon, Alisa. 1993. "An Army of Others: Why the Gay Ban Makes the Man." *Village Voice,* 9 February, 25.

Sontag, Susan. 1989. *AIDS and Its Metaphors.* New York: Farrar, Straus and Giroux.

Sosnoski, James J. 1991. "Postmodern Teachers in Their Postmodern Classrooms: Socrates Begone!" In *Contending with Words: Composition and Rhetoric in a Postmodern Age,* edited by Patricia Harkin and John Schilb. New York: Modern Language Association.

Spear, Karen. 1988. *Sharing Writing: Peer Response Groups in English Classes.* Portsmouth, NH: Boynton/Cook.

Spellmeyer, Kurt. 1991. "Knowledge Against 'Knowledge': Freshman English, Public Discourse, and the Social Imagination." In *Composition and Resistance,* edited by C. Mark Hurlbert and Michael Blitz. Portsmouth, NH: Boynton/Cook.

———. 1993. "Being Philosophical About Composition: Hermeneutics and the Teaching of Writing." In *Into the Field: Sites of Composition Studies,* edited by Anne Ruggles Gere. New York: Modern Language Association.

Thompson, Karen, and Julie Andrzejewski. 1988. *Why Can't Sharon Kowalski Come Home?* San Francisco: Spinsters/Aunt Lute.

Tracey, Liz. 1990. "School Gayze." *Outweek,* 12 September.

Vance, Carole S. 1983. "Gender Systems, Ideology, and Sex Research." In *Powers of Desire: The Politics of Sexuality,* edited by Ann Snitow, Christine Stansell, and Sharon Thompson. New York: Monthly Review Press.

———. 1989. "Social Construction Theory: Problems in the History of Sexuality." In *Homosexuality, Which Homosexuality?*, edited by Dennis Altman, Carole Vance, Martha Vicinus, Jeffrey Weeks, and others. London: GMP Publishers. Amsterdam: Schorer, 1988.

Villanueva, Victor, Jr. 1991. "Considerations of American Freiristas." In *The Politics of Writing Instruction: Postsecondary*, edited by Richard Bullock and John Trimbur. Portsmouth, NH: Boynton/Cook.

Vygotsky, Lev. [1934] 1986. *Thought and Language*. Revised ed. Translated and edited by Alex Kozulin. Cambridge: MIT Press.

Watney, Simon. 1989. *Policing Desire: Pornograpy, AIDS, and the Media*. 2d ed. Minneapolis: University of Minnesota Press.

———. 1991. "School's Out." In *Inside/Out: Lesbian Theories, Gay Theories*, edited by Diana Fuss. New York: Routledge.

Weeks, Jeffrey. 1991. "Writing About Sex." In *Against Nature: Essays on History, Sexuality, and Identity*. London: Rivers Oram Press.

Weiss, Andrea, and Greta Schiller. 1988. *Before Stonewall: The Making of a Gay and Lesbian Community*. Tallahassee: Naiad Press.

Weston, Kath. 1991. *Families We Choose: Lesbians, Gays, Kinship*. New York: Columbia University Press.

Wieringa, Saskia. 1989. "An Anthropological Critique of Constructionism: Berdaches and Butches." In *Homosexuality, Which Homosexuality?*, edited by Dennis Altman, Carole Vance, Martha Vicinus, Jeffrey Weeks, and others. London: GMP Publishers. Amsterdam: Schorer, 1988.

Williams, James D. 1992. "Politicizing Literacy." *College English* 54(7): 833–42.

Wolff, Robert Paul. 1965. "Beyond Tolerance." In *A Critique of Pure Tolerance*, edited by Robert Paul Wolff, Barrington Moore, Jr., and Herbert Marcuse. Boston: Beacon Press.

Yaeger, Patricia. 1991. Afterword to *Feminism, Bakhtin, and the Dialogic*, edited by Dale M. Bauer and Susan Jaret McKinstry. Albany: State University of New York Press.

Yee, Marian. 1991. "Are You the Teacher?" In *Composition and Resistance*, edited by C. Mark Hurlbert and Michael Blitz. Portsmouth, NH: Boynton/Cook.

Yeskel, Felice. 1992. "The Price of Progress." *The Women's Review of Books* IX(5): 21.

Zevy, Lee, and Sahli A. Cavallero. 1987. "Invisibility, Fantasy, and Intimacy: Princess Charming Is Not a Prince." In *Lesbian Psychologies*, edited by the Boston Lesbian Psychologies Collective. Urbana and Chicago: University of Illinois Press.

Zinn, Howard. 1980. *A People's History of the United States*. New York: Harper and Row.

Zitter, Sherry. 1987. "Coming Out to Mom: Theoretical Aspects of the Mother-Daughter Process." In *Lesbian Psychologies*, edited by the Boston Lesbian Psychologies Collective. Urbana and Chicago: University of Illinois Press.

Index